Ideas and Poli...
Modern Britaiɪ

Edited by
J. C. D. Clark

Foreword by John Patten, MP

MACMILLAN

First published 1990

Published by
THE MACMILLAN PRESS LTD
Houndmills, Basingstoke, Hampshire RG21 2XS
and London
Companies and representatives
throughout the world

Printed and bound in Great Britain by
WBC Ltd, Bristol and Maesteg

British Library Cataloguing in Publication Data
Ideas and politics in modern Britain.
1. Great Britain. Politics
I. Clark, J. C. D. (Jonathan Charles Douglas)
320.941
ISBN 0–333–51550–1 (hardcover)
ISBN 0–333–51551–X (paperback)

Contents

Foreword

The political scenery in 1990, and the political agenda for the decade that follows, are both very different from those to be found in the mid-1970s, when Macmillan also published a set of brief essays, edited by Robert Blake and myself, entitled *The Conservative Opportunity* (1976).

Then the concerns were not just of post-imperial decline after the loss of empire, but whether the country was governable and, if so, by whom. The first decade of Conservative Government under Margaret Thatcher has resoundingly resolved that set of questions. We have one of the most strongly governed countries in the world, democracy combined with direction.

The preoccupations of the 1980s were somewhat different to those of the 1970s, economic revival and a reduction in unemployment being to the forefront. They were combined with the laying of foundations for personal development by individuals in the families and communities in which they live; for example, by fundamental changes in education.

Now, the 1990s have a new agenda, still dependent on economic success, but focusing on the creation of a country which is safer for its citizens, cleaner and better managed, contributing to environmental improvement not economic dereliction, helping individuals, families and communities to lead more contented and happier lives with healthier children and old people. Quality of life and quality of thought march together, or should, in the 1990s.

But one thread runs through each of these phases and that is how public and private enterprise and public and private cooperation can fructify. This debate centres on the role and relations of the state and the community it both governs and serves.

So this book ranges widely over these and related themes, and shows, above all else, both that conservatism flourishes in Oxford and that conservative thought continues to make the running as it has throughout the past two decades. It is the only contemporary political philosophy with real moral and practical coherence.

No other political party or school of thought in this country has managed to produce a 'big idea', or set of 'big ideas' knitted together, to challenge it; the hegemony of the right of centre in political thought continues. This is clearly illustrated in what fifteen distinguished

writers and thinkers from a variety of points on the political spectrum
contribute in this thought-provoking, entertaining, and sometimes
authoritative set of essays.

Political thought is more than alive and well in Oxford and its
intellectual networks. Thinking across a range of disciplines – from
history and economics to philosophy and theology – is evolving
rapidly as account is taken of the ferment of ideas which emerged
from the right of centre since the mid-1970s. The opportunity is
seized in this volume to re-examine some familiar topics in the light
of new thinking, new evidence and the passage of the last ten
or fifteen years. Familiar arguments are applied to contemporary
problems, and in some cases found wanting. Conversely, new
arguments are measured against the yardstick of the old and found
to be a bit less revolutionary than was first thought. How old, or
new, for example, is economic liberalism? And do the arguments
about church and state necessarily reflect reality? These are searching
questions posed – and sometimes answered – in its pages. The
analytical approaches brought to bear on the different topics by their
groups of authors, itself a most interesting approach, vary widely.
The philosophical and theological are interposed with the practical.
For example, the intensely practical world of welfare policy is debated
against the background of morality, as it should be, making for most
stimulating argument.

Nathan Glazer's 'American View' includes surprise at the vigour
of contemporary Conservative thought even after ten years of putting
that thought into practice (and, one might add, four years of prior
soul-searching, debate and planning in opposition). I think this book
remains just such a surprising contribution.

JOHN PATTEN

Hertford College, Oxford
Minister of State at the Home Office
and MP for Oxford West and Abingdon

Notes on the Contributors

Jonathan (J. C. D.) Clark has been a Fellow of All Souls College, Oxford, since 1986. Born in 1951, he was educated at Downing College and Corpus Christi College, Cambridge. After returning to academic life from a career in the City, he was elected a Fellow of Peterhouse, Cambridge, in 1977, and subsequently held a Research Fellowship of the Leverhulme Trust. As well as articles on eighteenth-century British history in learned journals, he is the author of *The Dynamics of Change* (1982); *English Society 1688–1832* (1985); *Revolution and Rebellion* (1986); and (as editor) *The Memoirs and Speeches of James, 2nd Earl Waldegrave* (1988). He is currently writing two books: on Britain's relations with America, and on England's relations with Scotland, Ireland and Wales, in the seventeenth and eighteenth centuries.

Nathan Glazer is Professor of Education and Sociology at Harvard University and co-editor of the quarterly *The Public Interest*. Born in 1923, he was educated in the public schools of New York City, the College of the City of New York, the University of Pennsylvania and Columbia University. Among his books are *Beyond the Melting Pot* (with Daniel P. Moynihan, 1963); *Affirmative Discrimination* (1975); *Ethnic Dilemmas* (1983); and *The Limits of Social Policy* (1988). He is presently working on a book on New York City.

John Gray has been a Fellow and Tutor in Politics, Exeter College, Oxford, since 1976. Born in 1948, he was educated at Exeter College, Oxford, where he took his DPhil, and was formerly lecturer in Government, Essex University, 1973–6. His books include *Mill on Liberty: A Defence* (1983), *Hayek on Liberty* (1986); *Liberalism* (1986); *Limited Government: A Political Agenda* (1988); and *Liberalisms: Essays in Political Philosophy* (1989). He is currently writing a study of post-totalitarianism, and a volume of essays on post-liberalism.

S. J. D. Green has been a Fellow of All Souls College, Oxford, since 1982. He was born in 1959, and educated at Hampton Grammar School and Balliol College, Oxford, where he was a Brackenbury Scholar in Modern History. Subsequently, he was a research student in sociology at Nuffield College, Oxford. He is the author of numerous articles on various aspects of political theory and public policy, and has in preparation a study of life and thought of R. H. Tawney.

Stephen Grover has been a Fellow of All Souls College, Oxford, since 1985. Born in 1959, he was educated at Maidenhead Grammar School and Trinity College, Oxford. He is the author of articles on the philosophy of religion in learned journals, and is currently working on a study of philosophical atheism.

Martin Holmes is currently Senior Visiting Research Fellow at Mansfield College, Oxford. He was born in 1954 and educated at Bursar Street School, Cleethorpes and University College, Oxford, where he was awarded his doctorate in 1981 for a thesis on the economic and industrial policy reversals of the Heath Government. Dr Holmes is the author of many scholarly articles and three major books – *Political Pressure and Economic Policy: British Government 1970–4* (1982); *The Labour Government 1974–9: Political Aims and Economic Reality* (1985) and *The First Thatcher Government, 1979–83: Contemporary Conservatism and Economic Change* (1985). He is currently writing a book on the political economy of the 1983–7 Conservative Government.

Terence Kealey is a University Lecturer in Clinical Biochemistry in the University of Cambridge. Born in 1952, he was educated at Charterhouse, Balliol College, Oxford and St Bartholomew's Hospital Medical School. He was formerly MRC Training Fellow, in the Department of Clinical Biochemistry, University of Oxford, 1976–80; Clinical Lecturer in the same department 1980–2; Senior Registrar in the Department of Clinical Biochemistry, Newcastle-upon-Tyne 1982–6; and Wellcome Senior Research Fellow, Department of Clinical Biochemistry, Oxford, 1986–8. He has published extensively in biochemical and medical journals, and is also the author of *Science Fiction: and the True Way to Save British Science* (1989). As well as his biochemical research, he is currently researching an international comparison of government science funding policies and their economic outcomes.

Oliver Letwin is currently Head of the Utilities and Privatisation Team at N. M. Rothschild and Sons Ltd. He was born in 1956, and educated at Eton and Trinity College, Cambridge, where he received BA, MA and PhD degrees. He has been a Visiting Fellow in the

Philosophy Department at Princeton University; a Fellow of Darwin College, Cambridge; a Special Adviser to the Secretary of State for Education and Science, and a member of the Prime Minister's Policy Unit. In 1987, he stood as a Conservative Parliamentary Candidate. He has published widely in journals and newspapers, and is the author of a number of books and pamphlets, including *Ethics, Emotion and the Unity of Self* (1987) and *Privatising the World.*

Patrick Minford has been Edward Gonner Professor of Applied Economics, Univerity of Liverpool since 1976. Born in 1943, he was educated at Winchester, Balliol College, Oxford, and the LSE. He was formerly Economic Assistant to the Finance Director, Courtaulds Ltd; Economic Adviser, Ministry of Finance, Malawi; Economic Adviser, Ministry of Overseas Development; and Economic Adviser to HM Treasury's External Division, serving with HM Treasury's Delegation, Washington DC, 1973–4. He was Visiting Hallsworth Research Fellow, Manchester University, in 1975, and started the Liverpool Research Group in Macroeconomics in 1979. From 1988 he has been a Board Member of the Merseyside Development Corporation and edited the *Review of the National Institute for Economic and Social Research* in 1975–6. He is the author of *Substitution Effects, Speculation and Exchange Rate Stability* (1978); *Unemployment: Cause and Cure* (1983); *The Housing Morass* (1987); *Rational Expectations and the New Macroeconomics* (with David Peel) (1983); and publications on trade, monetary economics and the UK and international economies. He contributes actively to the macroeconomic policy debate in the UK, including a regular column in the *Daily Telegraph*.

Raymond Plant has been Professor of Politics at the University of Southampton since 1979. Born in 1945, he was educated at King's College, London University and from 1967 to 1979 was Lecturer and Senior Lecturer in Philosophy in the University of Manchester. His publications include *Hegel* (1973); *Community and Ideology* (1974); *Philosophy, Politics and Citizenship* (1984); and *Conservative Capitalism in the U.S. and Great Britain: A Critical Appraisal* (with K. Hoover) (1989). His current work includes a book on the foundations of political thought, and the forthcoming 1990 Sarum Lectures in the University of Oxford.

John Redwood has been Member of Parliament for Wokingham since

1987. In 1989 he became Parliamentary Under Secretary of State for Corporate Affairs in the Department of Trade and Industry. Born in 1951, he was educated at Kent College, Canterbury, Magdalen College and St Antony's College Oxford. From 1972 to 1986 he was a Fellow of All Souls. In 1977 he joined N. M. Rothschild and Sons Ltd of which he is currently a non-executive director. From 1983 to 1986 he was a member, and then head, of the Prime Minister's Policy Unit; in 1986–7 he led Rothschild's Overseas Privatisation Unit. His publications include *Public Enterprise in Crisis* (1980); *Value for Money Audits* (with J. V. Hatch) (1981); *Controlling Public Industries* (with J. V. Hatch) (1982); *Going for Broke* (1984); *Equity for Everyman* (1986) and *Popular Capitalism* (1988). He is currently revising the latter in the light of world developments, and writing on privatisation, the economic performance of the Thatcher governments, planning and the single European market of 1992.

Roger Scruton has been Professor of Aesthetics at Birkbeck College, London, since 1985. Born in 1944, he was educated at Jesus College, Cambridge. From 1969 to 1971 he was a Fellow of Peterhouse, Cambridge, and from 1971 to 1985 Lecturer and Reader at Birkbeck College. His publications include *Art and Imagination* (1974); *The Aesthetics of Architecture* (1979); *The Meaning of Conservatism* (1980); *From Descartes to Wittgenstein* (1981); *The Politics of Culture* (1981); *Kant* (1982); *A Dictionary of Political Thought* (1982); *The Aesthetic Understanding* (1983); *Peace Studies: A Critical Survey* (with Baroness Cox) (1984); *Thinkers of the New Left* (1985); *Education and Indoctrination* (1985); *Sexual Desire* (1986); *A Land Held Hostage* (1987) and *Untimely Tracts* (1987). His current research is addressed to the concept of culture.

John Stevenson is Reader in History at the University of Sheffield. Born in 1946, he was educated at Worcester College and Nuffield College Oxford. He is the author of *The Slump* (with Chris Cook) (1977); *London in the Age of Reform* (editor) (1977); *Popular Disturbances in England, 1700–1870* (1979) and *British Society, 1914–1945* (1984), as well as a number of essays on planning and the history of social policy. He is currently working on a study of the life and times of William Cobbett and a major new social history of modern Britain.

S. W. Sykes became Bishop of Ely in 1990, having been Regius

Professor of Divinity in the University of Cambridge, and Fellow of St John's College, since 1985. Born in 1939, he was educated at St John's College, Cambridge; he was formerly Lecturer in Divinity at Cambridge and Professor of Divinity at Durham University. His publications include *Friedrich Schleiermacher* (1971); *Christian Theology Today* (1971); *Christ, Faith and History* (editor) (1972); *The Integrity of Anglicanism* (1978); *Karl Barth* (editor) (1980); *New Studies in Theology* (editor) (1980); *England and Germany, Studies in Theological Diplomacy* (editor) (1982); *The Identity of Christianity* (editor) (1984); *Authority in the Anglican Communion* (editor) (1987) and *The Study of Anglicanism* (editor) (1988).

Adrian Wooldridge has been a Fellow of All Souls College, Oxford, since 1980; he currently writes on education and health for *The Economist*. Born in 1959, he was educated at Balliol College, Oxford. As well as articles in learned journals, he is the author of a forthcoming study of educational selection in England from 1880 to the present. His current research is into the meritocracy, education and the welfare state.

Introduction
Jonathan Clark

This book explores some of the relationships between ideas and politics in Britain during the last three decades – between the evolution of thought in a variety of academic disciplines, and analogous events in the public arena. Some disciplines are clearly progammatic; others (theology, history) are as obviously resistant to assimilation in present-day political progammes. Yet few disciplines escape the influence of the world of affairs, and the ferment of ideas which accompanied and drew encouragement from the breakup of the post-war political consensus produced a moment in British intellectual life of exceptional interest. It was, of course, a time of profound disagreement. This book reflects a continuing controversy as the outlines of new understandings emerge, not the sweeping victory of a pre-formed consensus.

Partly for that reason, the role of ideas in modern British politics has not been to reformulate great systems in succession to those whose passing is so widely acknowledged. Successive Conservative ministries were still unlike their Socialist or Liberal precursors in having no classic books to define a modern ideology: the writings of F. A. Hayek and Milton Friedman, for all their obvious functional and symbolic importance, acknowledged in these pages, never functioned in the same was as the texts of Jeremy Bentham or John Stuart Mill, let alone Marx and Engels. The evolution of ideas recorded in these pages was complex: it did not proceed by deduction from a single discipline, not even economics. Present politics, and Conservative politics in particular, have been charged with being unduly ideological for different reasons. First, a perceived loss of the intellectual initiative on the Left, in quarters where this sense had been an essential moral aid. Second, the rise of bodies of ideas which were consciously antithetical to collectivist moral liberalism and to socialism. Third, the consequences for our map of British development. Those two ideologies had generated among their subscribers a deep sense that history was evolving in their direction, that a logic had been identified in events which guaranteed the ultimate outcome: when history took a contrary course, it seemed to follow that something illegitimate was taking place. An assault on the sacred

1

teleologies of liberals or socialists could only be described as motivated by a prior commitment to another ideology.

The familiar scenario of British history had been open to two different emphases. In reality, they were inconsistent; yet since they were expressed in a common idiom and articulated common values, the degree of inconsistency was overlooked. According to one emphasis, a bourgeois revolution in the seventeenth century had met the social and cultural preconditions for industrialisation: Britain thereafter pursued a path which increasingly diverged from that of her continental neighbours, taking the role of pathfinder by breaking decisively with the values and practices of the ancien regime. Instead, in this scenario, Britain early embraced the values of liberal capitalist individualism; but although these market-oriented values were appropriate to the technologically-simple Industrial Revolution of the eighteenth century, they were claimed to be inappropriate to the science-based industrialism of the late twentieth century. Such technologies demand a corporate state and central planning, practices adopted with success in continental economies but which Britain's archaic individualism obstructed. Similarly, predicted this theory, Britain would be unable to integrate into the EEC because of the British doctrine of unlimited parliamentary sovereignty, itself indebted to Benthamite individualist utilitarianism and its dismissal of fundamental rights. For both these reasons – Britain's basic values and her Westminster model of government – no cultural revolution of the scale achieved in the seventeenth century had been possible in the late twentieth, and Britain had been unable to break from her pattern of economic decline.

This scenario achieved its most cogent expression in the work of David Marquand, a Labour MP in the 1970s and a founder of the Social Democratic Party in 1981.[1] Such a view explained why economic recovery built around radical individualism was impossible: it was therefore wholly unable to explain what happened after 1979. Marquand's analysis indeed captured the pessimistic perspective which seemed persuasive at the time he left Parliament in 1977; its failure to allow for or explain what happened since that date highlights the historical premises of its analysis in the Marxist historiography of C. B. Macpherson and Christopher Hill.[2] The discrediting of that historiography has gone hand in hand with the practical disproof, in the public arena, or many of the predictions which had been based on it.

In this first scenario of British history, then, radical change was impossible because of a too-successful revolution in the seventeenth century. From a political standpoint decisively to the left of Marquand's, a similar long-term scenario was given a different emphasis. In this version, it was emphasised that radical change was now impossible because the 'bourgeois revolution' of the seventeenth century had been incomplete and partly frustrated. Hence, in the twentieth century, it was claimed that

> No recovery from industrial 'backwardness' has been possible, precisely because no second revolution of the state has taken place in England: only the state could have engendered such a recovery, by revolution from above – but the old patrician structure of England's political system, incapable of such radical action, has also resisted every effort at serious reform up to the present day.[3]

This was a perspective widely accepted on the Left in the mid- and late 1970s; but after 1979, just such a second revolution was being claimed, and being more often dispraised than denied by its opponents. The categories employed by the Left had been vulnerable only to this, the unthinkable. But if the unthinkable had actually happened, then the whole scenario which had confidently predicted its impossibility was called in doubt.

From an American perspective (see Chapter 1), the 'British' experience seems far more homogeneous than it does from the European. In the European context (Chapter 2), one distinctive (and unAmerican) form of challenge to collectivism has come from resurgent nationalism in Poland and Hungary, the Baltic republics, and among the Basques. Within these islands, too, the assertion of Welsh and Scots separatism has challenged each of the overarching ideologies (liberalism, socialism, imperialism) which acted as doctrines of national unity. Their disintegration re-opens the question of nationalism within political philosophy also. It is re-opened as much for Roger Scruton (Chapter 3), who disavows liberalism, as for John Gray (Chapter 4), whose position is much closer to some aspects of it. For Scruton, the cultural substance given to race by the credence generally attached to the concept gives it a reality as a way of conceiving social unity, and in this sense Arabs and Jews equally defend it. Contract theory, he argues, cannot explain the principle of national unity which draws and holds the people who are hypothetically supposed to sign the social contract. For Gray, meanwhile, hegemonic radical individualism seems to have nothing to say which could prevent such a process, precisely because of its neglect of the

'cultural inheritance' which might stabilise civil society. If individualism is to be consistent with conservatism following liberalism's demise,
as Gray suggests, then individualism may have to be consistent
with nationalism also, including the nationalisms of Britain's new
immigrant minorities. It may be that radical individualism has
identified the lowest common denominator in a plural society; it
remains to be seen just how low that denominator is, and whether,
as Gray asks, government proves able to safeguard the 'cultural pre-
conditions of liberalism'.

From an American perspective, Britain developments in recent
decades seem more readily intelligible because (as Nathan Glazer
observes in Chapter 1) British policy options are focussed with greater
clarity by Britain's simpler, more centralised system of government.
At its most basic, growing scepticism about the effects of public or
corporate provision, and growing confidence in the efficacy of
individual motivation, were common to both cultures. Yet one source
of confusion has been an ambiguity about terms, especially the
multifarious meanings of the term 'liberalism'. Like all portmanteau
terms, it has grown by accretion to include a number of doctrines,
not necessarily compatible. First appearing in Britain in the 1820s, it
initially signified the policy stance of those members of the opposition
who conceived the most bitter hatred of the then-existing establishment in Church and State: religion, but especially religious hetero-
doxy, was central to their vision. Individualism was not. Later, the
individualistic economic components of *laissez-faire* came to dominate
the moral vision (chronology alone establishes that neither John
Locke nor Adam Smith were preaching liberalism). The reassertion
of free-market doctrines in modern Britain and America has attracted
the same nineteenth-century label; but it is now clear that its economic
overtones conflict with the moral commitments of the Left.

Indeed, its moral component has been torn apart by the practical
political problems now faced by western societies. Pluralism means
more than interesting ethnic and cultural diversity: it means the clash
of irreconcilable ideals in faith and morals. Such clashes reveal that
liberalism had always contained two inconsistent elements. One
element attached supreme importance to toleration: moral pluralism
was valued as an end in itself. Equality of esteem for individuals
meant that all individuals had to be free to act out their morality
within their own sphere. The other element attached overriding
significance to liberty: certain libertarian rights should be guaranteed
to all, if necessary by the intervention of the state. Yet these two

elements quickly become profoundly inconsistent if fundamentally different values are entrenched within the boundaries of race, family or religion. Are fundamentally different practices to be tolerated within different ethnic groups, or are western conceptions of civil and religious liberty to be imposed?[4]

It is the collectivist moral meanings of the term liberalism that have come under assault, turning the word itself into a taboo (wryly and obliquely invoked as 'the L word'). Similar problems have beset liberalism in the realm of theology, its original home. Stephen Sykes (Chapter 5) deploys an argument that the United Kingdom is still, despite obvious difficulties, 'a Christian state'. Yet he recognises that theologians have recently made a weak case for this claim, a weakness stemming from ignorance of the Christian tradition consequent upon the introduction of 'pluralism' into theology syllabuses. Liberalism, according to Sykes, undermined Anglican identity and self-confidence at exactly the point, from the 1960s, when ecumenical opportunities demanded both.

This 'massive failure of nerve' was promoted by the eclipse of socialism. The Christian socialist tradition had been a powerful one within the twentieth-century Church of England and among other churches, as Raymond Plant demonstrates; as in all declining institutions, Anglican defensiveness tended to shield it from fundamental reconsideration and led certain churchmen into spectacular conflicts with the Conservative governments of the 1980s. Thus, as Sykes sees, anti-collectivists have sometimes preferred secularisation to the socialist values still embedded within certain areas of Anglicanism; as Plant (Chapter 6) reveals, socialist Anglicans have preferred to see in Thatcherism an essentially economic doctrine deriving from Hayek and Friedman rather than a restatement of certain pre-socialist aspects of historic Anglican teaching. Plant condemns the individualist critique of the collectivist notion of distributive justice as if it were a negation of all social justice: such a critique would mean that the concept 'cannot yield detailed rules to guide public policy'.

Yet, in fact, a similar moral has to be drawn from the course of modern philosophy. If politics has lost much of its former ethical identity in favour of a pervasive utilitarian idiom, some reasons may be sought within theology. Wittgensteinian philosophy has left theology in a position in which (as Stephen Grover shows in Chapter 7) many argue that there cannot be a Christian ethics of a form so specific that it could be bid for by, or become the property of, any particular party. Socialist and liberal ethics have been dismantled by a process which seems to dismantle all other Christian ethics, too. The breakup of the moral consensus entailed by a plural society is thus a theme which can be illustrated in the realm of theology, as in other areas. Grover still wishes to find a route to 'a Christian ethics which is genuinely humanitarian', but his arguments against Don Cupitt on the one hand and Edward Norman on the other appear – as philosophy is now structured – to make such a hope vain. Moral arguments are now as common in the political arena as they are inconclusive, since their theological basis is so much contested.

Liberalism, as Grover establishes, is clearly a phenomenon arising from *within* theology, not illegitimately imposed upon it by any brand of modern philosophy. Such an insight dovetails exactly with the historical recovery of liberalism as, at its inception in the 1820s, essentially theological (heterodox) rather than political (libertarian). The profound sense of dissatisfaction expressed within philosophical theology at the extent of liberalism's dominance informs the chapters of Grover and Sykes equally, even if that dissatisfaction is only in the process of finding a voice.

Meanwhile, we see that atheism need not point in the direction of liberal humanism: if theism is abolished, there is no particular reason to expect that it will be replaced by kindly neighbourliness. It is more likely to be replaced by a host of ugly social problems, on a few of which the chapters of Simon Green and Adrian Wooldridge (Chapters 8 and 9) have touched. Those 'liberal, humanitarian or democratic concerns' which Grover recognises have been unnecessarily imposed upon Christianity since the nineteenth century still inform many of our attitudes towards public provision. A retreat into the private realm, for Grover, is permissible for a Christian but not compulsory. Meanwhile, in the public realm, social problems accumulate. Welfare policy, as Green demonstrates, has been dependent on a view of human nature and motivation which has led it, at times, into a 'crass moralism'. A failure of moral diagnosis has demonstrably led to a 'problem of social pathology' in society at large; in the schools, as Wooldridge argues, policy premised on such liberal assumptions of 'the elasticity of human nature' has been markedly unsuccessful in meeting its targets.

As Minford observes, all policy has theoretical premises and may equally be described as ideological. Those theoretical premises in the realm of economic management are explored in chapters by Patrick Minford, Martin Holmes and John Redwood (Chapters 10, 11 and 12). Common to their insights is the perception that the experience of the 1970s destroyed a previous consensus and greatly extended the territory of fundamental controversy. In economic theory, the premises of the corporate state have been destroyed; and thanks to the greater extent and apparent success which the corporate state had enjoyed in the Britain of *c*. 1945–79, its dismantling too was paradigmatic, as Redwood illustrates.

Britain had, indeed, long been a strong, unified and centralised state. These features were, historically, called in question not directly, but by those who objected most strongly to the content of the policies which the state promoted. In the 1980s, the progressive deregulation of the economy highlighted the extent to which authority was left unchallenged in other areas. Some commentators tried to elevate this into a paradox, insisting on a contradiction between moves towards 'a more competitive, more open economy and towards a more repressive, more authoritarian state'. Eric Hobsbawm warned: 'One should not forget that Britain is, in theory, an absolutism for governments with unshakeable majorities'. It was an ancient feature of the state which had evoked little disquiet on the Left when the majorities had been those of Attlee or Wilson; in the 1980s, it consorted ill with the discovery that, as other elements of socialism fell away, what remained was, essentially and non-negotiably, a commitment to state-directed planning.[5]

'Planning' (see Chapter 13) was a concept loosely based in economic theory, but exactly reflecting pervasive liberal assumptions about the malleability of human character – assumptions which, before the 1980s, were widely shared across the political spectrum. It is the distance now opening up between our intellectual world and its predecessor that allows the major premises of its social order to come into focus: Oliver Letwin's characterisation of them as 'myths' (Chapter 14) reminds us that those premises had an historical trajectory as well. If so, it follows that excellence in science and education is not (as Wooldridge and Kealey (in Chapter 15) both emphasise) chiefly determined by the amount of resources devoted to those activities. And, taking the argument a stage further, it would then be less surprising if government expenditure on universities in general and pure science in particular were not closely linked to economic growth.

The sense of the dissolution of familiar frameworks of thought, and the shifting of ancient landmarks, produced some statements which, take out of context, seem too sweeping. As a sociologist of religion noted at a conference in 1981,

> We have all of us – interested scholars from a variety of disciplines –
> virtually boxed the compass in our interpretations. We have begun
> to repeat ourselves as well as others. We seem to have exhausted the
> conceptual and ideational resources of the technological revolution,
> the industrial revolution, the enlightenment, the renaissance and
> perhaps even of mediaeval thought as well.[6]

Yet such statements were symptomatic, even if they exaggerated the
extent of change. An intellectual landscape is not reconstructed
overnight. But the sense of change was heightened by a contrast
between new thinking in some quarters and an absence of new
thought in others.

Socialism and liberalism now converge in an agenda which has
little to do with the positive affirmations of the parent ideologies:
green issues, anti-racism, feminism, the nuclear phobia, the defence
of minority cultures and alternative lifestyles. But the defence of the
pluralism of a plural society is less effective in Wales, Scotland and
Northern Ireland: to a far greater extent, they still see themselves as
unitary societies, united by shared culture and open to mobilisation
by nationalism. Nationalism and socialism now pose real, and
competing, alternatives in both Scotland and Wales. In England it is
more true that

> the problem with the Left's traditional economic agenda is that it
> has lost its traditional electoral base, that it no longer appears to
> address the reality of the social and industrial structure as it actually
> is. Whereas the new social movements have at least the potential
> to address an increasing proportion of the actual labour force as it
> develops in the real world.

With that candour, it could be admitted that 'the effort to bring about
the synthesis of the modern social movements and the traditional
socialist agenda surely remains the Left's most urgent political task'.[7]

One consequence of this weakening of old guidelines was a repeated
call for a fundamental reconsideration of opposition ideology. No
such reconsideration was forthcoming. As one candid observer
admitted, 'It is as though the moment we stray, even for a moment,
from the straight-and-narrow path of conventional Left wisdom, the
big, bad wolf of Thatcherite revisionism is waiting to gobble us up'.
The problem was that the categories in which the debate had been
conducted – categories formulated in the nineteenth century and long
unchallenged – were now in question. Professor Stuart Hall noted:

the underlying social, economic and cultural forces which are bringing the era of 'organised capitalism' to a close, coupled with the vigour of Thatcherite restructuring, have decomposed and fragmented class as a unified political force, fracturing any so-called automatic linkages between economics and politics: if, indeed, any such 'unity' or 'automatic linkage' ever existed (which I beg leave to doubt).[8]

Few retractions have been more extensive in their implications.

Notes and References

1. David Marquand, *The Unprincipled Society* (London, 1988). The extent of the corporatism that such an analysis would entail should not be underestimated: 'Politicians and public would have to accept that, in complex industrial societies, parliamentary election should not be the sole channel of representation: that, in their capacities as producers, "the people" are likely to be represented better by groups organised on functional lines than by members of parliament elected on a territorial basis; and that it is therefore right, as well as expedient, for governments emerging from territorial elections to share power with functionally based producer groups'.
2. These are the historians whom Marquand acknowledges. For a critique of their account of English history, cf. J. C. D. Clark, *Revolution and Rebellion: State and Society in England in the Seventeenth and Eighteenth Centuries* (Cambridge, 1986).
3. Tom Nairn, *The Break-Up of Britain: Crisis and Neo-Nationalism* (London, 1977; 2nd edn, 1981): 22.
4. E.g., Alan Ryan, 'Liberals on the fence', *New Society* (22 May 1987): 29. The dilemma is there posed as an acute embarrassment for liberals.
5. Cf. Eric Hobsbawm, 'Out of the Wilderness', *Marxism Today* (October 1987): 12–19.
6. Kenelm Burridge, in Bruce Lincoln (ed.), *Religion, Rebellion, Revolution* (London, 1985): 221.
7. David Edgar, 'When the Hardline is Right', *Marxism Today* (February 1988): 30.
8. Stuart Hall, 'Thatcher's Lessons', *Marxism Today* (March 1988): 20–9.

Part I
Contexts: Britain, Europe and America

1 Ideas and Politics in Britain: an American View

Nathan Glazer

One difficulty in discussing 'an American view' of Mrs Thatcher's Britain is that the great majority of Americans have no view or any bases for a view, and this is true even of the best informed. In general, the view of Mrs Thatcher and what she has meant for modern Britain is positive, but less because of what is most interesting about her – the introduction of radical new ideas on how to remake Britain, its economy, its social services, and its social institutions – than because her foreign policy has been so supportive of that of the United States. But most Americans know little of all this because their newspapers and magazines tell them little. The American newspaper and news magazine is events-based, as is not surprising: something has to happen to draw any attention to a foreign nation, even one so large and important, and one so closely connected with us, as Britain. The things that have happened during Mrs Thatcher's ten years and have been 'news', and which have therefore received attention, are her three electoral victories (but British campaigns are short, and don't give American reporters much opportunity for coverage), and the Falklands war. As for the rest, if one doesn't read the section on Britain in *The Economist*, as some of its 140,000 American subscribers must, one will not know much.

Of course it is the same in the other direction. In a front-page story in the *New York Times* on the government's new health plan (a unique case, for there never has been front-page coverage, I believe, of any British domestic policy initiative), Craig Whitney writes, in connection with the fear that Mrs Thatcher's government 'wants to make over the health service along American lines', that 'in the British public mind, this means snarling doctors turning indigent patients untreated onto the streets, personal bankruptcy for the uninsured middle-class patient, and superb care depending on ability to pay. No one has heard of Blue Cross, charitable in-patient admissions or municipal hospitals'. Well, no one aside from the experts — which is the same when it comes to knowledge of British social policy for the United States.[1]

Nevertheless, there are a number of groups of Americans among whom there has been great interest, and informed interest, in the remarkable developments in Britain over the last ten years. Among these are economists who study problems of economic growth and the effect of alternative policies, and social policy analysts in the universities and in the various research institutes such as Brookings and the Urban Institute, for whom developments in British social policy, and social policy in Europe more generally, have in the past served as a benchmark against which to measure American progress, or lack of it, in the development of a welfare state. Along with them have been other economists and policy analysts, of a somewhat different stamp, associated with free-market-oriented or conservative think-tanks such as the American Enterprise Institute, the Heritage Foundation, the Manhattan Institute in New York, and others. (I concentrate in this chapter on social policy, rather than economic policy.) As the most accessible and best-known of the welfare states of Europe, Britain's health and social services and educational system have been steadily studied by American experts both liberal and conservative as examples to be followed, and among some as examples to be avoided.

The international movement in ideas on the progressive approach to health and educational and social services has in general moved from Britain to the United States. But in the past twenty years, this international traffic has also included a stream of criticism of British welfare, health and educational services, flowing from Britain to the United States and surprising American analysts whose standard posture was admiration for how Britain managed these things, whether in its National Health Service, voluntary non-profit blood services, infant schools, council housing, or general social services. The role of the Institute of Economic Affairs is particularly important. Its work and publications precede those of most of the conservative American research institutes; its free-market orientation has been intriguing to many American policy analysts, particularly those, like the present writer, who have wondered whether there are not some good reasons, as well as bad ones, for the failure of the United States to develop its social services in the pattern of Britain. American policy analysts had been raised on work that applauded the huge British investment in council housing, comparing it with the paltry quantities of public housing we built in the United States; on admiring analyses of the National Health Service and its success in bringing a good standard of care much more economically and efficiently than our fragmented and costly health services in the United States. Even British schools, despite the class divisions that marked them more sharply than those of the United States, came in for a flurry of approving books because of open classrooms and ungraded infant schools in the 1970s.[2]

But along with the news of British pioneering in the development of a fully-fashioned welfare state, which reached perhaps a crescendo in the middle and late 1960s as we entered our own distinctive efforts to complete the welfare state, there began to come a disturbing undertone of critique. Few of us were aware of it. As early as 1965, one could have read, in E. G. West's *Education and the State*, a powerful critique of the accepted wisdom that the state ought to provide education for all, and that in its absence the population would be illiterate and ill-educated. But it took a while for anyone in the United States to be aware of all this. It was only in the late 1960s or early 1970s that I heard the name of E. G. West from Professor Edward Banfield of Harvard, and that Professor Gertrude Himmelfarb gave me an interesting article by West disputing the conventional account of the forces behind the establishment of compulsory state education in New York State in the nineteenth century: teachers, trying to guarantee their incomes, were the most powerful advocates of compulsory state education, West argued. By then those of us who did not come out of any conservative background were beginning to raise questions about the great expansion of welfare and social services in the United States in the later 1960s and early 1970s and were perhaps ready for a critique of developments in Britain that we had previously admired.

This sketch of the traffic of ideas deals of course only with social policy. Economists had earlier noted that Britain was lagging behind reviving and prosperous Western Europe in economic growth. American economists analysed this lag quite early, and were already cautiously moving in the direction of urging greater use of market incentives and disincentives. A Brookings Institution study in 1968 of Britain's problems in economic growth notes that full employment (unemployment never rose above 2.5 per cent in Britain in the fifteen years before this study!) 'may have contributed via rising prices and money incomes to the deterioration of the current account of the balance of payments and impaired the efficiency of the economy and thus the rate of growth'. The economists saw problems in some social programmes:

> Public housing programs require appreciable change, not so much
> because they deter private rental housing as because they hinder
> labor mobility. Maintaining the performance of the National Health
> Service in the face of demographic changes will require a large rise
> in payments for medical staff . . . Greater selectivity in social
> security programs would yield a marked cut in the growth of such
> transfer payments.[3]

One final twist in the traffic of ideas might be noted: from the late
1960s, we can see some influence from American Great Society
programmes, particularly those – the poverty programme, the model
cities programme – addressed to the problems of the inner cities.
American policies emphasised the participation in the shaping of
these programmes of inner-city residents, and emphasised the coordination of many different kinds of programmes in a joint effort to
improve the physical and social fabric of declining inner-city areas.
These programmes did not show any marked success, or indeed in
sum any success at all, in the United States, and I believe equivalents,
in part based on American precedents, were no more successful in
the United Kingdom. This experience also contributed to a weakening
of the authority of enlightened social intervention generally.

Thus in both the United States and the United Kingdom, a period
of high confidence in expert understanding of problems in education,
employment, planning and social life was succeeded by a period of
great scepticism among a rising number of social analysts about such
public interventions, combined with high faith in traditional individual
human motives to self-improvement, if given the opportunity.

As the 1970s came to an end, two leaders, in the United Kingdom
and United States, came to the fore, neither particularly representative of their parties (though they were both to reshape them), arguing
in effect for the role of traditional motives for self-improvement, if
only government would allow them to operate, and for the freeing
of market forces to respond to them.

In both countries, the party of the Left had weakened its appeal
to the electorate by moving left. In both, the appeal to compassion,
sharing and redistribution had weakened because it was seen increasingly as the appeal of selfish interest groups – that is, primarily those
who provided the services of an expanded state, and specific groups
that benefited from them. The welfare state was increasingly seen as
benefiting its employees more than the public in general. Teachers

became the most numerous group in the Democratic party convention. Teachers and other middle class professionals became dominant in the Labour Party, and a force in moving it left and away from dominant public opinion on some key issues:

> Labour's . . . activists became, with time, increasingly middle class. They were not necessarily of middle class origin but many were people who had by education, occupational advance or housing location moved on from the working class . . . The growth of the middle classes was caused . . . primarily by the rapid expansion of public sector employment . . . The 'new class' consisted predominantly of teachers and administrators, lower managerial and professionals or semi-professionals. Its rise was reflected in the burgeoning bureaucracies of local government and the health service authorities in the 1970s and also in the rise or the rapid growth of middle class trade unions.[4]

One could say the same of the Democratic Party in the 1970s. Specific issues were different – they would have had to be in view of the different roles played by the national governments in the United States and the United Kingdom. But the divorce between the party of the Left and popular opinion on many issues was equivalent. Labour in Britain was seen as the pawn of labour leaders defending selfish and partial interests; the Democrats in the United States were seen too as the party of 'interests', organised labour, government employees, women, blacks. Admittedly it is a question of rhetoric just when an 'interest group' is seen as a special and partial interest, and when it is seen as representing the interests of all of the nation. But was it only rhetoric that made entrepreneurs and businessmen (who may be seen pre-eminently as exemplifying selfish special interests) heroes in Thatcher's Britain and Reagan's United States, and succeeded in demoting the representatives of organised workers and government servants to special interests? Clearly rhetoric and political skill was involved, but common experience was involved too. Responding to their constituencies, the parties of the Left in both countries seemed unable to control high inflation, and in both countries more people seemed threatened by that than by the means that a party of the Right might use to bring it down.

In both countries the malaise over the economic situation internally was heightened by a sense of relative decline, in comparison to other countries doing better economically. In both countries the party of the Left had gone through a similar evolution, for different reasons;

the leftist elements within the party of the Left had increased their
weight, and had alienated some part of their original supporters.

> On the eve of the 1979 [Labour] conference, Austin Mitchell . . .
> who had succeeded to Crosland's seat . . . published a Fabian tract
> which pointed out that 86 per cent of the electorate had wanted to
> see bans on secondary picketing, 75 per cent were in favour of the
> sale of council houses, 60 per cent wanted to bring back the
> grammar schools . . . On the other hand, only 24 per cent thought
> fee paying schools should be abolished, only 20 per cent wanted
> to abolish the House of Lords, and only 38 per cent wanted to give
> trade unionists seats on company boards. All these were conference
> policies.[5]

One could have found similar contrasts in the United States between
positions popular in Democratic national conventions, where party
activists, minorities, and women had expanded their weight on the
basis of party reforms, and the rank and file of Democratic voters.
Some of the issues that alienated them were different, but the
dynamics were the same.

One is surprised to discover that even issues one had thought were
distinctively American, and (whatever their weight in helping Reagan)
could hardly have played a role in Thatcher's victory, popped up in
Britain. One would think for example that race could not have been
much of an issue in Britain, where the numbers of non-white citizens
and residents, and the historical significance of race, is so different.
In both countries references to race in politics are scarcely blatant.
The issue operates below the surface of political discussion: it concerns
people deeply, but the language in which that concern can be put,
without political damage, has not yet been invented. Joel Krieger
finds race a very potent appeal in Mrs Thatcher's first victory (indeed,
along with the promise of home-ownership for council houses, the
'most catalytic issue'), even though he is hard put to find any language
in the campaign that might suggest a racist appeal. Mrs Thatcher had
given an interview in 1978 in which she referred to the possibility of
four million people from the New Commonwealth or Pakistan in
Britain: 'Now I think that is an awful lot and I think it means that
people are really rather afraid that this country might be rather
swamped by people of a different culture. . .'. Immigration policy
played no role in the campaign, for all these issues had apparently
been settled, but Mrs Thatcher defended her use of the word
'swamped'. Krieger finds 'subliminal racism', mysteriously, in Mrs

Thatcher's closing words of her final major address:

> Somewhere ahead lies greatness for the country again . . . Look at Britain today and you may think that an impossible dream. But there is another Britain which may not make the daily news but which each of us knows. It is a Britain of thoughtful people tantalizingly slow to act, yet marvelously determined when they do . . . Its message . . . says: Let us make it a country safe to grow old in. And it says, above all, may this land of ours, which we love so much, find dignity and greatness and peace again.

This reader searched the speech in vain for the racism Krieger found in it. He argues it 'represented the ideals of whites in East London (or South Boston) who feel swamped at the sight of black children outnumbering white. . .'. Well, perhaps, the fact is that the swing to Mrs Thatcher was strongest 'in those London constituencies that had witnessed the most sustained National front organizing'. In the areas where race was an issue, the Conservatives did best.[6] Krieger has thus made his point from the electoral statistics, if not from the electoral rhetoric.

But other similarities were more salient, such as the attack on the effectiveness of government, the promise that a party less beholden to labour would be more effective in curbing inflation, the rise of a large middle class which outweighed industrial workers, the common appeal to nationalism, particularly potent in a United States frustrated (as it still is after three Republican victories) by the holding of American hostages by fanatically anti-American Muslim groups, and the fact that despite drastic weakening in traditional extractive and manufacturing industries, some parts of the country were prosperous on the basis of the expansion of new high-tech industries and services. The United States was two nations as well as Britain, and this explains electoral victories in the face of high unemployment and the inability to deal with economic decline in large parts of the country.

The motivating ideas in the success of Margaret Thatcher and Ronald Reagan were remarkably similar. They had the same sources, and a similar means of transmission had moved them from men of ideas to men and women in politics. Mrs Thatcher was closer to the source of these ideas than Ronald Reagan. She had, after all, read Hayek's *The Road to Serfdom* at Oxford when it came out during the war, and later had even 'grappled with Hayek's other work, notably *The Constitution of Liberty*'.[7] Both believed as I have suggested in the effectiveness of the traditional motives that activate people, that is self-interest and commitment to family and nation, and thus both believed in the power of the free market. Perhaps it is representative of the difference between Eureka College and Oxford University that Mrs Thatcher was generally more hard-headed about these ruling ideas than Ronald Reagan. Reagan seemed to believe that reducing taxes to give a larger role to economic incentives would be costless. He could cut taxes, and have enough in increased revenue from a higher level of economic activity to increase spending on the military and to balance the budget. He had authority from some economists to believe this, a doctrine expressed in the famous Laffer curve, and which asserted that increasing taxes reduces revenues, that reducing them will bring an increase in revenues as economic activity rises and tax-avoidance schemes become less necessary. Reagan never gave up his faith, insisting that the enormous budget deficits which became a fixture of the Reagan regime – and remain a fixture of the Bush regime – were the fault of Congress, and that were his budget proposals to be accepted there would be balanced budgets.

Mrs Thatcher took balanced budgets more seriously. As Peter Jenkins puts it, in the introduction to the American edition of *Mrs. Thatcher's Revolution:*

> She had never been a supply-sider and it is this more than anything else that sets Thatcherism apart from Reaganomics. She remained an old-fashioned fiscal conservative. A tax-cutter, yes, for cutting taxes was a way to sharpen the incentives to enterprise, but she never came to believe, with the supply-siders around Ronald Reagan, that tax cuts would increase revenue to cover borrowing . . . 'We don't have to choose between inflation and unemployment – they go hand in hand', declared Reagan in 1981. In her seminal budget of that year Margaret Thatcher chose fiscal rectitude, and throughout her first term rising unemployment was one of the hallmarks of Thatcherism.[8]

Of course Reagan's economic advisers included fiscal conservatives too, but they were never able to break through his sunny insistence that no hardship was ever necessary. In the event, unemployment rose as the result of the effort to curb inflation in the first years of the Reagan presidency to the highest levels since the depression, and if it came down rapidly thereafter it was undoubtedly in part because of the enormous budget deficits, which still continue. In Britain on the other hand, unemployment came down much more slowly, deficits were more moderate, but a balanced budget, inconceivable in the United States, eventually became a budget surplus.

Mrs Thatcher is harder-headed, and harder, than Ronald Reagan. But she would have to be. The difference reflects the differences between two individuals, but they also reflect the fact that they were operating in very different political systems, and in nations with very different locations on the curve of decline in world influence. These differences undoubtedly played a major role in bringing two such different persons to leadership in two nations, each coming with similar ideas and a similar mission, that is to reduce the state's role and to enhance individual and private enterprise. It is the difference in hard-headedness and hardness, not so much in the master ideas, that most sharply strikes the American.

Three elements of difference in the situation of Britain and the United States are particularly evident to the American observer. One is the role of Parliament and party in Britain, compared to Congress and party in the United States. The second is the difference in relationship between national and local government in Britain, and national and State and local government in the United States. The third is the difference of role in the world. The first two differences, one would expect, should naturally lead to a more decisive role for leadership in Britain than in the United States, and greater opportunity to implement a programme. The third, one would expect to lead to more decisive leadership in the United States. The expectations resulting from the first two differences were fulfilled: Mrs Thatcher was an infinitely tougher and more energetic leader, implementing almost unrelentingly the programmes she had said she would carry out, refusing to flinch in the face of great hostility, following a course which never brought her the support of the majority of public opinion. The expectations resulting from the third difference were quite belied by the course of events: the contrast is as enormous as that between the scale of effort and the danger involved in retaking the Falklands and invading Grenada.

The leader of a party in Britain runs for office on the basis of a party manifesto which is taken very seriously: victory means there will be a majority in the House of Commons bound to follow the party position and the party leader as Prime Minister. There is no such accumulation of power and responsibility in the hands of the President. He does not even play any substantial role in shaping the party platform, though by the time it is drawn up it is known who the party candidate will be. The party platform is a combination of carefully calculated electoral appeals and sops to various party elements. As it is irresponsible, so may the President who runs on it be irresponsible. It is not taken seriously, except as it indicates what kind of appeal the party is making, whom it hopes to attract, whom it is willing to give up. Since it is likely that the Presidency and the Congress (or at least one house of it) will be in the hands of separate parties, and since in any case the President cannot control Congressmen of his party, there is no real commitment that the platform on which the President runs can or will be carried out, though it is true that a statement in the platform will give the interest group most involved in putting it there some talking points in pushing the commitment with the new administration. And of course Congressmen wield much greater independent power than the British MPs and can ignore party platforms.

An American visitor is astonished to see that party manifestos are front-page news in Britain, but then quickly realises why it must be so: the party *may* win, and if it does, that will be *policy*; a Prime Minister, with a Cabinet entirely subject to the programme and the leadership of the Prime Minister, and a parliamentary party representation that almost never breaks with party leadership, are all in hand to put the policy into effect. It is rather sobering. There is nothing like it in the United States. It must, one would think, lead to greater sobriety in party leaders. They know what they are bound to, and they know that if they win they will have the power to do it, except insofar as they can plead international pressures (balance of payment crises, for example) which make it impossible. But much of the manifesto will not be subject to such influences.

Thus one would think ideas have to be taken more seriously. They cannot be used only to attract votes, because one must face the consequence that one will be expected to implement one's promises if one comes to power.

The promises in American party platforms are generally vaguer and more evasive, vaguer because the political situation of divided powers will not permit decisive action, more evasive because in the absence of this ability to act decisively one might as well make an electoral appeal even if there is little intention or will to carry it out (e.g., a promise to move the American Embassy in Israel from Tel Aviv to Jerusalem).

On occasion in the United States the platform and campaign speeches seem to make an unambiguous promise, and the power exists to carry it out, or so it appears, simply with executive and

Presidential power alone. What happens in such cases in the United States is revealing. One issue that has persisted in American politics now for almost twenty years is that of affirmative action, preferences in the employment or promotions of persons on the basis of race or sex. The strongest support of affirmative action is an Executive Order and supporting regulations, going back to the time of Presidents Johnson and Nixon, affecting all Federal contractors, that is, all those who do business with the Federal government (which includes not only all large businesses but hospitals, colleges and universities, etc.), and requiring them to have affirmative action plans, overseen by an agency of the Department of Labor, the Office of Federal Contract Compliance Programs. There are other supports of affirmative action: sometimes Congress requires that a certain percentage of contracts in a programme go to minority contractors or subcontractors; many states and cities have similar requirements, adopted on the basis of local minority political weight; in cases of demonstrated discrimination courts will impose hiring and promotion quotas on public and private employers, and even in the absence of such demonstrations employers will accept supposedly voluntary 'consent decrees' to hire or promote fixed percentages or numbers of minorities, enforced by courts, to avoid litigation.

There is thus the characteristic mix of powers — executive, Congressional, judicial, state and local – that we find in almost all policy domains in the United States. But one key actor, the Federal government, has the power to modify its executive orders and change its practices. All it requires is a 'stroke of the pen'. That phrase is taken from a promise by Senator John F. Kennedy when he was running for President, to eliminate by a 'stroke of the pen' all racial discrimination in Federal and Federally-assisted housing programmes. He was criticised and mocked because it took more than two years to get him to lift his pen, and even then the modification in Federal rules disappointed many civil rights advocates. The 'stroke of the pen' refers then to a Presidential action that is solely within Presidential power – neither Congress nor courts can prevent him.

In eight years of the Reagan presidency, however, on an issue on which promises had been clear, about which he himself was deeply concerned, nothing was done, and the Federal Executive Order and regulations were identical when he left office to what they were when he entered office. As Gary L. McDowell writes:

Ronald Reagan pledged to eliminate racial quotas when he ran for the presidency in 1980. The Republican Party platform unambiguously criticized 'bureaucratic regulations which rely on quotas, ratios, and numerical requirements to exclude some individuals in favor of others.' The party's candidate was even more forceful. 'We must not allow,' Ronald Reagan said, the 'noble concept of equal opportunity to be distorted into federal guidelines or quotas which require race, ethnicity or sex – rather than ability and qualifications – to be the principal factor in hiring or education' . . . It is therefore ironic that President Reagan left intact a federal policy of racial quotas.[9]

What happened reflects both forces common to American and British politics, and some differences: in this case, the Labor Department resisted the Justice Department's efforts to change the Executive Order, arguing that the issue had been losing saliency, that it could modify the effects of the order through its enforcement procedures, and that the political costs – the attack that could be expected from civil rights advocates in Congress and the national press – would be too great. The issue thus never came before President Reagan for decision. Undoubtedly the elements of political prudence that prevented the commitment from being carried out would have weight even in Britain. But it is inconceivable that such an issue would not have been brought to Mrs Thatcher and it is likely, in view of her record, that she might have said, prudence be damned. The great distance of President Reagan from issues as they were being fought out in his administration was in part owing to his own temperament, as Mrs Thatcher's deep involvement in issues was in part owing to hers. But might one not expect a system in which the Prime Minister is a parliamentary leader engaged in debate and give-and-take, face-to-face with opponents, to shape a leader very different from a system in which the President has never been involved in such an experience, whether as a Congressman, or state governor, or appointed official?

The second difference I have referred to is the role of state and local government. There is of course no independent constitutional role for local government in Britain. The matter is more complicated when it comes to Northern Ireland, Scotland, and Wales, but whatever the force of regional differences these historic nations are constitutionally in a much weaker position than the 'sovereign states' of the American union. What is striking, aside from the constitutional difference, is the deference to local powers in the United States even in the absence of constitutional protection. States are sovereign, and thus may reshape local government. They almost never do so in the United States. It is inconceivable that states would redraw the boundaries of local communities for greater efficiency, as was done when metropolitan authorities were created in Britain, or for political reasons, as was done when they were abolished by Mrs Thatcher. Whether this was right or wrong, better or worse for local services, would not enter into the situation in the United States: it just would not be done. Thus the United States has a complication of local government and local powers that can be found nowhere else. Some local governments are run by mayors, some by commissions, some have councils elected from districts, some have councils elected at large, most school boards are elected, but some are appointed, some have taxing power and some do not, and so on, and the state rarely intervenes in all this.

There can be national policies in Britain to reform education, or the medical profession and the hospital system, or the legal profession, and thus the initiatives now being carried out to reshape the great historic professions of medicine and law must strike an American with amazement. Even our states, despite the fact that they have such powers in these fields (or they might – we would have to have that tested in the courts, as everything is), would not dream of such sweeping reforms. States would never dictate a curriculum for schools, though they fuss around at the edges – they may approve textbooks, or require a course in American history, or one on drug education, or driver training, but most of the curriculum is untouched. That has recently changed somewhat. Our own great wave of education reform in the 1980s may have been stimulated to some extent by the report of a presidential commission which received great publicity, but the commission proposed no specific measures for the Federal government, or indeed state governments. The reforms that have taken place make a very ragged progress through the fifty states. Many states now require passage of state tests for high-school diplomas, some now require certain high-school subjects for admission to public colleges and universities. Nor are the reforms led by the Secretary of Education, but rather by some progressive state governors who reflect public and business opinion and have been influenced by a few conservative educational reformers, who, as in England, are divided between those calling for more freedom from government requirements, and those calling for higher common standards.

The federal government has, it is true, drawn great powers to itself since the 1930s, and they were increased in the 1960s and 1970s as an American modified version of the welfare state came into being. But there is little that the Federal government administers directly itself, aside from Social Security (old age and disability pensions). Almost everything else – welfare and social service programmes, housing programmes, education in all its spheres, health programmes – despite the substantial Federal funds that flow to these areas, are in the hands of the states, or local government. Federal regulations can go far toward implementing a vision, and indeed they have. But the Reagan vision has operated more by cutting funds than by introducing sweeping reforms. If one takes a somewhat conspiratorial approach, one can argue it has engineered such a huge deficit that it is hard for Congress to add more funds to old programmes and start new ones. To some extent the Reagan administration has modified social policies in the direction of its free-market philosophy and its espousal of traditional values. We have had a slow movement toward imposing more responsibility on parents receiving welfare, and we have had the encouragement of housing vouchers rather than publicly-financed building in housing, though the scale of this is small, and one cannot say any great changes have been implemented.[10]

The greatest impact of the Reagan reforms has indeed been through the restriction of funds, and one result, which I think is quite different from Britain, has been a surprising creativity in states and local government in adapting to the decline of Federal funds and their associated requirements. States and local government have been doing things they would never have attempted had the Federal funds continued to flow. Thus they have devised means to launch great enterprises of urban renewal and large housing programmes, and have discovered to their astonishment that using state powers of assemblage, tax incentives, some modest grants, and working with local private entrepreneurs, they can launch enterprises that they once believed only the Federal government would make possible. Of course in our diversity of states and cities it is hard to make generalizations, but certainly this is true in New York State and City, where Battery Park City has been developed entirely without Federal funds or oversight, as has been a 5 billion dollar city housing rehabilitation and building programme. Canary Wharf and other major urban redevelopment undertakings in Britain and the successful privatisation of huge public enterprises demonstrate the same in

England. It has turned out we do not need great public funds to redevelop cities. We have discovered, as we have seen in privatisation and large corporate takeovers, that huge private reserves of capital can be tapped, if government allows more market freedom.

As in the case of the separation of powers at the Federal level, the separation of powers horizontally has the same effect in shaping different leaders in Britain and the United States, and along the same lines: British leaders cannot so easily escape power and responsibility.

Because of the differences in political structure, the role of ideas in politics in Britain and the US seems to me quite different. British think-tanks emphasise pamphlets, American ones studies. The 'transmission belt' from ideas to implementation is shorter and more direct in Britain than the United States. In the United States, we seem to favour more analysis, and at length. One reason must be that our political diversity makes matters so much more complex that we have to study not only what the Federal government does or might do but what the courts are up to, what Congress is doing, what fifty states are doing, what hundreds of cities are doing, how what the Federal government does may influence states and local government. Because there is one strong centre for policy in Britain, the discussion is sharper and more focussed. To move from the lengthy monographs favoured by Brookings and the American Enterprise Institute to the crisp papers and proposals of the Institute for Economic Affairs, the Centre for Policy Studies and the Social Affairs Unit is like a dash of cold water in the face for an American, and rather refreshing. We do not debate policy proposals in the United States in pamphlets. One reason must be the differences in the structure of government.

The third difference I have referred to in the situation that faces a leader in Britain and the United States is the difference in international role. The United States, whatever its relative decline in economic and military power, still plays a world role far more extensive than that of Britain. American presidents tend I think to become absorbed with international affairs not only because they cannot avoid them but also because this is an area in which they have relatively a greater freedom to act, even if one steadily circumscribed by Congress. But whatever the institutional and situational differences between Britain and the United States, one cannot ignore the individual factor. Having devoted so much space to the institutional and constitutional factors that make a British Prime Minister different from an American President, one cannot avoid noting that this British Prime Minister was characterised by a steely determination to carry out policies she thought right, and that this President was a rather hands-off leader, pointing out a direction, occasionally insisting on it, but hardly committed to doing the unpopular thing even if he thought it right. Grenada was just the right crisis for such a President: there was no conceivable danger in taking strong action. One hesitates to imagine what a Reagan reaction to something equivalent to the Falklands crisis would have been.

The ideas on economic and social policy that dominated the Thatcher and Reagan administrations bore a great similarity. They had been shaped by policy analysts in the United States and Britain who had been influenced by the same thinkers, who had fairly close relations with each other, and who influenced each other. The ideas they propagated, largely developed in the two great English-speaking democracies, have had a remarkable influence, finding a sympathetic response in France, even though it elected in 1981 (and has since re-elected) a Socialist President, and some response in the rest of the European community. Some of these countries, however, seem able to combine a highly developed welfare state and a strong government role in the economy with a high rate of economic and productivity growth, and have not been afflicted by the decline in manufacturing exports that has characterised both Britain and the United States.

The general argument in favour of giving greater freedom to traditional human motives for self-improvement, providing incentives to encourage it, and depending to a greater extent on the free market and individual entrepreneurship, has had perhaps its most surprising influence on Communist nations, which now struggle to overcome their economic backwardness. Perhaps as surprising has been the influence of these ideas in some developing countries. 'Desperate, Latin Nations Discover the Free Market', reads a headline in the *New York Times*, and Mrs Thatcher is given proper credit:

> The shift toward the free-market approach comes after Latin Americans watched from the sidelines as the world economy grew during the 1980s . . . In Latin America, as Europe, free-market ideology is called liberalism . . . Said Roberto Campos, a Brazilian senator who has long advocated privatization, 'Liberalism was implanted as a theory in the 1970s. It came to power with Reagan and Thatcher in the 1980s. Now it may be Latin America's turn in the 1990s'.[11]

The power of liberalism as an idea was based of course on the failure of other ideas. Communist state direction and control as a means to a growing and productive economy failed. The ideal of the all-embracing welfare state failed to hold public opinion in Britain and the United States (matters were different on the Continent). Dependency theory and dependence on foreign aid failed as a means to economic growth for developing countries, as P. T. Bauer has relentlessly demonstrated. But resurgent liberalism, as the French and Latin Americans call it, has not yet decisively demonstrated its superiority. It did better than its critics expected in the 1980s in the United Kingdom and the United States, but great problems still face the economies of those countries. Whether they can continue to have growing economies as they lose much of their manufacturing base to other countries, developed and developing; whether a growing and productive economy can be based to a large extent on services; whether their depressed areas can make the shift from obsolete manufacturing industries to new industries; how they will deal with the social problems that are in some degree an accompaniment to greater freedom and individualism and the weakening of traditional social norms: these are all questions to which there is no answer yet. An *Economist* survey of 'Business in Britain' (20 May 1989) was titled 'The End of the Beginning', following Winston Churchill. It is not at all clear what follows now, and whether the surprising economic recovery of Britain in the 1980s – and the more ambiguous record of Reagan in the United States – can be sustained in the 1990s.

After their great success of the 1980s, the ideas that played so large a role in determining the content of both Reaganism and Thatcherism have the problem of maintaining their vigour after ten years of closeness to power, and of adapting to an ever-changing set of issues in society, the economy, and in politics.

One wonders about their adequacy for these new tasks. One element of difference between the Thatcher and Reagan epochs was the presence of the 'moral majority' in the United States, and the surprising power of such issues as abortion, and moral issues generally, based on a powerful Christian fundamentalism in America. There was no real equivalent in Britain. A key challenge for the 1990s, which this movement emphasised, even if it had no really effective policy to deal with it, is the upsetting and devastating change in social behaviour that afflicts the big cities of the United States, and perhaps in only slightly lesser degree Britain's big cities. The American visitor in Britain reads of and sees on television stories of crime in the underground, of the spread of drugs, of graffiti and crime in council housing estates, all of which he finds familiar, but which is, blessedly for Britain, on a much smaller scale than in the United States. The revival of conservative thought, whether in Britain or the United States, has had little to offer for such problems, except for exhortation and a nostalgia for a time when all this was different. (Leftists and liberals have had even less to offer.) Nor is it the kind of issue that traditional conservative thought and free-market economics has ever had occasion to address. These upsetting changes in behaviour influence the quantity and quality of the labour force and the ability of nations to compete internationally. They offer a new challenge to the revival of conservative thought, which may on occasion get to the margins of such issues, but has nothing like the fully formulated positions it has developed in the sphere of economics. The debates over education and social policy in Britain and the United States will test to what extent those who so successfully promoted their vision for the economy can respond to what are truly new challenges.

Notes and References

1. Craig R. Whitney, 'Thatcher's New Health Plan: An Outcry on All Sides', *New York Times* (24 June 1989): A1.
2. For example, Joseph Featherstone, *Schools Where Children Learn* (New York, 1971).
3. See Richard E. Caves and Associates, *Britain's Economic Prospects* (The Brookings Institution, 1968): 493–4.
4. Peter Jenkins, *Mrs. Thatcher's Revolution* (Cambridge, Mass., 1988): 111. The criticism that the Labour Party was more responsive to government employees than the great majority of the people was also made from the left: 'Labour leaders did not see education as a *popular activity* to stimulate and guide, but as state institutions for the professionals to run', Richard Johnson, 'Thatcherism and English education: breaking the mould, or confirming the pattern?', *History of Education*, 18 (1989): 96, Johnson's italics.
5. Peter Jenkins, *Mrs. Thatcher's Revolution*: 111.
6. Joel Krieger, *Reagan, Thatcher, and the Politics of Decline* (Oxford, 1986) : 76–8, 80–1.
7. Hugo Young, *One of Us* (London, 1988): 22.
8. Jenkins, *Mrs. Thatcher's Revolution*: xii.
9. Gary L. McDowell, 'Affirmative Inaction', *Policy Review* (Spring 1989): 32.
10. See Nathan Glazer, *The Limits of Social Policy* (Cambridge, Mass.,

1988) Chapter 3.
11. James Brooke, 'Desperate, Latin Nations Discover the Free Market',
    New York Times (30 July 1989): E2.

2 The History of Britain: a Composite State in a *Europe des Patries*?

Jonathan Clark

For most people, a sense of national identity is now formed less by economics, social policy or theology than by history, our shared understanding of collective origins and long-affirmed purposes. This shared understanding is of ancient growth, and is not easily or quickly reformulated. Nevertheless, it has ultimately depended on academic enquiry, and academic history can be an important analogue or anticipation of public events. So it has been in the last decade. Is Britain special? Can she integrate into continental Europe? Does Scots or Welsh nationalism threaten the essence of an English achievement? Has traditional class-based politics disintegrated? New answers to these questions were to be found in the historiography of recent years.

The history of the British Isles is obviously too diverse to be bound by a single formula or fashion: scores of scholarly initiatives in specialised areas are always threatening to create new patterns of interpretation, even if most of these initiatives take place at some remove from the public arena. Others, however, break the surface of general attention, not only revealing to an alarmed public some unsuspected hazards to navigation, but reminding us of that submarine geography of reefs and shoals which influences the tides and currents of national events. This chapter explores the implications of three such controversies.

They were part of a much wider rethinking. In the 1980s, British historiography found the conventional landmarks shifting. One commentator observed:

> The state of political and ideological flux today, the disillusionment with many inherited political programmes and their theoretical supports, seems reflected in the individual historical eclecticism of some flexible or younger historians, in their willingness to discard old alignments wholesale and rewrite, and in their reluctance to allow themselves to be categorized into some of the old left and

right positions which have ossified under the weight of decades of common room or pub chat. [New approaches] all diverge significantly from the compartmentalization, periodization, and emphasis on watershed or revolutionary bench marks of much historical writing of the '60s and '70s.[1]

Three historical initiatives in particular have recently intruded into public attention and provoked reflection, or excused controversy, on the relation between academic scholarship and the present-day commitments of its audience. It was not least their modern implications and resonance which linked seemingly far-removed discussions of the existence or absence of a mediaeval peasantry; of the parliamentary origins of the Civil War; and of the claims of Hanoverian England to rank as an ancien-regime state. Each of these three controversies had implications for England's relations with Scotland, Ireland and Wales, and for the place of these four societies within an EEC conceived in rival visions either as a *Europe des patries* or as a supranational unity.

All three controversies took their rise from the intellectual climate of the late 1970s, a time when a certain consensus was painfully disintegrating in many areas of national life. The first was triggered in 1978 by Alan Macfarlane's systematic denial of the main prop of the orthodox Marxist model of English feudalism,[2] the idea that mediaeval England was a 'peasant society' of a classic type: communal, technologically backward, a subsistence economy of self-sufficient local units structured by the extended family, its members tied to land held in collective ownership, without geographical mobility, their standard of living held down by the inexorable pressure of population on resources; a static and restrictive society which was finally transformed by a series of revolutionary changes as part of a process of 'modernisation'.

Macfarlane's picture of mediaeval English society was quite different, and strikingly modern. Land (the chief factor of production) was held in full private ownership, treated as a commodity and exchanged in an active land market. Rational accounting procedures went with the profit motive and an acquisitive ethic: men were market-oriented, thrifty, accumulators of capital for their farms or small businesses.[3] The labour market too was already developed: upward and downward social mobility were matched by geographical mobility as men adapted themselves to the market in search of employment. Wealth was widely diffused, and an unusually large middling order bridged the gap between rich and poor.

Far from 'capitalism' emerging in a transition from 'feudalism' in the early modern period, these reified categories dissolved under examination into truisms: capitalism existed in England, since the thirteenth century at least, in what Macfarlane implied were its essentials: possessive and affective individualism. It was a thesis supported by quantifiable data on, among other things, the nuclear family, and the family was conspicuous in its proof. Macfarlane accepted the thesis of Wrigley and Schofield[4] that the dominant variable in English demography had been not mortality, but fertility; and fertility (governed by age at marriage and the percentage of the population marrying) was related to the Reverend Thomas Malthus's 'preventive checks'. Since the thirteenth century, marriage had been based on the choice of the two parties and on their mutual love, rather than on the demands of community or kin, property or production.[5] Moreover, Christianity made a marriage indissoluble, even if childless. Such conventions amounted to a powerful system of moral and customary constraints, accurately codified by Malthus. England evidently succeeded as a society by its disciplines and by the integrity of its family structure, as family limitation made possible standards of living far higher than those known elsewhere. If Malthus were right and Marx wrong, claimed Macfarlane, 'there is only a choice between war, famine and disease on the one hand, and individualistic capitalism on the other'.[6] It was a conclusion on which hostile reviewers seized. 'Mrs. Thatcher could not have put it better' was Lawrence Stone's verdict in the *Times Literary Supplement*.

If these insights into the social structure of mediaeval England are valid, our view of the wider nexus of ideas known as 'individualism' is modified. No longer can we posit its emergence as a process chronologically located in some period of transition from 'feudalism' to 'capitalism'. Rather, individualism in respect of ownership, economic enterprise and the family was there all along, fully consistent with strong structures and ideologies of political authority in a variety of forms over several centuries. The traditional dichotomy between individualism and collectivism is, therefore, largely a false antithesis: a strong state has been more the political guarantor of economic individualism than its subverter. The antithesis could more accurately be reframed as one between economic individualism and the corporatism of intermediate agencies, from mediaeval barons and guilds to twentieth-century local government units and trade unions.

If there was no transition from 'feudalism' to 'capitalism', how did that square with the traditional Marxist scenario of the civil war of the 1640s as a 'bourgeois revolution' of the classic type? Here again, historians of early-Stuart politics have been dismantling the key components both of Whig–Liberal and of Marxist orthodoxies:[7] the idea that the early-Stuart House of Commons organised itself and stood forward to seize initiatives, culminating in a bid for sovereignty on behalf of the 'rising' capitalist middle class. Democratic self-government combined with popular sovereignty was the evolving goal, it was once assumed, as 'the people' increasingly used the Commons as the natural instrument for the redress of grievances. From R. H. Tawney's famous study *Religion and the Rise of Capitalism* (1926), socialists too had accepted this Whig account of 'superstructural' parliamentary politics as the natural symptom of 'underlying' causes, as the rise of a (capitalist) bourgeoisie challenged and finally unseated a (feudal) aristocracy. Thanks to these disruptive forces, claimed the Old Guard historians, England's institutions of government collapsed *before* the outbreak of fighting in 1642, not as a result of the war.

These Whig and Marxist theses had been contested by Geoffrey Elton and Hugh Trevor-Roper since the 1950s, but the historiographical revolution really dates from 1979. In a consensus-breaking book, Conrad Russell demoted early-Stuart Parliaments from the role conventionally assigned to them and inaugurated another classic historiographical controversy.[8] Its side-effects were apparently varied but unexpectedly coherent. First, it focused and made inescapable for political historians the mounting evidence that the Civil War was not a conflict between two types of men or two economic forces, north and south, stagnating and prospering, feudal and capitalist: religion rather than economic function emerged as the major variable in explaining allegiance. Social hierarchy complemented economic endeavour rather than being antithetical to it. Political conflicts were rooted in ideology rather than in objective, structural, class identity. Second, the traditional grievances against early-Stuart government, including the nature and incidence of taxation, assumed a much lesser significance. Taxation controversies now appeared as symptoms rather than causes. Third, it displaced the Whig-constitutionalist scenario which credited the Westminster Parliament (and, especially, 'the Opposition') with a linear urge to seize and implement popular sovereignty: parliamentary forces opposed to the King's ministers were revealed as fragmented, unconstructive, lacking a credible ideology, preoccupied with their internal conflicts. Executive authority was rehabilitated as a lasting principle in national life, no longer discredited by an ancient democratic critique or open to dismissal as reactionary absolutism. Fourth, the institutions of local government were revealed as inefficient, recalcitrant and a source of conflict both with the executive and in Parliaments. Fifth, if domestic English discontents were insufficient of themselves to produce a rebellion *in England*, attention now moved to the real rebellions in Scotland and Ireland which provoked a breakdown of English government. England's relations with Scotland, Ireland and Wales returned to the historical agenda.[9] The resonance of these five conclusions with the political conflicts of the 1980s was remarkable.

Such an outcome focused attention, too, on one feature of Alan Macfarlane's work: it concerned England alone. Its claims of long continuities in English social history, strong though the case was, were strengthened by the omission of the different and more discontinuous track records of Scotland, Ireland and Wales. These differences highlighted themes which Macfarlane's analysis had omitted: the social forms which he reconstructed on the basis of data on demography, property ownership and law took on a much more specifically English connotation once issues of religion, ethnicity and politics were added. These considerations made it less convincing to describe Macfarlane's middle ages as 'modern' in a way which removed the need for explanations of fundamental change. The problem area therefore shifted into a later age. If England's seventeenth century was as described by Russell and the 'revisionists' rather than Christopher Hill and Lawrence Stone, what were the implications for later centuries?[10] An attempt was indeed made to save the Marxist analysis by re-locating it chronologically, making 1688 perform the role previously performed by 1642:[11] but if this were unsuccessful, another alternative opened up. The eighteenth century might be redescribed as a traditional society, proceeding by devolution from mediaeval and seventeenth-century England instead of divided from it by a transformative revolutionary experience which reduced the Hanoverian era to a seedbed for the Victorian.[12] The whole notion of revolutionary modernism was being forced into later and later timeframes.

Here began a third historical controversy[13] which therefore impinged directly on modern problems. A reformulation of English history in the period 1660–1832 had a special significance: it threatened, by explaining historically, a series of dominant intellectual categories on the timeless validity of which the success of social democracy since 1945 had been premised. Radicalism and liberalism, democracy and class all assumed a different appearance when viewed from the perspective of the world before 1832. A range of institutions and policies stood to lose their mandate if their validating categories could be delegitimised.

In an exactly analogous process, the same had happened in the historiography of the French Revolution: 'What has been displaced', noted one historian succinctly, 'is the idea of a "bourgeois revolution" in which "capitalism" overthrew "feudalism" ';[14] and similar implications might be explored for continental Europe also. Did the old order, then, survive? It was an unwelcome conclusion. From the viewpoint of post-1945 historiography and values, the ancien regime had a particular connotation: social hierarchy appeared as inequality rather than mobility; the dominant religion of a confessional state appeared as a threat to moral pluralism rather than an affirmation of widely sanctioned values; a strong monarchy seemed to be an agency of executive tyranny rather than a referee guaranteeing fair competition within the law. Now these perspectives on social formations were called in question. So too were assumptions about parliamentary politics. The model of English politics sustained by political scientists since 1945 had been secular and consensual: a two-party system had given expression to minor swings in the pendulum of class politics, but the consensus was undisturbed by religion, ethnicity, nationalism or doubts about the exercise of executive power.[15] Now these problems returned to the historical agenda at the same time as they returned to the agenda of political scientists.[16]

It might be concluded, from these three historical controversies, that England had built a strong centralising state on a dynamic, individualist society. Yet these features of dynamism and individualism clearly had to be consistent with manifest evidence throughout English history of the changing forms of authority and hierarchy, status and deference. Along with individualism in the realm of property, law and the family went firm social control, as firm under Reformation Protestantism as under mediaeval Catholicism, as firm again under ancien-regime Anglicanism.[17] The manorial court closely supervised the economic life of the mediaeval village, as the church court did its social life; both forms of supervision were concentrated after 1660 in the hands of the Anglican JP, the archetypal commercialised landowner. Status and custom retained their hold in England because they were largely consistent with the imperatives of the market.

The most generally prevalent England images of the social order, as illuminated by the new scholarship already noted, were ones of hierarchy rather than class or caste: a hierarchy divinely or meritocratically sanctioned, accommodating extreme diversity and mobility, rather than the Marxist concept of objectively and inescapably determined class or the Whig assumption of indelible, imprescriptable caste. Since the 1970s, the weakening of both socialist and Whig–Liberal analysis, and voting figures in successive elections, have encouraged speculation of the end of class-based society.[18] From the perspective of present-day historiography, it can be claimed that neither class nor caste were ever objective realities in England: they were assumptions and descriptive categories which were propagated as part of distinct ideologies. As those ideologies disintegrated, their images of the social order similarly dissolved and revealed a far more ancient pattern beneath.

Historians who recorded that pattern increasingly dispensed with the ideas of England's alleged uniqueness which both Whig-constitutionalist and Marxist scenarios had sustained: as Macfarlane characterised the assumption,

> England starts in the century after the Norman invasion as a poor, rural society, thinly inhabited by 'peasants' and lords, similar in many ways to its Continental neighbours. Then, by some strange accident which has never yet been satisfactorily explained, sometime between the later sixteenth century and the mid-eighteenth it took a different course from its neighbours.[19]

True, England differed from the 'classical' peasant societies of eastern Europe, Russia and Asia; but the removal of the peasant model from English historiography reopened the question of England's affinities with the equally nucleated societies of central, northern and western Europe.[20] So too did the thesis that the political and ideological structures of the England of 1660–1832 were those of an unrevolutionised monarchical absolutism: if so, England may have had stronger similarities than dissimilarities to the ancien-regime states of the same region. These possible affinities reopened the question of the nature of English nationalism: 'English' and 'British' were no longer synonymous.

This train of argument led to the conclusion that the British state had one important feature in common with many of its continental rivals. Like France, Spain, and Austria, it had been constructed from a number of disparate components, as an ancient heartland had been reinforced by the addition of marches, principalities or provinces.[21] Assembled in a dynastic age, and complete only with the Union with Ireland in 1801, the United Kingdom has been defended with the quite different ideologies of liberal constitutionalism and socialism in the subsequent decades. After their fading, the state is again perceived to confront its component parts with a claim of absolute sovereign authority. Yet how could it be legitimate unless that authority had survived the vicissitudes of the Civil War and Glorious Revolution? Historical scholarship on the eighteenth century now offered an answer.

Even G. M. Trevelyan, the archetypal Whig historian, did not hesitate to write of 'the English people' as 'a racial and cultural unit'. Patrician Whig and Liberal assumptions about caste were part of the same set of attitudes. In recent scholarship, by contrast, it appears that English national consciousness had more to do with a shared history and with religion (once in terms of formal sectarian allegiance, now in terms of subliminal assumptions about human nature and values), less to do with doctrines of race (caste) or imperialism (class). The shared history in turn had most to do with the rule of law, the defence of the individual by the state, rights of private property, freedom of trade, a stable currency, a legal system premised on Christian morality, and a nuclear family in which patriarchal authority was bound up with affection and wise rule rather than the automatic tyranny of the eldest. It had little to do with such cultural formations as popular sovereignty, class consciousness, the cultural hegemony of the masses, devolved power, or the historical rootedness of such social formations as now characterise the 'plural society'.

Consequently, the social structure of such a society might well be summed up in the phrase 'authoritarian individualism',[22] a formation sustained by a variety of political systems from medieval mixed monarchy through Tudor and Stuart absolutism and the ancien regime of 1660–1832, and only obscured in the increasingly corporatist society of the twentieth century. The transitions between those systems were real, and involved fundamental changes in political structures and religious professions.[23] But beside them ran deep continuities which were merely reformulated in changing circumstances. Some of these continuities are quantifiable, like the stable long-term bastardy rankings of many regions,[24] or openly affirmed, like the lasting cultural traditions and identities of various immigrant groups. Others, and these by far the more important, were often overlooked because they are so prevalent, ordinary, the possession of the mass of

Englishmen.

Burke's doctrine of prescription appealed to just such an idea of long continuities in political and social life. There was a presumption in favour of established practices over untried projects of reform, because

> a nation is not an idea only of local extent and individual momentary aggregation, but it is an idea of continuity which extends in time as well as in numbers and in space. And this is a choice not of one day or one set of people, not a tumultuary and giddy choice; it is a deliberate election of ages and of generations; it is a constitution made by what is ten thousand times better than choice; it is made by the peculiar circumstances, occasions, tempers, dispositions, and moral, civil, and social habitudes of the people, which disclose themselves only in a long space of time.[25]

This was political rhetoric; historians in the last decade have sought ways of testing its validity as analysis.

These continuities became fully visible as distinct and special, not merely ordinary, once England's relations with Scotland, Ireland and Wales returned to the centre of historians' attention.[26] Far from England standing proxy for her three neighbours by virtue of having first blazed the trail (whether Whig-constitutionalist or Marxist) of historical evolution, it began to seem that England's distinctiveness could best be appreciated by the way she had impacted upon Scotland, Ireland and Wales. In the 1980s, historical attention turned to those aspects of Englishness which had been imposed on England's neighbours in past centuries. Apart from religion, little of this had to do with the deliberate imposition of representative democracy, language or culture; in general, it related to the introduction of English legal institutions, the elimination of local sources of authority like Scots clans, the extension of English commercial practices. This was most clear-cut in the case of Ireland, where memories of common clan-ownership of land persisted through the eighteenth century as an atavistic hatred of the expropriating English and an undying commitment to repossess ancient patrimonies. Capitalist agriculture failed over large areas to delete such political aims, rooted as they were in culture, language and religion.

Before the 1830s and after the 1970s, such confrontations might have an additional starkness: before, and after, the prevalence of Whig or Marxist analysis, such an imposition of a nexus of ideas was not mediated through the practice of compromise which was professed by English liberal constitutionalism, and any resentment it aroused was not capable of diversion against a reified international capitalism. In the 1970s and 1980s, the potential for Welsh and Scottish nationalism consequently grew.

The sources of Irish, Welsh and Scots nationalism have often been depicted by politicians in economic terms; but this has itself reflected the historiographical fashions of their times.[27] From today's perspective, ethnic, religious and cultural causes assume a greater prominence,[28] and despite the absence of any simple typology, economic arguments for national autarky have become more clearly visible as premised on the economic theories of protection, regulation, subsidy and control whose discrediting is explored elsewhere in this volume.[29] Such arguments have, as a result, not been particularly successful in inducing Welshmen and Scotsmen to demand political independence (as distinct from regional aid) in the 1980s: rather, they encouraged a residual support for the Labour Party. By the 1980s, even this was being eroded, as the Labour Party's continued refusal to exploit the national issue (even at a time of extreme tactical weakness) became inescapable.

In the world before 1979, the British gave their allegiance to a unitary state: but, according to conventional analysis, the working class gave allegiance to the state as reformable by socialism; the middle class, to the state as explicable by the liberal constitutional tradition. An indulgence of local customs and cultures merely acted as a safety valve. An element of devolution was not seen as a unique threat since the English heartland remained confident in its two ideologies, each of which explained the unitary outcome in advance. Where the Stuart and Hanoverian state had been repeatedly challenged by armed rebellion, this became much rarer after 1798. Apart from the independence of Catholic southern Ireland, Northern Ireland, Scotland and Wales remained remarkably quiescent until, in the 1970s, 'the threat of secession apparently eclipsed that of the class-struggle'.[30]

The agenda of English individualism had never been in itself sufficient, over many centuries, to reconcile England's provinces, neighbours or colonies. With it went another agenda, those unquantifiable achievements of culture and custom, art and affection, shared experience and historical rootedness that dignified an ancient state. Conquest was only part of English power: with the hope of military glory went the means of grace, as the English carried with them a view of man embodied in Anglican Christianity. This had been both a persuasive, and a barrier, to assimilation. It was the conception of the ultimate goals of life which at the same time provided the greatest impetus to English expansion, following the Reformation, and the greatest stimulus to Scots, Irish and Welsh resistance. Of these, the last was the weakest: with the Act of 1562 providing for the translation of the Bible and for services in Welsh, the principality was lastingly incorporated with the Anglican ascendancy. The Presbyterian settlement of 1689 imposed on Soctland a church well-affected to the Whig regime. The end of the era of Anglican ascendancy in Ireland was marked by disestablishment in 1871, in Wales by disestablishment in 1920. Thereafter, the public relations of these neighbouring societies were, ostensibly at least, secularised.

If religion had provided one major source of conflict and discontinuity, the long-term continuities in the relations between these four societies were not ones of shared culture, custom or formal religion: England's hegemony over Scotland, Ireland and Wales had most to do with the extent to which England sought, or failed, to impose the components of 'authoritarian individualism'. It was an attempt blanketed at certain periods by the fashionability of three other doctrines, each sustained by the intelligentsia but with shallower populist roots. The nineteenth-century doctrine of purposeful constitutional evolution towards limited monarchy, religious disestablishment, cabinet government and, ultimately, a wider franchise contained elements of truth as a partial account of the inner dynamic of domestic English politics but was, in its general outline, the polemical reification of the Westminster tactics and goals of one party, the Liberals. It gained less credence in Scotland, Ireland or Wales, though it was current in those political cultures also. Similarly, late-nineteenth- and early-twentieth-century imperialism explained how, despite obvious differences, the Scots, Irish and Welsh had something of overriding importance in common with the English: they were equally members of an imperial ruling elite, and stood to profit equally from the enterprise of empire. This too had elements of truth: Scotland especially was a partner in imperial commerce; but England was the senior partner, and the imperial ideal was not warmly received in Ireland.

It has been correctly observed that the goal of the British Labour movement was always to win control of the state, not to deconstruct it. Socialism, as much as liberalism or imperialism, acted as an ideology of national unity. Yet socialism was not as neutral, in respect of national cultures, as it professed to be. In retrospect, after its partial dissolution, it becomes more evident that the twentieth-century socialist doctrine of capitalist exploitation and the international class solidarity of the exploited was similarly devised on the basis of an English model (initially, a Manchester model) and proved markedly less successful when applied to the contrasting experiences of Scotland, Ireland and Wales (though it struck deeper roots on Clydeside and on the South Wales coalfield than anywhere in England). In the 1960s and 1970s the disintegration of these three doctrines allowed the reassertion of separatist aspirations;[31] from 1979 these aspirations were defined over against authoritarian individualism, the claim that the individual's interests and material prosperity were best advanced within a strong unitary state devoted to economic freedoms, the rule of law, and the individual's emancipation from intermediate powers whether trade unions, local government, or the threatened agencies of regional nationalism.

England's past political relations with Scotland and Ireland had explored the opportunities and difficulties created by the existence of just such subordinate powers. In particular, constitutional controversy had focussed on the role of subordinate legislatures: the Edinburgh Parliament and the Dublin Parliament.[32] The recent experiment of Northern Ireland's Parliament (1921–72) was exceptional in expressing the will to union of Ulster Protestants: both the Dublin and Edinburgh Parliaments had pursued an opposite path. In those two cases, devolved administrative power and legislative authority had led, at moments of crisis, to bids for national automony which Westminster could not ultimately accommodate. Their abolition, Edinburgh with the Union of 1707, Dublin with the Union of 1801, was the analogous outcome. The Dublin, Edinburgh and Westminster Parliaments shared common characteristics: they contained little inbuilt urge to representational democracy, but a considerable drive to assert procedural autonomy. In Westminster's case, this produced a series of constitutional crises, of which 1776 was only the most notable and, from the English perspective, the least successful, as metropolitan authority attempted to assert itself over colonial assemblies.

In the 1980s, authoritarian individualism found its most controversial expression in the community charge, whose popular title – the poll tax – aptly recalled the mediaeval origins of English individualism. The victory of the Scottish Nationalist Party's candidate in the Govan by-election of November 1988 was widely ascribed to the priority of this single issue. The growing reality of the EEC, and the survival of socialist corporatism as a gloss on its bureaucratic coherence, gave a new potentiality to nationalism: devolution might now extend to independence within the EEC. To the champions of free trade, competition, deregulation and individualism, however, the prospect of an EEC containing irremovable socialist and nationalist enclaves was not acceptable. The prospect that a devolved Scottish assembly would take this route directed attention to the role of the Edinburgh Parliament before 1707.

While Westminster remained the only parliamentary arena, Scotland and Wales receded since the 1970s into a psephological backwater. The ascendancy first of liberal-constitutionalist and later of socialist ideology had meant that English society could be fragmented: a majority divided on class lines could form an electoral coalition with a variety of minorities, and thanks to inbuilt majorities in Scotland and Wales a Liberal, then a Labour government at Westminster was a goal often realised. The fading of class analysis tended to dissolve this coalition, partly reunited an English majority behind the economic benefits of authoritarian individualism, illustrated the insignificance of England's minorities, marginalised Labour's Pavlovian electorate in Scotland and Wales, and made Labour's Scots and Welsh seats more vulnerable to nationalist challenge.

Since the 1970s under both Labour and Conservative governments, the growing strength of Welsh and Scots nationalism has, paradoxically, occurred despite a modest and muted racial or cultural assertiveness from those societies. Linguistic and ethnic nationalism undoubtedly exists there, but on nothing like the scale of late-nineteenth-century Ireland: the main reasons for the recent emergence of Welsh and Scots issues appear to be political, and to concern negative developments within England more than positive forces within Wales or Scotland.[33]

In such a setting, authoritarian individualism (which might, on the surface, be a culturally non-specific doctrine, exportable to all countries) can take on the air of an aspect of English cultural hegemony. If class categories were still valid, it might be described in non-nationalist terms either as the economics of the capitalist elite or the morals of the lower middle class.[34] But the etiolation of both caste and class reawakens nationalism. A more historical understanding suggests that English authoritarian individualism embodies more deeply-rooted and historically persistent traits of English character.

Reactions, too, take forms more ancient than liberalism or socialism. Labour party allegiance in Scotland and Wales draws on Scots and Welsh nationalism, though both those things are increasingly bid for by overtly nationalist parties;[35] republican allegiance in Northern Ireland after 1798 was always related to Catholic sectarian identity. It is remarkable that traditional Marxist or socialist organisations were relatively unsuccessful in explaining, and therefore in exploiting, these centrifugal forces.[36] Southern Ireland's independence had been won in 1921 on the basis of ethnic and sectarian nationalism; Welsh and Scottish heavy industry had locked them into classic Labour Party (and, in the case of Glaswegian Scotland, even Marxist) politics until the collapse of the traditional industrial base in the late 1970s.

English, Scots, Irish and Welsh nationalisms were realities into the 1980s, then, and their historical rootedness was increasingly at the centre of historical enquiry. Less and less could they be explained away as temporary phases of, or obstacles to, capitalist or constitutionalist development. But historical enquiry revealed also that there had been no inexorable logic in nationalism any more than in capitalism or democracy. Welsh, Scots and Irish self-images and self-awareness had risen and fallen over the centuries, always susceptible to redefinition in new circumstances. The mere existence of provincial nationalism had never predetermined its victory over the unitary state. British and Irish history over many centuries suggested that a more powerful formula than nationalism, and a formula with which English nationalism at least might indeed be consistent, was that nexus of ideas now identified from some perspectives as authoritarian individualism. On its future fortunes seems now to depend the United Kingdom's integrity in a Europe which is increasingly evolving a rival ideology of corporatist supra-nationalism.

Notes and References

1. K. D. M. Snell, 'English Historical Continuity and the Culture of Capitalism: the Work of Alan Macfarlane', *History Workshop Journal*, 27 (1989): 154–63, at 155.
2. Alan Macfarlane, *The Origins of English Individualism: The Family, Property and Social Transition* (Oxford, 1978). The debate is reviewed, and criticisms addressed, in the same author's *The Culture of Capitalism* (Oxford, 1987). This approach characterises the work of the Cambridge Group for the History of Population and Social Structure, a school of

thought which may be dated in England from Peter Laslett's *The World We Have Lost* (London, 1965; 3rd edn, 1983). Some of the arguments of Macfarlane's *English Individualism* were anticipated in *The World We Have Lost*; but it was Macfarlane's book which attracted a storm of indignant criticism, since its historiographical element made its consequences for the old tradition inescapable.

3. 'Throughout town and country there was a pervasive emphasis on monetary values, on trade, profit and accumulation . . . England was truly a nation not only ruled by shopkeepers but with a generalised shopkeeper mentality': Macfarlane, *The Culture of Capitalism:* 146.

4. Summarised in E. A. Wrigley and R. S. Schofield, *The Population History of England 1541–1871* (London, 1981) and Wrigley and Schofield, 'English Population History from Family Reconstitution: Summary Results 1600–1799'. *Population Studies* 37 (1983): 157–84.

5. Kinship was weak: 'people were early independent of parental power and most relied mainly on their own efforts': Macfarlane, *The Culture of Capitalism:* 146.

6. Alan Macfarlane, *Marriage and Love in England: Modes of Reproduction, 1300–1840* (Oxford, 1986): 344. Malthus had written to refute William Godwin, 'who had argued that the abolition of private property and the equalization of wealth would lead to a balanced and harmonious world in which trouble and strife would fade away . . . Malthus' reply was that the central features of capitalism guaranteed stability and happiness' (323).

7. The discussion is ably surveyed, though from a Whig-constitutionalist perspective, in J. H. Hexter, 'The Early Stuarts and Parliament: Old Hat and the *Nouvelle Vague*', *Parliamentary History*, 1 (1982): 181–215.

8. Conrad Russell, 'Parliamentary History in Perspective, 1604–1629', *History*, 61 (1976): 1–27, and *Parliaments and English Politics 1621–1629* (Oxford, 1979).

9. Conrad Russell, 'The British Problem and the English Civil War', *History*, 72 (1987): 395–415.

10. This question is answered at length in J. C. D. Clark, *Revolution and Rebellion: State and Society in England in the Seventeenth and Eighteenth Centuries* (Cambridge, 1986).

11. As is argued in J. C. D. Clark, '1688 & All That', *Encounter*, 67 (January 1989): 14–17.

12. This thesis is advanced directly in J. C. D. Clark, *English Society 1688–1832: Ideology, Social Structure and Political Practice During the Ancien Regime* (Cambridge, 1985).

13. The debate may be followed in: J. G. A. Pocock, '1660 And All That: Whig-Hunting, Ideology and Historiography in the Work of Jonathan Clark', *The Cambridge Review* (October 1987): 125–8; Joanna Innes, 'Jonathan Clark, Social History and England's "Ancien Regime"', *Past & Present*, 115 (1987): 165–200; J. C. D. Clark, 'On Hitting the Buffers: the Historiography of England's Ancien Regime', *Past & Present*, 117 (1987): 195–207; Jeremy Black, 'England's "Ancien Regime"?', *History Today* (March 1988): 43–51; J. C. D. Clark, 'On Moving the Middle Ground: the Significance of Jacobitism in Historical Studies', in Eveline

Cruickshanks and Jeremy Black (eds), *The Jacobite Challenge* (Edinburgh, 1988): 177–88; David A. Bell, 'All The King's Men', *The New Republic* (18 January 1988): 36–40; Patrick Bahners, 'Der Historiker als Rebell', *Frankfurter Allgemeine Zeitung* (12 October 1988): 35; Philip Lawson, 'Hanoverian Studies: The Impact of Recent Trends On Parliamentary History', *Parliamentary History*, 7 (1988): 130–8; 'Symposium: Revolution and Revisionism', *Parliamentary History*, 7 (1988): 328–38; and the articles by J. E. Bradley, J. Money, J. A. Phillips and J. C. D. Clark, in *Albion*, 21 (3) (1989).

14. Gwyn Williams, *Artisans and Sans-Culottes: Popular Movements in France and Britain during the French Revolution* (London, 1968; 2nd edn, 1989): ix. Similarly, the American Revolution has been claimed as 'a revolution concerned far less with democracy than with the issue of a government of laws': Ian R. Christie, *Stress and Stability in Late Eighteenth-Century Britain: Reflections on the British Avoidance of Revolution* (Oxford, 1984): 13.

15. Classically in Samuel Beer, *Modern British Politics* (London, 1965).

16. Cf. the retractions expressed in Samuel Beer's *Britain Against Itself: The Political Contradictions of Collectivism* (London, 1982).

17. The most obvious domestic achievement of the absolute state, in England as elsewhere, was its increasingly successful defence of the lives, liberties and properties of its subjects against murder, violence and theft. Thanks to this success, in England, the homicide rate dropped precipitously in the sixteenth and early seventeenth centuries; so too did the incidence of criminal execution (Lawrence Stone, 'Interpersonal Violence in English Society 1300–1980', *Past & Present*, 101 (1983): 22–33; Philip Jenkins, 'From Gallows to Prison: the Execution Rate in Early Modern England', *Criminal Justice History*, 7 (1986): 51–71). These achievements, in other words, predated those late-eighteenth- and early-nineteenth-century 'bourgeois' or bureaucratic reforms to which they were credited by an older historiographical tradition.

18. E.g., Mark Franklin, *The Decline of Class Voting in Britain: Changes in the Basis of Electoral Choice, 1964–83* (Oxford, 1985).

19. Macfarlane, *The Origins of English Individualism*: 61.

20. Macfarlane, *The Origins of English Individualism*, Chapter 7, argues a contrary thesis: that English society was in the relevant respects quite different from her neighbours in *western* Europe. This argument, which may be contested (on which Macfarlane is elsewhere noncommittal, e.g., *The Origins of English Individualism*: 200, n. 35, 204; and which he partly abandons in *Marriage and Love*: 337–8), is not necessary to or entailed by Dr Macfarlane's general argument of the contrast between England and *eastern* Europe, which should be accepted.

21. On this theme, see Michael Hurst (ed.), *States, Countries, Provinces* (Abbotsbrook, Buckinghamshire, 1986); M. Greengrass (ed.), *Early Modern State Building* (London, 1989); and the articles in *Historical Research*, 62 (June 1989).

22. For the same concept under the label 'authoritarian populism', see, *inter alia*, Andrew Gamble, *The Free Economy and the Strong State* (London, 1988) and Bob Jessop *et al.*, *Thatcherism* (Oxford, 1988).

23. 'We are not forced to return to a revised Whig evolutionism. Nor need we argue that there was no change': Macfarlane, *The Culture of Capitalism*: 158.

24. Peter Laslett, Karla Oosterveen and Richard M. Smith (eds), *Bastardy and its Comparative History* (London, 1980): 29–41, 280. 'The idea that the pattern of fertility itself should show marked localism in European countries is quite a familiar one, and there is a well-known story about a Spanish linguist who mistook a fertility map of his country for a linguistic one. No doubt a map of that country, or of any European country, representing its persistent illegitimacy pattern would also have cultural overtones' (39). The suggestion that some kinship groups were 'bastardy prone' (217–46) evokes recent emphases on social problems as moral, personal and familial more than environmentally determined: see, for example, James Q. Wilson and Richard J. Herrnstein, *Crime and Human Nature* (New York, 1985).

25. 'Speech on a Motion made in the House of Commons, May 7, 1782, for a Committee to inquire into the State of the Representation of the Commons in Parliament', in *The Works of the Right Honourable Edmund Burke* (12 vols, John C. Nimmo: London, 1887) vol. 7: 95.

26. For a review of some recent literature see J. C. D. Clark, 'English History's Forgotten Context: Scotland, Ireland, Wales', *Historical Journal*, 32 (1989): 211–28. On the same theme, see Hugh Trevor-Roper, 'The Unity of the Kingdom: War and Peace with Wales, Scotland and Ireland', in Robert Blake (ed.), *The English World* (London, 1982): 100–10; Richard S. Tompson, *The Atlantic Archipelago: A Political History of the British Isles* (Lewiston, New York, 1986); Hugh Kearney, *The British Isles: A History of Four Nations* (Cambridge, 1989).

27. Cf. the chapters of L. M. Cullen, Colin Baber, Glanmor Williams, Rosalind Mitchison and R. H. Campbell in Rosalind Mitchison (ed.), *The Roots of Nationalism: Studies in Northern Europe* (Edinburgh, 1980): 91–158.

28. E.g., Cullen, 94; Baber, 107; Glanmor Williams, 119, 128; Mitchison, 131, 141, 162, in Mitchison (ed.), *The Roots of Nationalism*.

29. E.g., Baber, 111, 113; Campbell, 143, 152–5, in Mitchison (ed.), *The Roots of Nationalism*.

30. Tom Nairn, *The Break-Up of Britain: Crisis and Neo-Nationalism* (London, 1977; 2nd edn, 1981): 14.

31. Within the Marxist vision, Scotland and Ireland were neglected. Only recently has this begun to be pointed out as a demerit within that tradition: cf. Willie Thompson's review of Geoff Eley and William Hunt (eds), *Reviving the English Revolution: Reflections and Elaborations on the Work of Christopher Hill* (London, 1988), in *Marxism Today* (September 1988): 47.

32. Traced in J. L. McCracken, *The Irish Parliament in the Eighteenth Century* (Dundalk, 1971); R. S. Rait, *The Parliaments of Scotland* (Glasgow, 1924); C. S. Terry, *The Scottish Parliament: Its Constitution and Procedure 1603–1707* (Glasgow, 1905).

33. I agree, to this extent, with Nairn, *The Break-Up of Britain*: 71. But Nairn, writing first in 1977, was preoccupied by England's 'slow

foundering' in the 1960s and 1970s; Welsh and Scots nationalism now has to be consistent with England's economic renaissance in the 1980s. My account, by contrast, avoids these reductionist proclivities and focusses on ideology.

34. Radical individualism is, of course, essentially undeferential, unlike the familiar picture of lower-middle-class mores. But the paradox is explained by the centre-and-periphery aspect: from Scotland and Wales, it seems that deference is being demanded to Englishness.

35. For the best attempt to explain these phenomena from the viewpoint of the *New Left Review*, see Tom Nairn, *The Break-Up of Britain*. Nairn explains 'neo-nationalism' as 'the extremely long-delayed crisis of *the* original bourgeois state-form', produced by 'renascent "bourgeois radicalism" (in the shape of Scottish and Welsh nationalism) rather than by the class struggle in the metropolis, although this may soon change' (19, 39) Nairn's italics. The suggestion advanced here is the opposite one: the characteristic problems of the 1980s were the result of a break-up of social democracy rather than of capitalism. Nairn's 1970s analysis depends on the premise that the 'English Revolution' of the seventeenth century destroyed absolutism and ushered in the bourgeois state (16), a premise destroyed by the three historical initiatives examined at the outset of this chapter.

36. For a restatement, from the perspective of the Revolutionary Communist Group, of Marx's argument that armed rebellion in Ireland is the necessary precursor of Marxist revolution in Britain, see David Reed, *Ireland: The Key to the British Revolution* (London, 1984): 372–96. Reed's analysis convicts the British Labour Party and trade union movement of 'moral and political bankruptcy' for their failure to exploit this opportunity since 1969, but offers little insight into the reasons for this failure other than to identify Labour doctrine as 'bourgeois socialism' (384–5).

Part II
Political Thought: the Nation and the Individual

3 In Defence of the Nation
Roger Scruton

Over the last decade it has ceased to be either polite or politic for British subjects to defend the 'national idea' as the foundation of political order. Or rather, you can defend that idea on behalf of others – at least if they are engaged in some 'struggle for national liberation' – but not on behalf of your own community and kind. Indeed, you should be careful not to use words like 'kind', 'race', or 'kin'. Loyalties, if they are not universalist, must be expressed surreptitiously, in the self-deprecating language of one confessing to a private fault. In a recent publication, Professor Bikhu Parekh shows why there is a need for caution. Parekh summarises a nationalist view (which he attributes to various people, including myself), in 'four basic premises':

> First, a State is held together by a sense of nationality; that is, the unity of the State is grounded in the unity of the nation. Second, the sense of nationality is only possible among people of a common stock and sharing a feeing of kinship; that is, the unity of the nation is grounded in the unity of stock or kind. Third, the black communities in Britain are incapable of developing affection or loyalty for it and sharing a unity of sentiments with the whites. Fourth, the preservation of nationhood is a supreme moral value and justifies such morally repugnant deeds as their repatriation and forcible assimilation.[1]

The first of those 'premises' is something that I shall indeed defend – as a conclusion – in what follows. The second is familiar from the literature of nationalism, being proposed in one form by Herder, and in another by Fichte.[2] A century ago it would have been possible to discuss its truth with open mind and open heart – as did Renan and Acton.[3] And of course it was possible, even then, to perceive that the 'common stock' invoked in this 'premise' is in part a metaphor, whose reality lies not only in descent, but also in language, proximity, faith and culture.

It is not for the sake of reviving that dead but interesting debate that Parekh offers his analysis. The two further 'premises' are the ones that have aroused his interest, as they naturally arouse the interst of all liberal readers. Are there really people prepared, in the modern world, to defend such things? And are they really permitted to retain academic positions? For the record, I should say that the peculiar belief that nationhood is a 'supreme moral value' is not one that *I* share. Nor do I think that repatriation or forcible assimilation are (unless perhaps *in extremis*) morally justifiable. Nor do I think the 'black communities' in Britain are incapable of developing loyalty to it – whatever 'it' may be. If I protest at the sentimentality which sees blacks always as members of 'communities' and never as individuals, it is not on grounds of 'liberal individualism' – for I am neither an individualist nor a liberal – but because the idea of 'community' here invoked runs counter to the national loyalty which it is my purpose to defend.

More interesting than Parekh's list of 'basic premises' is the theory that he opposes to them. He argues that defenders of the four premises fail to see that the modern state is founded in a new and autonomous principle of unity: a principle defined in purely *political* terms. The modern state, he writes, is 'not to subscribe to, let alone to enforce, a specific body of moral, religious or cultural beliefs, save those such as the rule of law which are inherent in its structure. Its job [is] to provide a framework of authority and a body of laws within which individuals and groups [are] at liberty to live the way they [want]'; and 'to be its member is to acknowledge the structure of its authority and to bide by its laws'.[4] That 'structure of authority' is the only source of unity which a modern state has, or ought to have. To accept this structure is part of what is meant by *Sittlichkeit*, and those who argue for the primacy of *national* ideas in establishing political unity are in effect asking us to relate to our neighbours (or at least to those of them who do not belong to our 'kind' or 'nation', through the more primitive, more entangled conceptions of *Moralität*, rather than as fellow citizens.

Parekh gives, as his single example of a 'modern state' constructed according to those enlightened principles, the United States of America, which, he says, is composed of many different nations, and which self-evidently derives its unity and legitimacy from the system of authority erected and maintained by the Constitution. And, he implies, the more mature a state, the greater its capacity to develop real political unity out of religious and cultural diversity.

If I were to judge from Parekh's other writings — witness, for example, his critique of Oakeshott[5] – I should conclude that he is in fact a critic, and even a severe critic, of the abstract liberalism that he here seems to be defending. I suspect that the liberal theory of the state appeals to him on account of its polemical utility, rather than its truth. Nevertheless, there is undeniably something very attractive in the extreme liberal theory, as Parekh describes it. It sets before us a picture of the state constructed entirely according to the abstract principles of a pure political science, in which legitimacy is unpolluted by the messy claims of prescription. And while it always astonishes me that those who endorse it, and who give the United States as their principal example (it would be hard to find another), are by no means uniformly pro-American – being often first in line to condemn the rootless, consumer-oriented chaos, as they see it, of 'capitalist democracy' – it is nevertheless true that no better theory has ever been devised with which to castigate obstinate reactionaries like myself, who freely admit to upholding Western institutions, Western values, and the features of political order which have been so powerfully realised in Amercia.

The 'full liberal theory of the state' originated as an account of *legitimacy*. It is invoked by Parekh, however, as a theory of *unity*. (The tendency to answer the questions of unity and legitimacy in the same terms, and through a single theory, is a recurring feature of liberalism, and can also be seen in Sidgwick and Mill.[6]) I shall consider the unity of the body politic, rather than the legitimacy of the institutions used to govern it. The full liberal theory sees the state itself as the source of that unity, whereas, I shall argue, unity is, in the normal instance, social rather than political, and ought also to be national.

The liberal theory has both a descriptive and prescriptive version. It tells us sometimes that this is how things *are* in the modern world, sometimes that this is how things *ought* to be. As a prescriptive theory it commands widespread acceptance, defended by Spinoza, Locke and Kant, and perhaps even embodied, as Parekh suggests, in the U.S. Constitution. A version has recently been advanced by John Gray, not in order to attack conservatism, but in order precisely to embody the insights of conservatism in a modified theory of the liberal state.[7] In all cases, however, an understandable concern for liberal ideas of legitimacy has given rise to a quite untenable theory of political unity – and one which, if upheld as *Realpolitik*, would almost certainly lead to the collapse of liberal jurisdiction.

Before considering the liberal theory of unity, however, it is useful to return to the theory of legitimacy from which it derives. The appeal of liberal theories lies in the ease with which they can be given a 'foundational' character, in terms which seem to presuppose no religious or metaphysical commitment on the part of those who subscribe to them. Two ideas have been particularly important in developing the 'deep' theory of the liberal state: the social contract, and the 'unconditioned rational chooser'. Defenders of the social contract argue that all obligation has its foundation in consent, and that we are under a political obligation only to the extent that we are bound by some contractual relation to comply with it. Those who base their liberalism on an idea of pure rational choice argue that a state is legitimate only to the extent that a rational being, consulting the principles of rational choice alone, and without reference to his distinguishing conditions, would choose to live within its jurisdiction. Sometimes the two theories are combined – as in Rawls, for whom, however, the second theory has gradually gained ascendancy. Both theories refuse to acknowledge 'prescriptive right' – i.e., obligations which were never 'undertaken'. And both are founded on a conception of the human person that is psychologically, morally, and metaphysically questionable.

The objection to the 'liberal individualist' conception of the person has recently surfaced even in the literature of liberalism, usually distorted, as in Walzer, Sandel and Charles Taylor, so as to seem like a further move in a 'leftward' direction.[8] But its original proponent – Hegel, invoked by Parekh in the reference to *Sittlichkeit* and *Moralität* – was no leftwinger. Indeed, in the matter under discussion, he was probably as reactionary as I. In Hegel's view man owes his identity as a rational chooser to a process of development that implicates him inescapably in obligations which he did not choose. These obligations of piety are both pre-contractual and pre-political. (Hegel assigns them to the 'family', though, as his own argument shows, that is too narrow a designation.) The legitimacy of the state depends in part upon its ability to recuperate and articulate these non-political obligations, which form the original of its own non-contractual order.

The person who, on releasing himself into the freely contracting world of 'civil society', dishonours the pieties that nurtured him is not more, but less rational than the one who respects them. The blithe momentary Benthamite cuts away the ground from the rational choices that he pretends to be making, by depriving himself of every value other than his own pleasure – a commodity whose worth vanishes in the possession of it. He may, once he has risen to full autonomy, possess himself of another source of morality – the universalising imperative of Kant, which derives its authority from reason alone. But the Kantian imperative sets a limit to goals, and does not provide them. Its capacity to become a *motive*, and so to be incorporated into the agent's acts and projects, depends upon what Hegel called a dialectical relation with those instincts, prejudices and pieties which it serves to qualify. Kant had imagined that reason could be its *own* motive: that the categorical imperative could be freed from all 'empirical determinations', and yet be sovereign. But in this he was wrong, for reasons which subsequent philosophers have made clear. Choice must start somewhere: and even if this starting point is later described, from the point of view of reason, as mere prejudice, this is not to condemn it, but on the contrary, to show the indispensability of prejudice in the make-up of a rational agent.

I mention those arguments only to remind the reader that the questions at issue are, at bottom, metaphysical, and that the assurance of liberals, that they have access to the truth of man's condition, ought to be set against the extreme implausibility of their metaphysical convictions. The same dubious metaphysics which informs the liberal theory of legitimacy motivates the liberal theory of unity. Every political order depends, and ought to depend, upon a non-political idea of membership. And to the extent that it emancipates itself from that idea, I claim, to that extent does it lose its unifying force, just as individuals lose their moral identity and will, to the extent that their prejudices, pieties and moral instincts are cancelled by the abstract imperatives of the 'pure rational chooser'. This is not to say that the full liberal theory of the state does not, in some sense, *describe* the society of the future. It prognosticates the death of political order, by its very ability to evaporate into abstract nothingness the prejudices upon which society depends. The result of this, I believe, will not be the birth of the liberal polity, but its final extinction. For as prejudice dwindles, tolerance is left unguarded by conviction, and falls prey to the ever-vigilant schemes of the fanatic.

MEMBERSHIP

It is often argued that the idea of the nation is a recent invention – coming to the fore either as a reaction to the Englightenment,[9] or as part of the Enlightenment itself: the necessary replacement for an aristocratic entitlement and a dynastic crown.[10] Certainly there is a

doctrine – 'nationalism' – which owes its being to the controversies
of the late eighteenth century.[11] But an idea is not born with the
doctrine that perverts it, nor does the fact wait attendance on our
first conceiving it. Nations were realities by the time Shakespeare
wrote his histories,[12] and the national idea is already luminous in
those histories, even if detached from the bellicose doctrines that
have polluted it in recent times. It was to the national idea that
Cardinal Richelieu appealed in 1617, when he ruled that, in matters
of state, no French Catholic should prefer a Spaniard to a French
Protestant.[13] It was a nation, in some sense, which established its
empire in South America. And, when the King James Bible has God
say to Abraham 'And in thy seed shall all the nations of the earth be
blessed' (Genesis 22: 18), this is surely not so far from the national
idea of recent history.

Nobody who defends the national idea is now likely to explain
himself in terms of kinship or race: and not only through fear of the
thought-police. The idea that mankind divides into biological 'races'
has been put to such absurd use by the Gobinistes and their followers,
and entangled itself with so much nonsense and pseudo-science, as
to have lost all credibility.[14] Even if there were some element of truth
in the theory, it could give no comfort to the nationalist, since races,
if they exist, are not confined within national boundaries, and have
no characteristic language, culture or history. Indeed biological races
are defined without reference to history: there is no other justification
for the concept. The idea therefore offers nothing to those searching
for an historical identity, upon which to found a state which owes its
legitimacy to birthright alone.

Nevertheless, it is difficult to avoid terms like 'race', not least
because they accurately reflect *ways of conceiving* social unity. The
Jewish self-identification as 'children of Israel' is an important
instance. That the Jews form no homogeneous genetic entity is
evident. Nevertheless, they identify themselves in terms of a common
descent, and this is a feature of their pre-political unity which cannot
be discarded without detriment to their cohesion. Our own terms for
'nation' also originate in ideas of common descent: *natio, patria,
národ*, etc. German has as its normal term for pre-political unity,
Volk, a word which is now neutral as to who begat whom, but which
originally had connotations of family and tribe. Interesting, too, are
the Arabic words for nation. One – *watan* – derives from *watana*, to
dwell, and identifies a people purely in terms of its dwelling place.
Another, *Umm*, the classical term still used in such phrases as *al-*

Umam al-mutahidah (The United Nations), derives from the same root as the words for 'source' and 'mother'. Yet another, *qawm* – the more usual term when it comes to questions of nationalism and national identity, and which means, in pre-political parlance, kinsfolk or fellow tribesmen – derives from the root *qama*, meaning to stand up, to arise, to be proud, to attack, to be. In this root – which occurs in the description of God as *al-qayyum*, the Everlasting one – is condensed a whole philosophy of man's social nature, and one that should be borne in mind by the student of modern 'Arab nationalism'. For a *qawmah* is also an uprising, a 'revolution', and it is through such a 'standing up' against adversaries, the Arab nationalist believes, that a people is born.

In a loose sense, therefore, the term 'race' may still perform a function, even for those who have discarded the eugenic supersititions of the racists. It denotes a continuity across generations, based in kinship and intermarriage, but supported also by a consciousness of common descent. This common descent creates the obligation of inheritance: we must receive from our forefathers what we also pass to our children. Only the idea that the inheritance is entirely *biological*, rather than cultural, renders the concept suspect to those of open mind. The belief in racial inheritance, construed as an endlessly transferable set of benefits and burdens, is universally encountered, and not to be despised merely because it seems to conflict with the liberal conception of politics: the fault may lie, after all, with the liberal conception of politics. It would not be the first time that the conflict between liberalism and human nature had to be resolved in favour of humanity.

Concepts of race are kind-concepts. As is evident, we are not dealing with a natural kind, nor indeed with any other kind usually studied by contemporary philosophy. A race is an 'intentional' kind – one formed partly in obedience to a conception of itself.[15] And the simplest way to understand it is through the notion of membership.

Membership comes in many forms, and I shall begin by considering the form which seems furthest from the liberal conception of citizenship: membership of the tribe, secured by birth and initiation. The ceremony of initiation ratifies the bond of membership, and transforms it from a natural condition into a conscious responsibility. The boy now becomes a man, and in doing so accomplishes in one moment a spiritual journey of bewildering immensity. After initiation, the experience of the tribesmen ceases to be preparatory: his changed sense of belonging is received as a changed perception of the world.

Circumstances provide occasion for action which previously wore only a neutral aspect; others speak of duties and freedoms which were before only guessed at; while others still, which were once awesome and intimidating, are now subdued to his will, and shorn of their old authority.

The ceremony of initiation is a threshold: but it is a threshold to which the tribesman constantly returns. He attends each year the initiation of those who grow behind him, and re-enacts as a man what he first underwent as a boy. The ceremonies are an important source of social renewal, and year after year, although he knows them inside out and can speak their every word, he returns to them with gratitude. The meaning that he first obtained from them has not been wholly separated from the experience. He comes back to it, as a person returns to his favourite works of art, for something important which he can describe only in halting and imperfect terms, and which he can best identify by a gesture – pointing to the ceremony itself.

The ceremony of membership has an important function, besides that of confirming rights and duties acquired by descent. It can be offered to strangers, and used to incorporate them as limbs of the collective body, despite their lack of kinship. Of course, this privilege is a rare one, and all tribes are sensible of the dangers which ensue, when membership is offered on easy terms to those who have not proved their capacity for a lifetime's commitment. But that membership can be extended in this way is an important sign that the natural has been transcended into the spiritual, and that the race has begun to define itself in terms of a common destiny.

As we know from the work of the great anthropologists, who arrived on the scene of history just in time to capture the last examples of a disappearing innocence, and who brought with them the liberal attitudes that were to undo the remaining happiness of mankind, the phenomenon I have described was once universal, and survives in secret in many of our sophisticated ways. It is in terms of such phenomena that we should identify the root characteristics of a 'common culture.'[16] Such a culture gives meaning to the world, by offering occasions for action, a right and wrong procedure, and those ready concepts which close the gap between thought and action – concepts of sacred and profane, of seemly and unseemly, of virtue and vice. A common culture impresses the matter of experience with a moral form.

There is only a limited scope, in a true common culture, for change and innovation. Indeed, innovation is never a value in itself, but at best a necessary accommodation to changes arising from outside. Too much innovation – especially in those customs and ceremonies which provide the core experience of membership – is inherently threatening to the culture. Tradition, on the other hand, is of the essence. One way – maybe the principal way – in which this kind of membership is understood, is as a form of union with the unborn and the dead. Through membership I see the world as it will be seen by those who are yet to be. Hence I rise to an exalted perspective – a perspective above my own perishable being. Through the ceremonies of membership 'my eyes are opened', and I see the world no longer as an object of my own paltry needs and appetites, but as it really and eternally is (or, to be more philosophical, as it really and eternally seems). Through the ceremony of membership, therefore, the gods enter the world, and make themselves known. Hence there is a close relation, which may verge on identity, between membership and religious faith.

The attitude of a common culture to innovation is necessarily one of suspicion and hostility. Much more is at stake than the scoffing rationalist can conceivably imagine. (If he *could* imagine it, he would cease to scoff, and cease thereby to be a rationalist.) Innovation can take place, if at all, only in the spirit advocated by Burke – the spirit of a reform which aims to conserve. Innovation must therefore be construed as a renewal of something more fundamental than the detail changed: a casting away of accidents and perversions. The innovation must prove itself, by showing that it already *belongs* to the tradition which it seems to violate. And by adapting itself to tradition, it adapts tradition to itself. Conservatism in politics – at least Burkean conservatism – is a sign of attachment to a non-political experience of membership. And it is this attachment which sets the conservative against the liberal reformer, rather than any repudiation of the liberal state.

As I noted, 'immersive' membership, of the kind exemplified by the practice of initiation, is closely tied to religion. (Etymologically, a *religio* is a 'binding'.) Communities which experience immersive membership tend to define themselves, like the Jews, in religious terms. But the Jews also display the *revisionary* potential of religion. The gods themselves, once seriously believed in, have a tendency to detach themselves from the localities which gave birth to them, and to exert their sovereignty more extendedly – perhaps over all mankind. Indeed, when a religion is monotheistic, directed towards an all-wise and all-powerful creator, worship must be open to all who have the capacity for obedience. A people can be 'chosen', like the Jews, as the instruments of God's purpose or as a 'race of suppliants', but not as solely entitled to worship him. In such a case, therefore, the experience of membership, and the religious doctrine, have a tendency to separate, and to acquire independent histories.[17] It is one mark of a 'nation', in the modern sense, that this separation has occurred, so that membership can be defined without reference to religious obedience (cf. the injunction of Cardinal Richelieu, referred to above).

At the opposite pole from tribal initiation stands the free contract of partnership, in which individuals meet on terms, and recognise no obligations that are not contained in the contract itself. In such cases association dissolves with the extinction of the mutual purpose. Such relations are only doubtfully described as relations of membership: for their character is entirely summarised by an agreement between individuals, who create no entity beyond themselves.

At the same time, however, there are associations, often verging on the contractual, which introduce new corporate entities, and which are rightly understood as forms of membership. Clubs, corporations and trusts are treated by the law in special ways which reflect their corporate nature. Legal personality (which is sometimes accorded and sometimes withheld) is not a convenient fiction, but the transcription of a real and independent moral identity created by the ties of membership. Even when the law recognises nothing but a contract (as in the 'unincorporated association'), the individuals may experience their relation as a form of corporate personality with a common will and common goals. Contracts are means; membership is always at least partly an end in itself; and what begins in a contract (joining a club, for example) may outlast the dissolution of the contractual tie.

From such examples one can without too much difficulty envisage an axial ordering of associations. Some are purely contractual, others purely immersive. But contract and immersion exert their gravitational force over the entire field of human loyalty, and each association will involve its own particular synthesis of their contrasting vectors. Here sociologists might follow Tönnies, in distinguishing *Gemeinschaft* and *Gesellschaft*; or Weber, in contrasting 'traditional' with 'legal-rational' forms of authority. Others may take from Hegel the distinction between instrumental and constitutive relations, or borrow similar ideas from Oakeshott and Horkheimer. And it is worth bearing those discussions in mind, since they add a certain authority to an argument which I shall nevertheless develop without reference to them. More useful for my purpose is another and earlier attempt to describe the 'innocent' form of social unity – the form from which man drifts away into politics. In *Muqaddimah* Ibn Khaldun writes at length of *'asabiyah*, which denotes the 'binding force' of society. *'Asabiyah* results, in the normal case, from ties of blood and marriage, and involves a 'willingness to fight and die for each other'.[18] Its strength and value depend on the virtue of individuals, and its natural tendency is to create a sovereign authority (*malaka*), and thereby to transform itself into law. With law, however, comes indolence, luxury, and a false sense that the individual can stand alone, neither needing nor knowing his kind. *'Asabiyah* then disintegrates, and social life is at an end. (*'Asab* means sinew – and Ibn Khaldun's imagery approximates to Homer's, as he describes the loosening of the sinews in death.)

Ibn Khaldun was feeling his way, I believe, towards a very modern – even proto-Hegelian – conception of the mutual dependence of political and pre-political loyalties, and his belief that the concept of the citizen cancels, at last, the experience of membership is one that has been confirmed by modern history, even if not confirmed before.

ALIENATION

For there is no gainsaying that 'modernity' has involved an attempt to revise the experience of membership in a contractual direction. But there is no evidence that mankind has become happier (even if it has become more prosperous) as a result. The complaint against 'alienation' may, of course, be so much self-indulgence: after all, it issues from people who are 'not at home in the world'. Nevertheless, we ought for that very reason to take it seriously: when self-indulgence becomes the norm, something is wrong with the society that engenders it.

Two things are usually identified as the root of alienation: capitalism, and scientific thought (including the technology that springs from it). For the liberal there is a certain paradox here. For 'capitalism' is (by and large) a rude name for the system of market relations – in other words, economic relations established by consent. And science is simply a name for the system of propositions thought to be true, and believed for no other reasons. Science and the market are the two fundamental forms of man's relation to an objective world: the two ways of recognising the world's objectivity, either as thing (and therefore object of knowledge and use), or as person (and therefore subject of consent). It is perhaps a sign of original sin, that these two indispensable links to an objective reality should be experienced as a 'fall' into something 'alien'.

One explanation of this 'fall' is provided by my discussion of membership. The relations established by a market, like those created by science, have a *universal* character. A contract requires no bond, no anterior attachment, between the parties, and its meaning is exhausted by its terms. Moreover, terms are dictated 'impersonally', by the rational self-interest of all who have access to the market. 'All' means everyone; defenders of the market are *ipso facto* defenders of free trade, wishing to multiply the benefits of a free economy through universal access. The alienating quality of the market consists partly in the fact that the 'alien' has utter equality with the friend. No *special* relationship exists to provide the meaning of the transaction, and I throw myself into the system only to set aside the claims of affection in the interests of agreement. There is a loneliness here, born of the very idea that consent is sovereign: the very same loneliness detected by Tocqueville, at the heart of American democracy.

The desire for some new kind of economic relation is therefore invariably couched in terms of a 'communitarian' ideal – such as 'market socialism' – in which cooperatives, and the relations of trust and loyalty among their members, are proposed as antidote. This involves a move away from contract, towards economic relations which are 'bonded' and circumscribed by duties, in the manner of a feudal tenure. It is also a move in a particularist direction. The market offends by its universality: it pays no attention to people, but only to the abstract person, the 'rational economic man'. The communitarian economy 'restores man to himself' by recognising his social nature, his *Gattungswesen*, his *membership*.[19]

Similarly with scientific thought. The categories of science arise directly from our rational interst in truth. Science is therefore *common* to all rational beings, and the peculiar possession of none of them. When I engage in scientific enquiry, I free my perception of the world from intentional concepts – and therefore from those categories whose sense derives from a particular community or particular way of life. I no longer see the world under the aspect of 'belonging'. I am not 'at home' in the world of science, for precisely the reason that I am just as much at home there, and just as little, as everyone else.

Two antidotes have been proposed to this condition: the search for a 'subjective' relation to the world (a search which begins in modern times with Kierkegaard, and which leads to Husserl, Heidegger and Patočka); and the search for a 'cultural' mode of knowledge, one that is formed in the image of membership. In the modern world, those two searches tend in a single direction. For the purely individualistic conception of 'subjectivity' again opens the way to solitude and alienation: it stands in need of 'redemption', and redemption either takes a religious form, as in the 'leap of faith' of Kierkegaard, or else involves a *Heimkehr* to the breast of some implied community – some Little Gidding of the imagination – as in the 'culture' of Arnold, Leavis and Eliot. In the opposition between science and culture, therefore, we find precisely the same contrast as that which exists between the free market and the 'moral economy' (to use E. P. Thompson's phrase): the contrast between a universalised relation to the world, and a relation circumscribed by some particular attachment. The same contrast galvanised and tormented the French Revolutionaries, who could never decide whether the 'nation' which they had so unwisely deified consists of a contractual partnership of all-comers, or of a 'people', bound by destiny and by the unchosen ties of membership.

The contractual view of society is in one sense supremely rational: it recommends a negotiated solution to every conflict, and suggests a path to every goal. Of course, it does nothing to *provide* goals, which must be brought ready-made to the contractual encounter. It is silent about the meaning of life, and has nothing to offer to the lost and the disaffected. That, for the liberal, is its strength. To demand anything else from politics is to demand what cannot be obtained, except at enormous human cost – and perhaps not even then. Political institutions exist in order to mediate and adjudicate, not in order to mobilise and conscript.

Unfortunately, however, the political sphere cannot stand so serenely above the loyalties which feed it. The spirit of contract enters human relations, precisely in order that the liberal state should stand in judgement over them. Those relations are therefore voided of their residue of membership, and become provisional, rescindable, uncertain of themselves, with no authority beyond the transient 'sovereignty' of choice. Such is the celebrated transition from status to contract, described by Sir Henry Maine.[20]

The sanctity of human bonds is, however, inseparable from their reality as *bondage*. Rebuilt in contractual form they become profane, a system of façades, a Disneyland version of what was formerly dignified and monumental. What meaning they have no longer inheres in them as an objective and personal countenance, but merely shines momentarily, as we sweep the light of our desire across their disenchanted surfaces. Nobody, not even the liberal, is happy with this: only the crudest reformer actually *welcomes* what has happened to marriage, for example, in the wake of its desacralisation. But the liberal sees no remedy to this misfortune: and for the true liberal there *is* none, besides some new habit of mind which enables us to live with the problem. Of course, there are those – Sandel, Walzer and Dworkin, for example[21] – who propose 'communitarian' ways of thinking, as a further move in the direction which a sophisticated liberalism requires. But none of them is prepared to accept the real price of community: which is sanctity, intolerance, exclusion, and a sense that life's meaning depends upon obedience, and also on vigilance against the enemy. Or at least, insofar as liberals have perceived this, they have deplored it, and tried to attribute these features to some *bad* form of community, in order to save the *good* form which is their heart's desire. If the 'nation' has often been identified as the *bad* form of social membership, this is partly because, in existing circumstances, loyalty to the nation is a real possibility. To fix one's desires on the irrecoverable enables one to persist in the liberal posture, of recommending nothing.

NATIONALISM

The experience of membership is precisely *not* political, but social. It arises, and ought to arise, independently of the state, and it should not be the state's concern either to impose or to forbid any particular form of it, or any particular experience of the sacred and the profane. So says the liberal, and the conservative partly agrees with him. Both are wary of the attempt to *achieve* social unity by political directives, even if they differ as to how it should be *safeguarded*. A core experience of membership, once lost, cannot be recovered by conscription. It is not for the state to manufacture the deeper forms of loyalty, and the attempt to do so is inherently totalitarian. It involves, and has always involved, the replacement of religion by ideology, of civil association by conscription and of law by conspiratorial power. This is so evident to us, in our time, as to go without saying. Nevertheless, the fault, I suggest, lies not in the national idea, but rather in the use that has been made of it. As an *ideology*, force-fed to the multitude, so as to enlist them in a new obedience, nationalism is the enemy of the liberal state. It is also the enemy of nationality, extinguishing, in its furious purposefulness, the purposeless bonding that holds men together in peace.

But the same is true of *every* ideology – including those universalist ideologies which are, in the modern world, set against the 'national idea'. As ideologies and instruments of conscription, 'equality' and 'liberation' have proved to be as much the enemies of freedom as the notion of a 'master race'. Indeed, it is only ignorance that could permit the belief that Soviet communism, founded on universalist principles, has involved less crime, less suffering, less insolence and indignity, than the particularist politics of the Nazis.

At the same time, there is little doubt that the ideology of nationalism has so formed contemporary perception of its leading idea, as to have made it difficult to separate the 'nation' from the tragi-comedy of pre-war Europe and of the present Middle East. Elie Kedourie and Kenneth Minogue have argued vigorously for the view that the ideology comes first, and has therefore given shape to the concept of nationhood. Minogue summarises what is now a familiar liberal argument in the following words:

> The point we have to emphasize about modern nationalism is that the politics comes first, and the national culture is constructed later. We have found nationalisms without nations, aspirations substituted for reality. Instead of a dog beginning to wag its political tail, we find political tails trying to wag dogs. The Irish government tries to promote an Irish culture, the Nigerian government tries to persuade Ibos, Hausa, Fulanis and Yorubas that they are part of a Nigerian or an African nation . . . This amounts to saying that the concept of the nation is almost entirely empty of content, until a content is arbitrarily supplied from local circumstances.[22]

As we shall see, Minogue's last claim is untenable. Nevertheless, he is right to suggest that the national idea has been used to *conscript* people to nationhood: to impose a social unity by political means. In this respect, however, the full liberal theory of the state makes a comparable error. It too believes that there is, or ought to be, no source of political unity other than the political process itself: it differs in claiming that unity cannot be imposed, and that, in the right conditions, it emerges from, and expresses, an act of common

consent. Until sustained by a national idea, however, the liberal state
is, I believe, a solvent of unity and therefore contains the seeds of its
own destruction.

WANDERING AND SETTLED PEOPLES

To establish that point, we need to make an important (although
again not hard and fast) distinction, between wandering and settled
peoples. Ideas of 'kind' are as important to the nomadic as to the
sedate – perhaps more important. It was the nomadic Bedouin who
provided Ibn Khaldun with his paradigm of *'asabiyah*. Lacking
territory, and lacking, in time, even the common language that may
have once united them, such people base their loyalty on ideas either
of faith or of kinship, and usually of both. Kinship becomes, as for
the Jews, a continuous and developing *story*, whose meaning is
religious, and whose aspect is that of a homeless culture, based,
however, in a consuming nostalgia for home. Religious conversion –
whereby an outsider claims protection from the tribal gods – may be
frowned upon or (when not backed up by marriage – i.e., by entry
into the kinship relation) subjected to rigorous proofs. Thus, following
the diaspora, and the birth of Judaism, Jews have less and less sought
conversions, and more and more devoted themselves to safeguarding
the faith among those required by birth to inherit it.

Nor are the Jews peculiar in this respect. Many of the 'confessional
communities' of the Middle East have the character of peoples
wandering or driven from their original pastures, holding on to their
identity through ideas of membership which are gradually shorn of
the transcendental convictions that once attached to them. The Druze
are a particularly interesting case. In some frames of mind, they seem
to believe that their membership has been fixed eternally, and can
neither grow through conversion nor decline through apostasy.[23]
According to certain of their authorities, every child born into a
Druze family is the reincarnation of another Druze, and therefore
stands in need of no further initiation. He does not need to discover
the form or content of the faith to which his inheritance attaches
him, for the simple reason that he can do nothing to lose it and is
saved in any case. This belief is in fact extremely functional: the long-
standing practice of *taqiyyah* (literally 'holiness' – but in fact denoting
the systematic concealment of doctrine for the sake of survival) seems
to have resulted in a near-universal amnesia among the Druze as to

what their religious doctrines are. The Druze are, in this instance, only an extreme case of a process that can also be witnessed among Maronites, Melkites and even Greek Orthodox in the region: the reduction of faith to ritual, and of ritual itself to a root relationship of kin. Such instances, while they show the vital importance of membership, also show again that it is quite different in kind from 'conscription to a cause' – i.e., from the *manufactured* loyalties of the ideological state.

So far I have given two examples of non-political unity: the tribal-racial and the religious. Both derive from a core experience of the sacred, in which membership is displayed as immersion (baptism). However, as I emphasised, religion and race may grow apart, and will tend to do so whenever God is one and infinite. Under favourable conditions, men advance towards the idea that this-worldly membership and other-worldly obedience are (*pace* the Druze and the Alawites) quite separate things. The way is open for a new kind of loyalty, one in which the individual is free to seek his god without consulting the gods of his neighbours. The way is open, too, to philosophy, theology and science: men can now *study* God and his works; they can put their beliefs to the test, since it is not on *belief* that political unity – and therefore peace and leisure – depends. This emancipation from dogma is one of the achievements of the *polis*, and causes liberals persistently to overlook the non-political loyalties upon which even the *polis* depends.

In a recent work Régis Debray has offered a powerful picture of religious doctrine (and its ideological substitutes, such as Marxism) as *formes a priori de la sociabilité (ou de l'existence politique)*.[24] Doctrine, he argues, is both necessary to the formation of a pre-political 'we', and also consequent upon it: *une idéologie est un drapeau, mais on ne se rallie pas à un drapeau au vu de ses couleurs, on adopte le drapeau parce qu'on s'incorpore à la troupe*.[25] As Debray notices, this resuscitation of the Marxian theory of ideology – not so as to criticise ideology, but rather so as to endorse it, in terms similar to those used by Burkean conservatives in defending 'prejudice' – has profoundly anti-liberal implications. If it is true, then what hope do we have of establishing the kind of polity esteemed by Parekh (and defended by Rawls as uniquely conforming to a pre-philosophical idea of justice), in which confession, doctrine and 'conceptions of the good' are all required to vacate their thrones to the sovereign rule of law?

But Debray's thesis is false: not because the foundation of loyalty is, or can be, purely political, as the full liberal theory requires, but because there are other forms of non-political unity than those founded in doctrine. Race is one of them; nationality another. *Pace* Kedourie and Minogue, there is a perfectly coherent idea of membership based in those relations between people which come from *occupying the same place*. People who are not, like the Jews, 'strangers and sojourners' in the land, may have things in common sufficient to constitute them as a 'kind'. The most important of these is territory. People gathered in the same place, must accord to each other rights of occupation if they are to live in peace. The network of those rights defines a portion of the earth as 'ours'. Peoples from elsewhere are strangers to our rights, uninterested in preserving them, and liable, in times of war, to cancel them. There arises a common interest in defence, which has territory as its object. Until territory is *ours*, there is no real 'mine' or 'thine'.

If territory is to fall, in this way, under a common but divisible right of ownership, there must be a content to the collective 'we', which settles the terms and the boundaries of membership. Certain factors, naturally associated with joint occupation, contribute to this 'we':[26]

1. *Shared language*:   There is no more dramatic mark of the stranger than his inability to speak my language. My language is not only mine. It is public, and shared, learned from and taught to those who are dearest. My language is always *our* language; the first thing that I inherit from my forefathers and the first that I pass on to my child. Attachment to language is the root of national culture, and, in favourable conditions, may be used to define the boundaries of nationhood. (Cf. the history of Polish, Turkish and especially Arab nationalism in our times.)[27] Language may also be imposed – either to break down loyalties inimical to the political order (Bulgaria, the Soviet Union, the USA until recently), or in order to consolidate a political order that has been newly established (Israel, and also Ireland – in which the attempt met with failure).
2. *Shared associations*:   Settled people have more opportunity for association than those who wander. They can meet not only in family, festival, team and army, but also in places given to membership: churches, clubs, schools, localities of work and leisure. They have an opportunity for institution-building, and for attaching their institutions to the land. Their mutual ties lose the

solemn and immersive nature of the ties formed by those who pass each other in the desert. They become looser, freer, and more 'civil', and at the same time fitted for corporate life. Societies differ, of course, as to which associations are permitted, and as to their ability to perpetuate themselves as institutions. The Hegelian idea of civil society is one of maximal association, under a rule of law which permits and encourages the incorporation of all lasting forms of membership. We can see a nation as partly constituted by the long-standing associations which are formed and inherited within it.

3. *Shared history*: People united by language, association and territory triumph and suffer together. They have common friends and common enemies. An historical *narrative* is manifest in the very associations which serve to combine them, and the memory of it is attached to the landscape, the towns, the institutions and the climate by which they are surrounded.

4. *Common culture*: There is both the desire and the need to consolidate community in the core experiences of membership, as these are safeguarded and enhanced by faith, ritual and worship. For a wandering people this is the root of identity, and the sole durable source of a pre-political 'we'. In certain circumstances, however, membership can develop away from its 'angel infancy' and smile more inclusively, if also more coldly, on the surrounding world. The process – described by Spengler as a transition from 'culture' to 'civilization' – may perhaps foretell (as Spengler thought) the ruin of a people. Nevertheless it is the process that formed the nation-states of Europe, and which conditions all that we may have or hope for in the modern world. It is precisely this which permits the full loyalty of nationhood, and, with it, the moderating institutions of a liberal state.

A nation, like a race, is a kind formed through a conception of itself. The members of a nation do not merely share those four things (or some significant sub-set of them), but also *concede* them to each other as of right. Membership involves an acquiescence in the claims of others, and a recognition of a shared identity. Others of my nation have a right to the common territory, provided, at least, they are prepared to risk their life in defence of it. This self-consciousness of a nation is part of its moral character. It endows nations with a life of their own, a destiny, even a personality. People who think of themselves as a collective 'we' understand their successes and failures as 'ours', and apportion collective praise and blame for the common outcome. Hence there arises what Solzhenitsyn has called 'repentance and self-limitation in the life of nations':

> Those who set the highest value on the existence of the nation, who see in it not the ephemeral fruit of social formations but a complex, vivid, unrepeatable organism not invented by man, recognise that nations have a full spiritual life, that they can soar to the heights and plunge to the depths, run the whole gamut from saintliness to utter wickedness (although only individuals ever reach the extremes).[28]

There is something drastic in that utterance, as in the self-castigations which fill the Old Testament, and from which our forefathers acquired the idea of a collective and inherited guilt. But Solzhenitsyn's words correspond to a recurrent thought in the life of nations, one which reveals the force and the depth of every true non-political loyalty. Only when moderated by law, and by conceptions of corporate personality, do sentiments of such intensity become negotiable. And that is why the nation needs law as much as law needs the nation.

HOME AND PATRIOTISM

What holds together the features that I have identified as part of nationhood? Why is the emergence of this new kind of loyalty not just a passing accident? To answer those questions is difficult – for it is always difficult to give what Kant called a 'deduction' of a non-natural kind. However, something can be said to awaken the reader to the importance of nationhood as I have described it. We need only reflect on the difference of predicament, between a wandering and a settled people. What I have been defining is a special case of being *at home*, and of the attachment to home which is common to all people fortunate enough to have one. This attachment is sometimes referred to as patriotism, and has been so described and defended by one left-wing author, in terms which hearken back to, and indeed are largely taken from, Burke:

> At its core, patriotism means love of one's homeplace, and of the familiar things and scenes associated with the homeplace. In this sense, patriotism is one of the basic human sentiments. If not a natural tendency in the species, it is at least a proclivity produced

by realities basic to human life, for territoriality, along with family, has always been a primary associative bond. We become devoted to the people, places and ways that nurture us, and what is familiar and nurturing seems also natural and right. This is the root of patriotism. Furthermore, we are all subject to the immense power of habit, and patriotism has habit in its service.[29]

Hence 'the theme of homecoming is the central motif of patriotic discourse'.[30] John Scharr goes on to emphasise the importance of 'patrimony' – meaning the inheritance of benefits and obligations which we cannot refuse without dishonour to ourselves and our children. This element of patrimony is, however, *common* to all forms of non-political loyalty, and not peculiar to the national idea. It implies that there will be a racial element in all national sentiment – an element of 'birthright' and 'birthduty'. In reminding the reader of this obvious fact, it is useful to be able to call on an established left-wing authority.

But this now brings me to the question of what we might actually mean by 'patriotism', and how, if at all, we might distinguish it from other forms of national loyalty. Because no particular use of words is forced on us, I shall make a proposal, in keeping with what I think are popular sentiments in the matter. I shall distinguish three 'moments' within non-political loyalties: attachment, patriotism, and ideology. The attachment is simply the relation of membership itself – the tribal, confessional, racial or national bond. National attachment defines a home; confessional attachment does not. Loyalty to the *polis* also defines a home, as is clear from the famous funeral oration of Pericles. Pericletian loyalty stands to the city state as national loyalty to the nation-state: neither need be felt with any strength or deliberation and neither need be patriotic.

Patriotism consists in the extent to which the obligations of patrimony are *acted upon*. There is a patriotism of the 'little platoon', and a patriotism for every kind of membership, even those without a 'home'. Wandering peoples also have patriotism: the Jews more than any other. The manifestations of patriotism are many. First among them is the 'public spirit' which becomes an active force only when people live their lives in honourable recognition of the unborn and the dead. Throughout the middle ages the Jews gave to the *kuppah*, and to other charitable works, a considerable part of all their earnings, and offered shelter, employment and ransom to others of their kind. They were right to do this then, and are right to do it now, buying

the oppressed members of their race from governments degraded
enough to sell them. Such charitable works are one part of the public
spirit which is the guarantee of national freedom. Another part is
the willingness to die for the sake of the group. That willingness
depends upon a commitment to the dead and the unborn; hence
liberals have great difficulty in seeing how it might be justified, the
dead and the unborn being excluded, in the nature of things, from
the social contract among the living.

The ideology of a pre-political attachment is a kind of emergency
measure, a response to external threat which should not outlast the
time of present danger. The ideology of the nation is nationalism;
that of the tribe is tribalism. Ideologies can be used to conscript
people to an artifical unity; but they are neither substitutes for, nor
friends of, the loyalties on which they meditate.

Armed with those distinctions, we may return to the concept of
'home', as this is advanced through the national idea. It is one
consequence of the analysis that I have given that there can be
'nested' nations – that is, nations which contain other nations as
parts. An example is Czechoslovakia, in which two nations, with
separate but related languages, customs and faiths, have merged to
form a single more comprehensive nation, whose sense of identity,
in the face of communist enslavement, is at least as strong as the
separate identities of the Czechs and the Slovaks. A less clear example
is the United Kingdom, in which separate but vestigial nations have
been merged into a union which used to be called (in the eighteenth
century) an 'empire'. This nesting of national loyalties is the unsurpris-
ing consequence of the fact that territories also nest within one
another, and are captured or defended together. The sentiment of
'ours' leaks easily across the borders of Wales and England, or those
of Moravia and Slovakia, and people from one side of the border
feel equally 'at home' on the other.

It is impossible to separate the sense of home from that of family.
To acquire a family is to 'settle down'; and a person who settles in a
place wishes also (as a rule) to breed there. No settling of territory
can occur, therefore, without establishing family bonds; the mingling
of the two ensures that territorial loyalties will be experienced in the
patrimonial fashion that I have described. Moreover, territory must
be defended, and people die in the defence of it: a sense of sacrifice
therefore attaches to the soil and to the memory of those who fought
for it. A prolonged peace may erode this sense. But it is always
renewed in a time of crisis, and, when it ceases to be renewed,

'*asabiyah* is at an end, and the nation must die.

A nation may last, however, as long as the land provides a 'home' for it. Nations have an identity through time which is distinct from that of the state, and independent of institutions, even those dearest to its people. A nation can outlast the demise of its system of government, and its ancestral laws, even though it lives on, like the Russians and the Poles, in a state of deep unhappiness. It is not right to attribute full moral personality to nations – to regard them as Solzhenitsyn does in the passage quoted earlier. Only in the political sphere does corporate personality emerge, and the non-political stands to the political as the body to the soul. It is the source of life upon which rational discourse is predicated. Nevertheless, the identity of a nation through time has a clear moral aspect, and the reaffirmation of this identity, through acts of pride and contrition, is a part of belonging, and of living under immovable obligations.

The liberal state has no home, and generates no loyalty towards generations which, being either dead or unborn, form no part of the contract. Without such a loyalty there is neither honourable accounting nor provision for the future, but only a squandering of resources in the pursuit of present goals. The liberal state must depend therefore upon some other loyalty than loyalty to itself. More than any other system of government, the liberal rule of law depends upon the renewal of public spirit, and therefore on patriotism. Burke was wrong to speak of a *partnership* between the living, the unborn and the dead – for that is to raise the feelings of piety from the realm of social membership into the conscious light of politics, and so to make them rescindable, defeasible and insecure. But he was right to suspect that without loyalty to the dead, and to the land that houses them, the whole project of liberal politics is endangered. For a liberal state to be secure, the citizens must understand the *national* interest as something other than the interest of the *state*. Only the first can evoke in them the sacrificial spirit upon whicn the second depends.

LOYALTY AND JURISDICTION

If we consult the standard works of liberal theory, we do not as a rule find any discussion of social membership or social unity. It is assumed that the principles which determine the legitimacy of the ruling institutions will also settle the question as to who is governed by them. Advocates of the social contract, for example, suppose men to be gathered together by the very contract which settles their future obligations. But how were they gathered, and who did the gathering? On what basis are those unborn to be admitted to the contract? How do we distinguish those who are entitled to contract, from those who are 'barging in'? There is no satisfactory position for the contract theorist to take, short of universalism: if the contract is open to anyone, it is open to all. Anything short of world government is therefore tainted with illegitimacy. That is just another way of saying that, until moderated by a non-political loyalty, the contractarian view of the state is without application.

Similarly for democracy. When politicians address the people at an election (when they 'go to the country' as it is said in British parliamentary discourse), they ask a definite question: what do *we* want? The 'we' in question is the class of those entitled to vote. But how they acquired that entitlement, who conferred it and what justifies it, are questions whose answers are inseparable from the history of a nation.

Nor are liberals consistent in their repudiation of the national idea, as is shown by a characteristic liberal attitude to immigration, and to those like myself who wish to prevent or limit it. The argument is advanced that we have no right to close our doors against immigrants from our former colonies, since it was we who exploited them, or who reduced them to the state of economic and cultural dependence which ensures that their best – perhaps their only – prospects are now on British soil. If you examine the use of 'we' in that sentence, you will find a perfect instance of the national idea, as I have described it: the idea of a moral unity between people, based in territory, language, association, history and culture, and so bound up with the self-consciousness of those who are joined by it, as to make subsequent generations answerable for the sins of their forefathers, and entitled to the benefits which their ancestors forewent.

Supposing we accept the need for a non-political loyalty. Why should that loyalty be *national*? The answer is contained in the nature of the modern state. All law requires jurisdiction: that is, a principle for determining who is, and who is not, subject to its edicts. It is a peculiar feature of wandering peoples that they tend to be governed by laws which are coterminous with their religious confessions, and which derive their authority from the same divine source. When the people are 'strangers and sojourners' this gives rise to an enormous problem of law-enforcement, as instanced by the Jews. (Consider the case of Noah Raphael da Norsa in sixteenth-century Ferrara, which had to be tried innumerable times, all over the diaspora, before the culprit was forced by the pressure of public opinion, and the judgement of fifty rabbis, to yield.[31]) When a wandering people establishes an empire, and enforces its law over subject territories, the result is never a liberal *Rechtsstaat*. The *shari'a* of the muslims, for instance, makes little provision for the legal rights of non-muslims. Despite the ingenious arguments of the various schools of jurisprudence, it has never been decided whether the law really applies to non-muslims, or whether their affairs are to be dealt with under treaties of pacification.[32] The name for the non-muslim communities which enjoy protection is *dhimmi*, meaning those governed by treaty, as opposed to those governed by the holy law. (*Dhimma* – covenant, treaty, protection.) How to adjudicate a contract between a muslim and a *dhimmi* is a question that still has no answer. There thus emerged the pattern, institutionalised under the Ottoman *millet* system, and still persisting (just) in modern Lebanon, whereby each confession governs its own relations of matrimony, family and inheritance, while one by one the transactions of civil society are removed from confessional adjudication and made subject to the secular law of the state. In modern Lebanon, legal order rests on appeals to Rome, to the Sunnite Mufti, to the Shi'ite *'ulema* and the Druze *'aql*. This undermines the idea of political unity, while establishing in the minds of the people the idea that those who do not share their religious beliefs and customs are in some important sense outside the law. Such an idea of jurisdiction is incompatible with the emergence of a state in which rights are offered regardless of confession. The emergence of a Jewish *Rechtsstaat* in Palestine was made possible partly by the fact that the law prevailing there is *not* Jewish law, but the law of the British mandate, established according to a territorial concept of jurisdiction.

The safety, continuity and stability necessary to a rule of law are unobtainable until territory is secure. And in the modern world only a territorial idea of jurisdiction will permit the final separation of law from confessional attachment. Territorial jurisdiction exists in two forms: that of empire, and that of the sovereign state. The first is parasitic on the second, since only if there is a 'metropolitan power' can there be an empire. Empires provide the most striking examples that the world has known of trans-national rules of law: the Roman Empire, for example, the Russian Empire during the nineteenth century (especially in Finland and the Baltic states), and the British

Empire in India and Africa. Even the Ottoman Empire, despite its disabilities and the imperfection of the *millet* system, made moves towards the rule of law, while the Austro-Hungarian Empire (to which I shall return) is the true paradigm for which Parekh is looking in the passage which I began by quoting, of a political unity which casts its mantle over many nations. There are two reasons, however, why liberals should be reluctant to countenance empire as their preferred form of jurisdiction. First, empires have now ceased to be founded on the rule of law: the Soviet Empire, for example, has persisted by extinguishing law and adjudication in all the territories which fall beneath its control. (Law is replaced by a Potemkin substitute, from which the sovereign Party is exempt; and to the extent that a rule of law can be reasserted – as in modern Hungary – to that extent is the Empire threatened.) Secondly, an empire imposes law on its subject peoples. The unity between them is an artificial unity, dependent upon the force exerted by the central power. This force in turn depends upon the cohesion of that power, and its territorial jurisdiction at home. And this depends upon a loyalty adapted to the defence of territory: in other words, on the persistence of something like a national idea. Hence the appeal to empire as the foundation of law may not, in the end, be distinct from the appeal to nationality. The collapse of the Roman Empire was caused precisely by the collapse of Rome – by the loosening of '*asabiyah* in the Empire's heart.

It is at this point, I think, that a liberal ought to bite the bullet, and confess to the advantages of the national idea. It establishes a social loyalty suited to territorial jurisdiction; and without territorial jurisdiction, there is no possibility of a liberal state. It is for this reason that the history of the *Rechtsstaat* and the history of the national idea are inseparable. In trying to understand this fact liberals have sometimes distinguished – as does Lord Acton in a famous essay – between nationality based in race and language, and nationality 'formed by the state', which is 'the only one to which we owe political duties . . . and the only one which has political rights'.[33] It seemed to Acton that the coincidence of national loyalty and legal obligation could be secured only if the nation were in some sense the creature of the law which governs it. (At the same time, he advocated empire as the best guarantee of the freedom of nationalities, and therefore of the rights of individuals.) But the question is not which comes first – the law or the nation – but rather what determines the unity and durability of each. The national *Rechtsstaat* should be seen in terms of a continuing process of interaction, between a national loyalty and a territorial jurisdiction. The first is social rather than political, just like the loyalty of the Jews. Nationality and jurisdiction interpenetrate, and it is not absurd to envisage their relation in terms of that between body and soul (a special case, for Aristotle, of the relation between matter and form). To notice, as Acton does, their inseparability, is not to deny their distinctness. And to assign the unity of the body politic entirely to its legal part (as the liberal theory does), is as grave an error as to suppose, like Locke, that personal identity has nothing to do with the identity and continuity of the body.

SOME EXAMPLES

This brings me to what is most objectionable in the standard liberal view of politics, namely the refusal to perceive men and nations as they are: the refusal to clothe in flesh the abstract rational chooser who sits on the liberal chessboard. Consider, again, the all-important example put before us by Parekh. If the United States really is a multi-national state united by a single rule of law, whose authority is sufficient to establish political unity, then this would merely show that the United States is a peculiar exception among modern political systems. But, of course, Parekh's description of the United States is a fantasy.

Although it is true that the US Constitution has a unifying power, it owes this power to the fact that it draws upon, defines and upholds a national identity. Even though Abraham Lincoln declared the American 'nation' to be distinct from others, in being founded on a 'covenant', he did not mean to discard the national idea, but on the contrary to endorse it. Modern presidents and politicians make free use of this idea, and almost all children are inducted into citizenship by means of it. The most rebellious of leftist journals in the US calls itself the *Nation*, in order to emphasise the fact that the country has a *national* and not just a political interest, and that the Left is its true custodian. As the United States now exists – the most stable liberal polity in the mdoern world – it has all the characteristics of nationhood, and actively renews itself from its own national consciousness. America is first of all a territory, possessed through a 'union' of states. It has a common language, common habits of association, common customs and a common Judaeo-Christian culture. It is

intensely patriotic, and – in its healthy part – determined to defend
its interests against the world. As all readers of Tocqueville know,
the process of association is hyperactive in the United States,
proliferating its 'little platoons' which add their fund of local loyalties
to the larger loyalty upon which the political order depends. There
is also a strong religious dimension to the American idea. A
strange hybrid monotheism has grown from the thousand churches of
America – Christian in form, Hebrew in content – and each new
generation is absorbed into it by the process of national loyalty. And
this loyalty has its own historical myths, its own 'dreams', its own
sense of mission, its own powerful self-image, in which the American
land is the last refuge of the dispossessed, and also the birthplace of
a new and unfettered enterprise and will.

I do not say that the national loyalty is shared by *all* Americans.
But whoever travels away from the universities (centres of disaffection
in any state) will discover a process of nation-building that is second
to none in the modern world. And those who stand *outside* the
national loyalty – who attack their country's traditions and ridicule
its culture, who scoff at its simplicity, despise its leaders and reject
its God, who, in short, lack all vestige of American *'asabiyah* – who
are they, in general, if not the liberals themselves, those iinhabitants
of ivory towers who wrinkle their noses at the surrounding swamp of
moral bondage? And, by their single-minded attachment to the
'constitution' as the source of all political order, the liberals have
changed this instrument of national government into an instrument
of national interrogation: a means to question the legitimacy of
American traditions, and to break down the American culture. Only
the amazing strength of the national idea has maintained unity (and
therefore the rule of law) against a constitution now bent on
destroying it. And it is partly because America exists so *manifestly*
as a nation, in a world where national loyalties are falling or in
disarray, that there is such hostility to America in the modern world.

Which brings me again to the example that Parekh should have
chosen: the Austro-Hungarian Empire in Europe. On the surface
this offers a paradigm case of the multi-national *Rechtsstaat*: where
pre-political loyalty, such as it was, was owed not to a nation but to
a *crown*. But the Empire was not always liberal: it became so during
the eighteenth century, by virtue of the transformation which affected
all of Europe, and which awoke the sleeping consciousness of nations.
As the Empire moved in a liberal direction, so did its peoples begin
to define their loyalty in territorial and linguistic terms; and their

whole conception of themselves was gradually turned upside down. For many years the national loyalties which grew in central'Europe coexisted with the Habsburg obedience: but how long did it last, and how long was it likely to last? The Empire entered the First World War only to collapse in ruins. For the loyalties upon which it depended were by that time – thanks to the very liberal institutions which had been built on them – at variance with the imperial sovereignty. A similar collapse, accompanied by terrible civil war, followed the ending of the British Empire in India, peace being restored only when the rival confessions had formed themselves into separate states.

Why was the Ottoman Empire for so long the 'sick man of Europe'? Surely because its subject peoples, having (apart from the Turks and the Lebanese) no national but only a confessional identity, showed no disposition to defend their territory collectively, or to recognise a common jurisdiction over the people who resided there. At the collapse of the empire only two fragments of territory showed any lasting disposition to govern themselves by law and to permit the emergence of democratic institutions: Turkey and Lebanon, the two incipient nation states. In the case of Lebanon, however, national loyalty proved too fragile a thing, and gave way, in the face of external emergency, to confessional loyalties which have split the country and all but abolished its law.

Such examples remind us of the value of the national idea: not only as a source of unity, but also as a pre-condition of territorial defence. (It was his experience of the helplessness of Germany before the Napoleonic armies that inspired Fichte's nationalism: without an effective 'we', defined over territory, he realised, nothing can ever be defended.) In the modern world, it is precisely national loyalty that the liberal state requires, and national loyalty cannot emerge in a state where other, tighter, and fiercer loyalties compete with it. However, for Parekh, the liberal state is conceived as a staging post towards his real goal, which is the 'multi-cultural' society. In such a society the process of nation-building is impeded, or reversed, by the growth of loyalties of a non-national or anti-national kind. Experience ought to warn us against such a society: experience not only of Lebanon, but also of Cyprus, and India. If we really are interested in the survival of the liberal state, then we should be doing our best to preserve the loyalties which sustain the liberal jurisdiction.

LEFT CHAUVINISM

In a striking work, Alain Finkielkraut has pointed to the peculiar paradox of the 'multi-cultural' vision.[34] On the one hand it defends the universalist values of the Enlightenment, and recognises the legitimacy of no exclusions, no loyalties, no claims of ancestral right. On the other hand it speaks out for minority cultures, defends their exclusivity and sense of inherited purpose, and makes space for them within the liberal state. To the question whether to be universalist or particularist, the multi-culturalist liberal has two incompatible answers, depending on who asks the question and why. He is universalist against Western loyalties, particularist for the loyalties of others. But this intellectual inconsistency hides a consistent purpose: which is to undermine the social loyalties of the Western states – the only loyalties which, in the modern world, have shown any tendency to sustain liberal (and universalist) jurisdictions.

Nor does this purpose go unperceived. The failure of the left in Western elections is the consequence of their perceived disloyalty. Parties which advocate the destruction of national defences, the surrender of national sovereignty, the relaxing of controls on immigration; which endorse the destruction of national culture, the liberalisation of mores, and the dominance of urban élites; which show no attachment to the customs and ceremonies of the country, or to the religion that prevails in it – such parties naturally fail to capture a majority. If they were to do so, social loyalty would first have to disintegrate. And with it would disintegrate both the nation and the liberal state.

But this raises a deep question concerning liberal psychology. Why do the defenders of the liberal idea turn so angrily on those who oppose it? Why do these advocates of tolerance show so little tolerance of those who *really* disagree with them, and why are they prepared, like Parekh, to make false and damaging accusations against those with whom they most need to enter dialogue? The fact is that the advocates of the pure liberal theory are rarely satisfied by it. Just as much as the rest of us, they yearn after an original innocence, an experience of membership that will open the heart, and also close the mind. At a certain point the strain of living without an 'us' and a 'them' becomes intolerable. On the lonely heights of abstract choice nothing comforts and nothing consoles. The Kantian imperatives seem to blow more freezingly, and the unfed soul eventually flees from them, down into the fertile valleys of attachment.

But where shall he rest? To whom shall his loyalty be owed? What flock or herd or army can he join, who looks on all of them with the merely vicarious loyalty of the envious anthropologist? The answer is this: to find an enemy, to create a new kind of membership in the spirit of the battle. The enemy is the one who believes what the liberal so tragically fails to believe – the one who feels the loyalties to which the liberal ought in conscience to attach himself but which his own thinking has destroyed. To turn on the conservative is, in a peculiar way, to partake of his conviction, just as the Huron Indian absorbs the courage of his vanquished enemy by eating his unvanquished heart. This is the process of 'moral inversion'.[35] And it provides an interesting proof of our need for membership, in a world which – thanks to liberalism – is increasingly deprived of it.

BACK TO HEGEL

This returns me, in conclusion, to the deepest question raised by Parekh in his article. The conservative view of nationhood, Parekh suggests, refuses to advance from *Moralität* to *Sittlichkeit*, in dealing with those who belong to other 'kinds'. The contrast drawn by Hegel was not, in fact, between *Sittlichkeit* and morality (which is a part of *Sittlichkeit*, and transcended in it), but between morality and abstract right. Morality consists in the sphere of particular obligations, arising among those who are brought together by the workings of history, destiny, and chance. It is a sphere of concrete duty and responsibility, in which our obligations are inseparable from the conditions of life as mortal and dependent creatures. Abstract right corresponds more closely to the idea of obligation that underlies the full liberal theory of the state. Right and duty are here defined universally, without reference to the historical circumstances of the individual agent. Nothing in the sphere of abstract right distinguishes me from you or you from your neighbour: like all abstract systems, Hegel suggests, this of right is purely formal, without content, offering no concrete answer to the question what to do. Content comes only when abstract right is *situated* in the sphere of morality, when its formal laws are 'determined' by reference to the circumstances of life.

The 'full liberal theory of the state' sees no necessity for that synthesis. It stays fixated in the idea of right, and in the purely abstract notion of the rational agent. It moves directly to the thought that government requires nothing else for its legitimacy. Its schemes for the regeneration of mankind make no reference to historical attachments or prescriptive obligations: government is legitimate only if it does not dirty itself with the messy particularities of the flesh. Abstract right, taken alone, points always away from the empirical world of politics, to the Kingdom of Ends. This phantom – appearing now as the 'just society' of the contractarians, now as the 'full communism' of Marx – poisons our attachment to the realities through which we might, in our fallen condition, live and find fulfilment.

For Hegel the reality of *Geist* – as we might say, of everything human – is acquired through a process of realisation, in which the abstract is fixed in the concrete, and the universal disciplined by the particular. Reason, Hegel believed, will accomplish this transition of its own accord: out of the cold absolute of abstract right the urge to morality is born. But neither abstract right nor morality are fully real, he argued, until overcome in *Sittlichkeit*, which preserves in more conscious, more concrete form the distinguishing features of each. And *Sittlichkeit* in turn is sundered into three moments: the immediate and abstract, the mediated and concrete, and the final fulfilment of both in a self-conscious act of recuperation. These three moments are family, civil society and state. The legitimacy of the state depends upon its ability to overcome the separation inherent in civil society, and to recuperate in free and legal form the sense of belonging which surrounds us at birth, and nurtures our identity.

I would not defend the Hegelian picture in all its detail. But is it not a more plausible résumé of the interpenetration of the political and social, and of the mutual dependence of political legitimacy and non-political unity, than we are offered by the full liberal theory of the state? To suppose that the national idea is somehow alien to the liberal state is to fail to perceive that our existence as political beings does not derive from the state, but from spheres of social loyalty, and that it is by means of such loyalty that the state persists.

Notes and References

1. Bikhu Parekh, 'The "New Right" and the Politics of Nationhood', in N. Deakin (ed.), *The New Right: Image and Reality* (London, The Runnymede Trust, 1986).
2. J. G. Herder, *J. G. Herder on Social and Political Culture*, trans. and ed., with an introduction, by F. M. Barnard (Cambridge, 1969).

J. G. Fichte, *Addresses to the German Nation*, trans. by F. R. Jones and G. H. Turnbull (London and Chicago, 1922).

3. Ernest Renan, *Qu'est ce qu'une nation?* (Paris, 1882); Lord Acton, 'Nationality' in *The History of Freedom and Other Essays*, ed. J. N. Figgis and R. V. Laurence (London, 1907).
4. Parekh, 'The "New Right"': 39.
5. See B. Parekh, *Contemporary Political Thinkers* (Oxford, 1982).
6. See Henry Sidgwick, *The Elements of Politics* (London, 1891); J. S. Mill, *On Liberty* (London, 1859).
7. John Gray, 'The Politics of Culture Diversity', *The Salisbury Review*, 7 (September 1988): 38–44.
8. Michael Walzer, *Exodus and Revolution* (New York, 1985). Michael Sandel, *Liberalism and the Limits of Justice* (Cambridge, 1982). Charles Taylor, *Philosophy and the Human Sciences*, 2 vols (Cambridge, 1985).
9. So argues, for example, Sir Isaiah Berlin, in 'Nationalism: Past Neglect and Present Power', in *Against the Current* (New York, 1980).
10. Such, perhaps, is the nationalism of Sieyès and the French revolutionaries.
11. See Elie Kedourie, *Nationalism* (London, 1960).
12. See R. A. D. Grant, 'Shakespeare as a Conservative Thinker', in R. Scruton (ed.), *Conservative Thinkers* (London, 1988).
13. See the commentary by H. T. Buckle, *History of Civilization in England*, 3rd edn., vol. 1 (London, 1864): 491.
14. See the painstaking demolition by Jacques Barzun, *Race: A Study in Modern Superstition* (London, 1938).
15. On intentional kinds, see my *Sexual Desire* (London, 1986) Chapter 1.
16. I have tried to explain this idea more fully in 'Emotion and Common Culture', in *The Aesthetic Understanding* (London, 1983).
17. The dilemma that this poses for the contemporary Jew is interestingly unfolded in Alan Montefiore, 'The Jewish Religion – Universal Truth and Particular Tradition', *Tel Aviv Review*, 1 (1988): 166–86.
18. Ibn Khaldun, *Muqaddimah*, trans. and abridged E. Rogerson, Chapter 2, sections 8, 19, Chapter 3, sections 1, 19, 24–6.
19. In order to save Feuerbach and Marx from any suspicion of 'race thinking', *Gattungswesen* is normally translated as 'species-being' – which does little justice to the climate of opinion that gave birth to the term.
20. Sir Henry Maine, *Ancient Law* (London, 1890).
21. See note 7 above, and also Ronald Dworkin, *Law's Empire* (London, 1986).
22. Kenneth Minogue, *Nationalism* (New York, 1967): 154.
23. I discuss the communities of Lebanon in more detail in *A Land Held Hostage* (London, 1987).
24. Régis Debray, *Critique de la Raison Politique* (Paris, 1981): 178.
25. Debray, *Critique de la Raison Politique*: 208.
26. The canonical Marxist theory of nationality acknowledges the same basic features as I do: 'The nation is a human community, stable and historically constituted, born from a common language, territory, economic life and psychological conditioning, which together are translated into a community of culture' – J. Stalin, *Marxism and the National Question*

(1913), reproduced in Stalin, *Marxism and the National and Colonial Question* (London, 1941): 8.

27. See especially Albert Hourani, *Arabic Thought in the Liberal Age* (Oxford, 1962) in which the reader can clearly see the way in which liberal conceptions of law, sovereignty, and national ideas of *'asabiyah*, have emerged simultaneously in the modern Arabic world, and stood always in a relation of mutual questioning and dependence.

28. Alexander Solzhenitsyn, 'Repentance and Self-Limitation in the Life of Nations', in *From Under the Rubble* (London, 1976).

29. John H. Scharr, 'The Case for Patriotism', *American Review*, 17 (May 1973): 62–3.

30. Scharr, 'The Case for Patriotism': 63.

31. See Paul Johnson, *A History of the Jews* (London, 1987): 238.

32. See Antoine Fattal, *Le statut légal des non-musulmanes en pays d'Islam* (Beirut, Imprimerie Catholique, 1958).

33. Acton, 'Nationality': 294.

34. Alain Finkielkraut, *La défaite de la pensée* (Paris, 1987).

35. The term, but not the theory, comes from Michael Polanyi.

4 Conservatism, Individualism and the Political Thought of the New Right

John Gray

Perhaps the most remarkable and among the least anticipated developments in political thought and practice throughout the Western world in the 1980s was the conquest of conservatism by the ideas and doctrines of the New Right. This conquest was nowhere total, and it was not by any means universal. It can be justly termed hegemonic, nevertheless, in precisely the Gramscian sense, in that conservative parties, governments and intellectual journals came to be dominated by a discourse and an agenda of policy that emanated from thinkers of the New Right and embodied a searching and often harsh critique of conservative thought and practice during the thirty years or so that followed the Second World War. Indeed, the hegemonic character of the political thought of the New Right – a hegemony that may prove to have been fragile and ephemeral, but which at present shows only few and small signs of strain – was attested by the fact that during the 1980s the parties of the Left felt constrained to adopt much of the discourse, and many of the policies, that conservative governments had imbibed from the theorists of the New Right. In one case, that of New Zealand, it was the Labour Party that implemented the most radical and far-reaching programme of economic reform (on lines suggested by New Right thinkers) that has been attempted in any Western democratic state – a reform programme that, despite its upheavals and difficulties, has compelled the conservative National Party in New Zealand to adopt a rhetoric of economic liberty and market competition that is very different from the Keynesian and protectionist rhetoric and policy that are its historical inheritance. It would be rash to essay the judgment that the policy achievements of governments animated by the ideas of the New Right are irreversible. It is reasonable, at the same time, to affirm that a sea-change has occurred in political life in the western democracies, and more particularly in conservative thought and practice in the English-speaking nations, that has many of the marks of irreversibility.

The hegemony of the New Right within conservatism emerged in a very definite historical context. Even if, as I have intimated, it will probably have some consequences for both conservative and socialist policy and rhetoric that are irreversible, it is sensible to suppose that the hegemony of the political thought of the New Right, both within and outside conservatism, will be limited by the historical contingencies that brought it into being. This is so, most particularly, in regard to its domination of conservative thinking. For the relations of the New Right with the received tradition of conservative thought and practice are highly complex and controversial, but there can be no doubt that the novel orthodoxy of New Right thought within conservatism has initiated as much rupture with recent practice as it has (on some accounts) restored conformity with an earlier and supposedly a purer conservatism. My object in this exploration will be to attempt to define the content, limits and varieties of doctrine of the New Right, and to specify the affinities and tensions that have arisen between the New Right and the received inheritance of conservative practice. Except by way of an occasional comparison with conditions in the United States, I shall confine myself to the British experience. And I shall focus my inquiries around the central and fundamental question of the place and character of individualism within conservative doctrine – a question that has been answered very differently both by thinkers of the New Right and by their conservative critics.

A rehearsal, not of my arguments, but of my conclusions, may be apposite. I shall conclude that, whereas the New Right correctly perceived that a generation of conservative practice had led modern western democratic states into a dead-end of corporatist stagnation in which a ratchet-effect operated that moved the political centre steadily leftwards, its theorists consistently neglected the cultural inheritance which is the matrix of a stable capitalist order. In part because of their debts to the intellectual tradition of classical liberalism, the principal theorists of the New Right failed to perceive the dependency of individualist civil society on a dwindling but real patrimony of ideas, beliefs, and values. In some cases, they subscribed to the unrealisable and dangerous utopian project of a minimal or neutral state enforcing a regime of common rules that is not underwritten by a fund of common culture. In no case did the thinkers of the New Right undertake the historical researches necessary in order to illuminate the sources of the stability of the capitalist order in Britain or the United States. The political thought of the New Right, even in its subtlest expression (or in Hayek), transmitted to conservatism an abstract rationalism and legalism that occludes serious theorising of the conditions under which market capitalist institutions have for centuries enjoyed an almost unchallenged hegemony in Britain and the United States. In other words, the New Right has in its theorising failed to grasp the historical and cultural presuppositions and limits of the kind of civil society they seek to maintain, restore or enhance. And this theoretical neglect has disabled the policies of governments animated by the thinking of the New Right, in that policy (as distinct from rhetoric) has been concerned almost solely with securing the legal and economic conditions of market competition and thereby of general prosperity, and has only rarely and inadequately addressed the cultural conditions that undergird and sustain a stable market order. Insofar as the New Right ever nurtured a hegemonic project, this has been compromised in political practice by the blind-spot it has cocooned regarding the importance of the culture of the individualism of which a market economy is only the visible part.

It is to this culture of individualism, ancient in England and resilient if insulted and injured, even in our own times, that theoretical inquiry and historical research should now turn. Here the argument I develop diverges from that of conservative critics of the neo-liberal New Right, such as Roger Scruton, who have perceptively and powerfully criticised the neglect within neo-liberalism of the common culture that founds western civil society and enables it to reproduce itself across the generations. My argument diverges from this conservative critique, in as much as it maintains at once that our common cultural inheritance is individualist, and that its political embodiment cannot always, or even as a rule, coincide with that of the modern nation-state. The character of this individualist inheritance, as we receive it at present, and the forms in which it may enjoy a political embodiment, are very difficult issues, about which I can here only offer inconclusive speculations. The upshot of my reflections, however, is that, since individualism as a form of life pre-dates liberalism as a political doctrine by centuries, it is reasonable to expect (and to hope) that individualist culture will survive the demise of liberalism. And, since individualism and liberalism are not to be confused, it is a mistake on the part of conservative critics of the New Right to suppose that civil society can do without its individualist inheritance, or find a surrogate for that inheritance in the modernist project of integral nationhood.

What, then, was the New Right?[1] At the level of policy, it is not difficult to identify the salient themes of New Right thought. Policy animated by the ideas of the New Right sought to dismantle the corporatist institutions built up in Britain in the post-war period, to limit government and at the same time to restrain the power of inordinate organised interests such as the trade unions, to achieve a stable currency and abandon deficit financing and, in general, to engineer a transfer of initiative and resources from government to civil society that was massive and politically irreversible. In practical terms, such a policy orientation expressed itself in measures for the privatisation of state-owned industries, in the Medium Term Financial Strategy, tax reduction, a curb on public expenditure, and a variety of supply-side measures deregulating prices, wages, rents and some planning controls. It is not such detailed policy measures that will interest the historian of the New Right, however, but rather their philosophical and theoretical inspiration. The intellectual perspective which infused these policies was not that which had dominated post-war British conservatism; it came from outside the Conservative Party, from the works of F. A. Hayek and Milton Friedman, and from the free market think-tanks, above all, from the Institute of Economic Affairs.[2] The pedigree of this perspective on policy on society was classical liberal, not conservative. This is to say that it was strongly and sometimes stridently individualist, it sought to reduce government to an indispensable minimum, and (except, to some extent, in the work of Hayek[3]) it concerned itself very little with the cultural or social conditions of a stable restoration of market institutions. In economic policy, the impact of classical liberal thought, especially as developed and applied (during decades of neglect by the mainstream of academic life) by the IEA, was crucial and indispensable. The classical liberal inheritance, consistently and judiciously implemented in the early years of the Thatcher period, enabled government to act to dismantle, probably for good, a significant portion of the detritus of corporatist institutions left by a generation of passive and reactive conservative government and policy-making.

As it was embodied in the early years of Thatcherism, the classical liberal orientation of much policy could also legitimately claim a genuine conservative pedigree. The allegation of the Tory 'wets'[4] that Thatcherism represented a rupture in an otherwise unbroken tradition of conservative thought and practice does not survive historical scrutiny. Nineteenth-century conservative government, whether that of Disraeli or of Salisbury, conceived itself as superintending the institutions of civil society, and occasionally supplementing them, but not as being in the business of managing the economy. This is to say that, at least until the 1930s, British conservatives conceived government as the guardian of civil association (in Oakeshott's terminology[5]). The idea of government as an enterprise association – as a sponsor or pacemaker of economic growth, say – is in fact quite alien to the British conservative tradition. In this respect, then, Thatcherism can make a genuine claim to have revived or restored an earlier tradition of conservative government.

There is another, and more fundamental reason in support of the thesis that Thatcherism embodies a genuine British, or more precisely English, tradition, and is not an incursion into British political life of an alien liberal or conservative doctrine. This is in the historical fact, profoundly explored by Alan Macfarlane,[6] and deployed by Jonathan Clark in his contribution to this collection (Chapter 2), that English life, contrary to the traditional historiography of Polanyi,[7] and of Marx, has had an individualist character at least since the thirteenth century. The idea that there was, in the seventeenth century or earlier, a Great Transformation of English life from communal to individualist forms, an idea that has entered political thought from the work of C. B. Macpherson,[8] does not accord with demonstrable facts about English life – facts to do with personal mobility, land use and the pattern of family life. If, as Macfarlane has persuasively argued, England was an individualist society immemorially, then the project that animated Thatcherism – the project of limiting government and reviving civil association – is one that seeks to reassert the most ancient and fundamental English traditions.

Neo-liberalism and Thatcherite conservatism are, then, seeking to restore and reproduce an English individualist culture that is our historical inheritance. Where they appear to differ is in their recognition, or neglect, of the historical conditions and inheritance which allowed this culture to sustain itself for so long. As Jonathan Clark has argued in Chapter 2, English individualism – the culture that grounded English civil society – was not liberal but instead authoritarian individualism. This is to say that it depended on a nexus of beliefs, practices and inhibitions which conferred legitimacy on it and continued the corrosive tendencies about which the Scottish writers, and particularly Ferguson,[9] were concerned in their theorising about the potentially self-destructive effects of the anonymity and moral laxity that were latent in individualist life. These tendencies were inhibited in English authoritarian individualism by the strength in England of a common moral culture and, more particularly, by the authority of the Anglican church (and, later, by the moral discipline imposed by noncomformist Christianity). Similar religious traditions in the United States for a century or more constrained the tendencies toward anomie and hedonism which (as Tocqueville perceived) were otherwise present in the individualism of a culture lacking in the hierarchies that had structured individualism in England.

Thatcherite conservatism has distinguished itself from neo-liberalism, and has established its affinities with American neo-conservatism, by its reiterated emphasis on the familial and religious values that legitimated capitalist institutions in their Victorian hey-day. Thatcherite conservatism has the advantage over neo-liberalism, for this reason, is that it explicitly addresses the character of the cultural matrix of individualist civil society. It is far from clear, however, that the invocation of Victorian values – religious and familial – can do the job of legitimating market institutions that is required of such values by the Thatcher project. This is so for several reasons. In the first place, England is in the late twentieth century a massively secularised society. In this it resembles most closely the Scandinavian countries and Japan, and differs sharply from the United States (which in turn accounts for the non-existence in England of anything resembling the American phenomenon of the Moral Majority). It is wholly anachronistic to expect that Christianity, and particularly the Church of England, will ever have the political significance in England that it possessed throughout the seventeenth, eighteenth and nineteenth centuries. Indeed, insofar as the Anglican Church has had influence on political life in England, it has been to further the tendencies whereby market institutions and individualist civil society are delegitimated, since the dominant part of Anglican social theology has for decades been infused with the anti-capitalist mentality that pervades intellectual life in England more generally.

The second reason why the Thatcherite appeal to the common cultural inheritance of individualism cannot work is the substantial enhancement of various sorts of pluralism within English society. The mass immigration of the 1960s has contributed to English life an ethnic and a religious pluralism that is unalterable and irreversible in any foreseeable future. Given the self-assertion of British Islam, and its demands for separate state-funded schooling, it is likely that this pluralism will increase, rather than diminish, over the coming decades. A similar, though more diffuse and less politically visible pluralism is widespread in English society in attitudes to marriage, sexuality and other beliefs about dependent institutions and practices. If the English common culture were ever a seamless garment, it is no longer so. It is questionable whether a strong and resilient common culture any longer prevails in England. It is beyond reasonable doubt that its content has been attenuated, and its significance in performing a legitimating role in respect of civil society in England weakened. Nor is there any reason to suppose that Thatcherite rhetoric has had any transforming impact on the diverse and indeed fragmented culture which now exists in England.

What might supplement the dwindling common culture as the legitimating force that sustains a capitalist regime in Britain? In practice, both Thatcherites and neo-conservatives in the United States have relied – thus far successfully – on economic growth, and the manifest failure of both post-war macroeconomic management and of socialist command economies to sustain the electoral support needed for neo-liberal economic policies. Unless the most optimistic among the American supply-siders[10] are right, and the business cycle has been abolished, it seems imprudent and complacent to suppose that the hegemony of market institutions can rest forever on increasing prosperity. (Environmental concerns may in any case constrain the pursuit of constant economic growth.) In the context of the mass democracies of contemporary Britain and the United States, there is every reason to suppose that a period of protracted economic difficulty would swing the political pendulum back to interventionist, and in the United States protectionist, economic policies, and could well end the long tenure in power of the Conservatives and the Republicans. This is not to say that we need fear in England a return to full-blooded socialism. The intellectual hegemony of the New Right in economic theory, and the collapse of socialism as a doctrine in both Eastern and Western Europe, rule out any doctrinal survival of socialism. Again, many of the policies implemented under the incisive Thatcher Government are politically irreversible. (Most privatisations fall into this category). What is to be feared in the wake of protracted economic difficulty is not socialism, but a return to corporatist and interventionist policies that not only injure the autonomous institutions of civil society but also compound the economic difficulties that evoked them. In the United States, more than in Britain, the end of the long boom may well see a serious crisis in financial institutions weakened (as much of corporate America is) by inordinate debt, and a policy response which reinvigorates the American tradition of combining isolationism with protectionism. In the British case, where fiscal prudence has been maintained, we are likely to see a return to 'stop-go' economic management, against a background of high inflation, high interest rates and revived union power.

Exclusive or primary reliance on economic growth as the legitimating condition of market capitalist institutions in the context of mass democracy is unwise and will predictably fail. An alternative, suggested by High Tory critics of the neo-liberal components in Thatcherism such as Roger Scruton, is little more promising. Scruton argues in his contribution to this collection (Chapter 3) that it is nationhood that provides the indispensable foundation of liberal civil society in our time. Scruton's argument has considerable merit in exposing the insufficiency, and the inconsistency, of those such as Parekh[11] who have maintained that a multi-cultural society can be supported (as supposedly in America) solely by liberal legalism and constitutionalism. Scruton's positive endorsement of nationhood as the condition of a stable civil society is nevertheless unpersuasive. In historical terms, what has sustained the most successful civil societies has not been nationhood but monarchy (as in the British case) or empire (as in the Hapsburg Empire which Scruton discusses). If civil society has a future in contemporary Spain, again, it is in virtue of monarchy, since Spain as it now exists is little more than a composite state which itself is an artefact of monarchy. Scruton also underestimates the modernity of nationhood. As late as the 1870s a majority of French school children identified themselves by their provinces, and not as French. In Europe, nationhood is in most countries the construction of political élites, not the expression of the solidarity of a people. Ironically, the modern European nation-state is mostly the creation of nineteenth-century classical liberalism, which was an agency for centralisation and against localism.[12] Examples such as Poland and Japan, where nationhood and statehood coincide, are in fact highly exceptional, and not at all the rule.

Minogue and Kedourie[13] are closer to the mark than Scruton, when they observe that nationalism is a modernist project inspired by romantic doctrine. In the post-colonial world, it has acted as a destroyer of traditional forms of life and as a pacemaker for communism. Where it has expressed a genuine, pre-political or social popular solidarity, it has typically been one that was once embodied in statehood, and is preserved as such in popular memory – as in the Baltic states. (Only the Kurds come to mind as a possible exception to this generalisation.) Finally, when nationalism has arisen within a civil society governed by a rule of law, as in the Sikh phenomenon in India, it has acted as a threat to civil society. In all these respects, the modernist cult of nationalism is akin to the no less modernist phenomenon of fundamentalism. With rare exceptions, such as Poland and the Baltic states, it is characterised by enmity to civil society and not by support for it.

Neither neo-liberalism nor its conservative critics, if my reasonings are sound, recognise the cultural foundation and historical limits of individualist civil society. In this they may be influenced by a conflation of individualism with civil society that is valid in the English and American contexts but not in a world context. The English and European theorists of civil society – Hobbes, Locke, Hegel, Tocqueville and others – represented as an inherent and univeral truth the connexion between individualist culture and a civil society encompassing market institutions. The experience of the last decade or so, however, in which powerful and stable market economies have emerged in the non-individualist cultures of Japan and Korea, for example, suggests that the connexion between individualism and civil society is contingent and not necessary. This recent experience supports the Scottish and neo-conservative fear that, in slowly consuming its pre-individualist foundations, Western civil society may (as Schumpeter speculated[14]) be a self-limiting historical episode.

For the present, no doubt, such fears are exaggerated – although it remains to be seen how American culture responds to the novel experience of continuing, and probably inexorable, economic decline. The concerns I have explored suggest, however, that there are no easy answers to the question: What is now the content of the common culture that supports and legitimates market capitalism? And this in turn suggests that the policy agenda of post-Thatcherism will need to be judicious and balanced when it comes, as it inevitably must, to seek to retard or reverse the further erosion of the moral capital on which market institutions must rely. The crusade for Victorian values is, as has already been intimated, an exercise in anachronism. This is not to say that there cannot be serious policies aiming at strengthening what remains of the common individualist culture in England. In education, in social and welfare policy, there are desirable reforms, well within the limits of what is politically possible, which could well strengthen the family and reinforce the popular sense of individual responsibility. Enforcing the obligations of the delinquent parent in one-parent families, wherever this is feasible, is only one rather obvious example. In education, a National Curriculum which enforces literacy in English, which promotes an understanding of British history, and which perhaps incorporates a civic education, could do something to restore the fabric of the common culture.

No government can create a culture where it is absent, or engineer the renewal of a culture where it is moribund. As Wittgenstein put it, deliberately continuing to renew damaged or weak traditions is as hopeless as trying to repair a broken spider's web with one's bare hands. Government has, nevertheless, and contrary to neo-liberalism, a vital role in regard to the culture of individualism. Negatively, it can refrain from damaging it, by abandoning policies which create dependency, overturn traditional disciplines and encourage irresponsibility.[15] Positively, it can provide a framework of policy and institutions within which individualist culture is protected and nurtured. In so doing, it is tending the pre-individualist forms of life – family and local life, for example – that are the soil on which individuality grows and thrives. It is only by addressing these cultural pre-conditions of individualism, and framing sensible policy in respect of them, that the current hegemony of market institutions can be preserved, and a secure future for civil society achieved.

The philosophical insight which such desirable reforms embody is that, even where (as in England) individualist culture is immemorial, it is not primordial, but depends on a background of beliefs, values and institutions which both form and constrain individuality. It is this cultural patrimony of individualism that neo-liberal thought ignores, and which Thatcherite policy has insufficiently addressed. Individuality, as we know it, is not a natural fact, but a cultural achievement. The persons who inhabit and reproduce a liberal civil society are not biological organisms but historical artefacts, products of a long and often arduous struggle to build up and maintain specific sorts of institutions and practices. With us, at any rate, individualism and civil society have always gone together, and civil society has no future apart from the culture of individualism. Ironically, it is this culture that is being threatened, especially in the United States, by a left-liberalism which regards the undergirding institutions of liberal civil society – marriage, private property and so forth – as constraints upon, and not as conditions of individual freedom. The irony in intellectual history is that it is liberalism, at least since Mill,[16] that has transmitted the enmity to civil society and to the moral traditions that support it that has long been evident in modern Europe in the antinomian character of the anti-individual (in Oakeshott's expression[17]) – the dislocated, anosmic character, typified by Rousseau, who seeks a release from the burdens of freedom in the recreation of a form of communal solidarity that, in England at any rate, was always largely imaginary.

Individualism in England is not – as it is in Turkey, say – an imposition from above, generated by legality and military force. It is our common cultural inheritance. But, as I have argued throughout, the renewal across the generations of this individualist tradition cannot be left safely to chance. Government has a vital role in preserving, or repairing, the framework of practices and replenishing the fund of values, on which individualism depends for its successful reproduction. If Thatcherism was ever an hegemonic project – and that it how it should rightly have been conceived – it condemned itself to failure by its faulty grasp of the cultural pre-conditions of market liberalism. It may be that, despite its continuing economic success, Western civil society is in an irreversible decline, which government can retard but not reverse. Even in this worst case, it remains the intellectual responsibility of conservatives in the era of post-Thatcherism to theorise the conditions under which civil society in England may retain its vitality. In this task they are distracted by neo-liberal and holistic High Tory doctrine which fails to attend to the minute particulars of our individualist inheritance and which does not illuminate the deeper tradition that it expresses. Civil society – which is to say a society that, under a rule of law, allows the great majority of transactions to be conducted in autonomous institutions, and in which the bulk of economic life is realised in market exchanges among legally recognised owners of private property – is the only form of life in which civilisation has been enjoyed by modern Europeans. Oakeshott has characterised civil society in the English form with unsurpassable clarity:

> What, then, are the characteristics of our society in respect of which we consider ourselves to enjoy freedom and in default of which we would not be free in our sense of the word? But first, it must be observed that the freedom we enjoy is not composed of a number of independent characteristics of our society which in aggregate make up our liberty. Liberties, it is true, may be distinguished, and some may be more general or more settled and mature than others, but the freedom which the English libertarian

knows and values lies in a coherence of mutually supporting liberties, each of which amplifies the whole and none of which stands alone. It springs neither from the separation of church and state, nor from the rule of law, nor from private property, nor from parliamentary government, nor from the writ of *habeas corpus*, nor from the independence of the judiciary, nor from any one of the thousand other of the devices and arrangements characteristic of our society, but from what each signifies and represents, namely, the absence from our society of overwhelming concentrations of power. Similarly, the conduct of government in our society involves a sharing of power, not only between the recognised organs of government, but also between the Administration and the Opposition. In short, we consider ourselves to be free because no one in our society is allowed unlimited power – no leader, faction, party or 'class', no majority, no government, church, corporation, trade or professional association or trade union. The secret of its freedom is that it is composed of a multitude of organisations in the constitution of the best of which is reproduced that diffusion of power which is characteristic of the whole.[18]

If conservatives are serious in the commitment to the project of achieving a political hegemony for this form of life, they must return their theorising to history. For, in returning us to a self-understanding hitherto clouded by defective history – liberal, Marxist or High Tory-holist – they will thereby strengthen the intellectual hegemony which the thought of the New Right has achieved in economic theory and policy. And, in so doing, they will make a small, but vital contribution to the success of the political project of securing hegemony for civil society – by creating a discourse in which its most central institutions can be theorised as historical achievements.

Notes and References

1. For an excellent survey of the New Right, see Norman P. Barry, *The New Right* (London, 1987) and David G. Green, *The New Conservatism: the Counter Revolution in Political, Economic and Social Thought* (New York, 1987).
2. A good account of the role of the IEA in successfully promoting a counter-revolution in economic thought can be derived from several of the essays in A. Seldon (ed.), *The 'New Right' Enlightenment* (Sevenoaks,

1985).

3. So, especially, Hayek's essay, 'Individualism: true and false' in F. A. Hayek, *Individualism and Economic Order* (London, 1976).

4. For an exposition of Tory 'wet' views, see Ian Gilmour, *Inside Right* (London, 1977).

5. See Michael Oakeshott, *On Human Conduct* (Oxford, 1975).

6. Alan Macfarlane, *The Origins of English Individualism* (Oxford, 1978) and *The Culture of Capitalism* (Oxford, 1987).

7. Karl Polanyi, *The Great Transformation* (London, 1948).

8. C. B. Macpherson, *The Political Theory of Possessive Individualism: Hobbes to Locke* (Oxford, 1962).

9. I discuss this concern of Ferguson's briefly in my *Liberalisms: Essays in Political Philosophy* (London, 1989): 268–71.

10. The writings of Paul Craig Roberts are among the best of the supply-side argument for the eliminability, or radical reduction, in the business cycle.

11. See B. Parekh, 'The New Right and the Politics of Nationhood', in M. Deakin, *The New Right: Image and Reality* (London, 1986).

12. This point is well developed in Norman Stone's *Europe Transformed 1879–1919* (London, 1984): 201 *et seq.*

13. See E. Kedourie, *Nationalism* (London, 1960) and K. Minogue, *Nationalism* (New York, 1967).

14. See J. Schumpeter's classic work *Capitalism, Socialism and Democracy* (London, 1943).

15. I consider some such desirable measures in my *Limited Government: A Positive Agenda* (London, Institute for Economic Affairs, Hobart Paper, 113, 1989).

16. On the failings of Millian individualism, see Chapter 12 of my *Liberalisms*.

17. For Oakeshott's account of the emergence and character of the anti-individual, see his *On Human Conduct*.

18. M. Oakeshott, *Rationalism in Politics* (London, 1962).

Part III
Theology: the Vision of Man

5 Theology, Toleration and Conflict

S. W. Sykes

The purpose of this Chapter is to unravel some complications in the status and content of Christian theological contributions to the public discussion of political and moral ideas in Britain today. It is, regrettably, no more than a prolegomenon to the case for arguing that it would be both coherent with the traditions of this country, and humanly, that is, morally satisfying, to act on the assumption that the United Kingdom is a Christian state skilled in the politics of toleration. Such a case has been dismissed mostly by default, and the theological contribution to it, for reasons we shall need to explain, has been less than impressive. The attractiveness of such a conclusion in the context of contemporary debate grows with increased appreciation of the bleakness of the alternatives, an experience constantly reinforced by exposure to the incantatory vacuousness of the phrase 'a modern pluralist culture'. On the contrary Christianity remains, as the Education Act 1989 affirmed, the dominant religious tradition in the United Kingdom. But it is a tradition whose history demonstrates a lack of homogeneity, and which has continued to change in significant ways in the last twenty years. The same period has seen growth and increasingly vigorous participation in public life from the non-Christian religions, and a large percentage of the population (as much as 28 per cent) declare themselves to be of no religion.[1] A great deal, therefore, turns on how the dominant religious group treats both religious minorities and secularists. The character and fate of Christian toleration matters to British culture, to say nothing of the Irish context.

Part of the complexity of this history emerges with an examination of the study of theology in British universities.[2] Already in the late nineteenth century a separation had begun to take place between the academic study of theology in universities and its practical or pastoral application in denominational seminaries. By a series of deft accommodations what in England had been designed as a syllabus for the education of Anglican clergy was turned into the undenominational study of the Bible and Church History. Scottish universities retained their rôle of training Presbyterian ministers for the parishes, and church representatives still sit on key appointments committees. But in England, apart from Durham and Oxford, the Faculties and Departments of theology have entirely abandoned any form of denominational control over appointments.

Characteristically this situation has come about through a series of minor local adjustments, and not through any centralised enquiry or planning. The result is that what passes for a degree in 'theology' in a modern English university may bear startlingly little resemblance to the classic courses of study in the European context, Protestant or Catholic. Even the truncated three-year syllabuses of English universities in the 1950s seemed provincially narrow in their scope; more so the market-led cafeteria of options lacking any pretence at sequence or coherence designed to match the whims and fancies of the undergraduate of the 1980s.

One astonishing example of the defects of the theology syllabuses might be mentioned, the fate of the study of Christian ethics. In the classic Catholic and Protestant schemes of education Christian ethics was an essential part of the core curriculum, closely associated with Christian doctrine, and thus strongly stamped by the characteristic traditions and teachings of a particular denomination. In the undenominational syllabuses of English universities, however, the study of Christian ethics has all but disappeared, its residual survival as an option resting upon precarious association with philosophical ethics. As a consequence modern theologians trained in English universities know virtually nothing about the traditions of Christian social and political thought since the days of St Augustine and are correspondingly unprepared for the ethical challenges of developments in modern biology, biotechnology, and economics.

Among the reasons for this state of affairs is the failure of theology to engage in criticial reflection on the basis for its very presence in the modern university.[3] In the 1960s a challenge to the Christian domination of theology emerged with the rise of 'Religious Studies', a phenomenon of North American provenance. Critical of the implicit Christian bias of syllabuses of theology, protagonists asked why, for example, British Jews should tolerate a biblical discipline entitled 'Old' Testament studies, or why there was virtually no place in Faculties and Departments of Theology for the study of Islam, Hinduism and Buddhism except as 'comparative' religion.[4] Taking their cue from departments of religious studies in state universities in the USA, syllabuses were devised so as to ensure that more than one religious tradition was studied in its integrity, and that the methods of study were phenomenological or (at least) religiously neutral. The University of Lancaster became the first to develop a large and successful Department of Religious Studies; other universities engaged in smaller and more tentative developments; others again characteristically adapted by adding religious studies to their existing theological enterprises.

The initial debate about theoretical principles was never especially profound, and the invocation of a 'modern pluralistic culture' as justification for the new development rested on a cluster of still-obscure assumptions. Theological study in universities survived the challenge for two pragmatic reasons. In the first place, student demand for 'proper theology' (a pious phrase frequently on the lips of candidates for admission to the more resolutely conservative Faculties of Theology in this country) continued. Whereas the theory of religious studies demanded that Christian theology should be a subordinate sub-discipline within an overarching, religiously plural scheme, in fact the modest adoption of religious studies as one part of a predominantly Christian studies programme has so far proved to match the needs and interests of the majority of current students. Secondly, the practical difficulties of doing justice to the study of three, four or five separate religious traditions with inadequate numbers of teachers has wholly overwhelmed the theoretical desirability of doing so.

The gains to theology from the implicit and explicit challenge of religious studies have nonetheless been considerable. Methods of the study of religions drawn from the social sciences and from phenomenology have counterbalanced the tendency of Christian theology to overstress the importance of explicit, propositionally formulated belief. More important has been the attention which religious studies has focused upon the needs and interests of religious minorities in Britain. If it has not led to a wholesale abandonment of Christian theological enterprise, it has none the less forced upon theologians of that tradition the question about Christian attitudes to other religions. Although this had been long debated in theology, especially in European Protestantism, against a background of radical doubt about the appropriateness of Christian missions, the British discussion took place in the unique context of an already existing set of compromises about undenominational religious education, and a searing controversy about the limits of unbelief.

The provision of the Butler Education Act of 1944 for undenominational but Christian religious education in state schools reflected what had proved to be an acceptable compromise within the universities.[5] The tolerance which had made it possible for established churches both in England and Scotland to coexist with other churches enjoying complete religious liberty and civil equality was celebrated by the Anglican historian Norman Sykes in *The English Religious Tradition* (1953) as an example of 'the English [sic] genius for compromise'.[6] Religious education meant Christian education (though Catholics did not participate); Jews, Muslims, Buddhists, Hindus – or atheists – were minorities whose religious liberty was protected, negatively, by the right to withdraw.

Since 1944 one notable advance has occurred broadly within this consensus. The modern emergence of Catholicism out of a partly imposed and partly self-imposed ghetto into participation in English cultural life is a story of considerable fascination.[7] The early 1960s had witnessed the early beginnings of English discussion of the possibility that Catholics might take full part in university theological education.[8] The ideological basis for such participation was provided by the Second Vatican Council's declaration on Religious Liberty (1965), which wholeheartedly endorsed freedom of conscience as a pre-condition of any Christian belief whatsoever.[9] It is sobering to recall that the Cambridge lay Anglican historian, Kitson Clark, had only a few years earlier in his *The Kingdom of Free Men* (1957) engaged with Cardinal Ottaviani, Pro-Secretary of the Holy Office, on precisely the question of whether it could be argued (as Ottaviani did) that religious error had no rights.[10]

The impetus which the Second Vatican Council gave to Catholic participation in the ecumenical movement greatly strengthened the central Christian liberal consensus of toleration, a movement with deep European roots, already formulated by Erasmus in the context of sixteenth-century European theological and political intolerance, and drawing on a broader humanism with both classical and Christian strands. In theory the 1970s should have been a moment when Anglicanism emerged as triumphantly vindicated by history, as the Catholic Church moderated the excessive papalism of the Counter Reformation and the First Vatican Council, endorsed the principle of lay Bible study, and introduced the use of the vernacular in the liturgy. In fact Anglicans, especially in the Church of England, together with the major Protestant denominations of the western world, and, eventually, the Catholic Chruch itself, began to taste the bitter fruits of liberalism, its sheer inability to provide an adequate positive basis for religious conviction, its tendency to be parasitic on, and reactive to, the profounder religious convictions of others.

The Church of England at this moment began to exhibit the symptoms of a massive failure of nerve about its own identity. The roots of this disease are by no means the simple desire to be ever more broadly tolerant, although it is the case that Erasmian humanism played an important part in the formation of Anglican 'comprehensiveness' in the sixteenth century. Paradoxically one of the least tolerant strands of Anglicanism, the High Church or Oxford Movement of the nineteenth century, played a major rôle in the history of Anglican deconfessionalisation. A characteristic of each of the churches of the Reformation was their formulation of a 'confession', as a public profession of theological identity and as a foundation charter for the life of the Church. Although at an early stage the Church of England produced its own Articles (later known as the Thirty-Nine Articles), and although these were extensively based upon the Lutheran *Confessio Augustana* of 1530, at no stage in the life of the Church of England have these articles had the exclusive status of the confessions of the Calvinist or Lutheran Churches. At the very least one must say that the Thirty-Nine Articles are supplemented by the Book of Common Prayer and by the Ordinal, and that these inclusions introduce an element of unclarity and ambiguity into the notion of a 'confessional basis', as compared with a single, homogeneous confessional text. But groups of late-eighteenth- and early-nineteenth-century Anglicans were determined to accentuate the distinction between Anglicanism and Protestantism; and some of the writers of the Oxford Movement began to denigrate the actions, theology, confessional and liturgical productions of the sixteenth-century Anglican reformers. Whereas eighteenth-century liberal Anglicans had deplored the act of affirming the Thirty-Nine Articles because they were too restrictive, nineteenth-century Anglo-Catholic Anglicans did so because they were too Protestant. The movement to separate international Anglicanism from its sixteenth-century 'confessional' basis can be traced through the Lambeth Conferences from 1867 to 1968, when a hastily constructed motion advising member churches not to print the Articles in their prayer books was passed with few abstentions.[11] The coalition which this represented between liberals and Anglo-Catholics was, of course, too unstable to provide any alternative confessional basis. And meanwhile the radical, historicist wing of theological opinion was arguing, on grounds of general historical relativism, that no confession of pre-modern date could possibly be adequate to, or binding upon, minds formed by the 'modern scientific view of reality'. The Church of England Doctrine Commission, presided over by the Regius Professor of Divinity in the University of Oxford, Maurice Wiles, and dominated by Anglican modernists, produced after many years of labour an astonishing document, *Christian Believing* (1976), which made clear the extent to which prominent scholars had lost confidence in the truth of the classical creeds.[12]

At once a chasm opened up. Were there no limits to liberalism? Did Christian toleration and hospitality extend to those to whom it had traditionally been refused, deniers of the doctrines of the Trinity and incarnation, and even of the classical doctrine of God? Prominent Anglican theologians appeared to belong to each of these heretical categories, and modern publicity ensured that their existence within the spectrum of Anglican comprehensiveness was well known. Suddenly, at a moment when the central Anglican tradition ought to have been celebrating its ecumenical and international coming of age, it was plunged into anxious and self-absorbed debate about its own identity.[13] The internal instability of liberalism was manifest.

The debate about sexual behaviour ran parallel to, and sometimes overlapped with, the theological discussion of the limits of unbelief. The connections between the two have been admirably identified by Bernice Martin employing *rites de passages* conceptuality from social anthropology.[14] The movements which in the 1960s strove for the breakdown of hierarchy and structure and for a more thorough realisation of human *communitas* (to use Victor Turner's word), attacked the conventional role-differentiation of the sexes. It was demanded of the churches that they should no longer seek to restrain or even to structure the life of the feelings, and the prohibition of adultery, fornication and homosexual genital behaviour came under attack. On the whole orthodox theology failed to perceive the general cultural background to this movement, which in its Christian guise presented itself as a new reformation overturning an oppressive and Pharasaic religious culture of sub-Christian origins.

The counter-attack against the liberal consensus has its own complexities and contradictions. Since the impact of the European Enlightenment, Catholic and Protestant churches have had a continuous history of forms of reactionary conservatism, national denominational confessional movements, romantic returns to a selectively reconstructed Christian past, and violent anti-modernist purges. Since churches live as much by the accumulation of memories as by the dissemination of ideas, it is hardly surprising that contemporary anti-liberalism should contain numerous echoes of older reactions, the apparent re-occupation of long abandoned fortifications. One such revival is the re-pristination of the relentless, two-hundred-year-old apologetic of European Catholics, that the Papacy alone is the bulwark against modern atheism, a force which is certain in due course to sweep away the paper structures of Protestantism.

The contradiction between such a position and the anti-collectivist strand in the modern reaction to the liberal consensus is patent. For on the standard account of Catholic apologetics it is precisely Protestant theology which is the source of that ruinous individualism which has aided and abetted the forces of secularisation. For the anti-collectivist, individual responsibility, independence and self-reliance is the very basis of a 'healthy society', and social structures must take account of the fact that human beings are so irrational, self-centred and fallible that welfare provision by the state will eventually destroy the will to be responsible for oneself and for others, as it undermines the incentive to profit from one's own activities. This pessimistic model of humanity is much more obviously characteristic of Protestantism, though it certainly has pre-Protestant sources in western Christian thought. Its deployment in anti-collectivist ideology is in plain contradiction to conservative movements in Catholicism, which identify Protestant thought as a major form of compromise with secularism.

A similar contradiction emerges in the very appeal to Christian values as the legitimation of anti-collectivism. Mrs Thatcher's celebrated address to the Assembly of the Church of Scotland in May 1988 made the characteristic division between the creation of wealth and its use. 'The Spiritual dimension comes', she said, 'in deciding what one does with the wealth'. The rôle assigned to churches by implication is that of teaching individual citizens to make personal, moral choices about the disposal of their own wealth, not about the processes and policies involved in the creation of wealth in the first place, nor about the state's collective distribution of the wealth accumulated through taxation. But this theoretical division closely matches and reinforces the processes of secularisation, which characteristically receive no analysis. Secularisation banishes religion from the centre to the margins of society, from technology, economics, and politics which govern the processes of commercial and industrial life, to the domestic sphere, to the context of individual and familial choices, to the realisation of personal values and goals. The collusion between anti-collectivism and secularisation was nowhere better illustrated than in the Conservative Government's assault upon the legislative boundaries marking off Sunday from weekday commercial and sporting activity. So long as the individual was free to choose whether or not to go to Church, it was implausibly argued, no spiritual harm could come to national life by the abolition of antiquated restrictions upon Sunday trading.

The relegation of religion to the private sphere enables a further, curious alliance to be made between anti-collectivists and exponents of the thesis that Britain now constitutes a pluralistic culture, in which, since religion is a matter of private choice, it is unfair to permit any one religion to make an impact upon public policy. The confusions to which such an association leads were exposed by the discussion of the Islamic response to Salman Rushdie's *The Satanic Verses*, and the feminist reaction to the demand for Islamic schooling. At once the question arises whether a 'modern pluralistic culture' can generate a set of values secure enough to resist the demands of a religion supposed to be included within the pluralism.[15]

It has recently been argued, in commentary upon these issues, that Protestant individualism is that form of Christianity which genuinely does express the way in which the premise of moral equality, claims for conscience and insistence on a range of basic human rights are inextricably bound up together.[16] The attempt to divorce these values from their Christian background is thus a disaster. The liberality of pluralism needs defending on grounds which implicitly privilege Christianity above other religions, as indeed modern Islamic critics of 'western values' have always feared.

The argument is beguiling. It is not Protestant in any sectarian sense, in that Siedentop draws attention to the sources of the idea of individual rights in mediaeval canon law. Nonetheless its construction needs supplementing by an important fact about Christian history, namely the failure of the post-Reformation enterprise to impose either Catholicism or various kinds of classic Protestantism upon whole nations, and the contribution of heretical independency to the formulation of democracy outside the context of western Europe. The development of religious toleration within Europe was the fruit of irresolvable conflict. The political toleration of differing forms of Christian belief within England developed in contradiction to the theory (and, in part, the practice) of Anglican comprehensiveness. A conflict theory of Christian identity is of help when the reasons for this state of affairs are considered. On this account, Christianity gives rise to and sustains a series of irresolvable social conflicts in reflection of the processes of its own internal dialectics. For this reason throughout history it has characteristically both supported and subverted numerous diverse political structures. Christianity is neither uniquely intolerant, nor uniquely tolerant, but both at once. It is thus perhaps uniquely maladapted to being a reliable source of social and political legitimation.

The focus of most of the above discussion has necessarily been upon liberalism, as defended and attacked within the last twenty years of public Christian theological controversy. One of the curiosities of the gathering anti-collectivist reaction against the politics of the welfare state has been its expansion and development during the years in which so-called 'liberation theology' has made its mark in Christian theological circles. Coming first to institutional focus in meetings of Latin American Catholic bishops in the late 1970s, liberation theology's major claim was that since God himself preferred the poor of the earth to the rich, no theology could claim to be true which was not rooted in activities on their behalf. Faith and love are inseparable from justice, and Christians have no alternative but to work for the radical transformation of the structures of society in the interests of the poor of the earth. The traditional theology of the academy was criticised for its failure to perceive the impossibility of political neutrality, and praxis (a term ambiguously lifted from its Marxist context) was elevated to a position of priority over mere theory.

A number of puzzles and confusions have arisen over the claims of liberation theology. Initially a strong emphasis was laid on its being context-related, that is, specifically Latin-American theology, as distinct from European or Western theology. Rather quickly, however, its association with nationalism was dropped, once its use of (European) Marxist social analysis became clear. Subsequently its supposed novelty was subjected to scrutiny. Could such a theology be consistently Catholic, when its formulation so obviously depended on dialogue with the economic and political theories of a nineteenth-century German? One of the earliest and most prolific Catholic expositors, the Chilean theologian, Gustavo Gutierrez, increasingly tends to deny the novelty of liberation theology, tracing its sources less to modern *Ideologiekritik* and the hermeneutics of suspicion, and increasingly to Judaeo-Christian sources on the doing of the will of God.[17]

It has to be said that liberation theology faces a difficulty in a post-

Enlightenment Western context if it presents itself in the guise of the exclusive claim either to see the action of God in the world through the eyes of the poor, or not to see at all. A hermeneutical veto on alternative perspectives simply joins the long list of competing forms of intellectual imperialism to which Christian theology has given rise over the centuries. A Vatican document critical of liberation theology, *Instruction on Christian Freedom and Liberation* (1986), wisely chose to focus its attack upon an extreme version, hardly different in kind from a form of fundamentalism. Needless to say, liberation theology is perfectly capable of more sophisticated and differentiated exposition, and is at its most powerful when it combines a biblical, especially Old Testament, tradition of protest against rank injustice and concern for the unprotected with a critical self-understanding of the liabilities of interpreters to partiality in their own interests. The moral basis for the latter is certainly older than Marxism, association with which is of dubious benefit when it comes to the identification and criticism of gross injustices perpetrated in the name of the people.[18]

   The application of liberation theology's challenges to the performance of academic theology in Britain raises further uncertainties. Though it is the case that British society is still only a single generation away from the experience of near starvation and the widespread prevalence of the sicknesses and debility of malnutrition, the shifting definition of poverty makes the transition from a Latin American to a British context highly problematic. The Church of England's attempt to identify and respond to urban deprivation in its Chruch Urban Fund, arising out of the Report *Faith in the City* (1985), shows at least a widespread perception of, and concern for, poverty within Britain. That report, however, explicitly denied the direct applicability of liberation theology to British circumstances; the attempt of the Conservative Central Office to rubbish it as 'Marxist' was as spectacularly wide of the mark as it was helpful to its circulation. The theoretical poverty of the report is now widely acknowledged. It is evident that the relative deprivation of the urban citizen of a modern democracy requires a much more complex analysis and is correspondingly more difficult to denounce than the gross political injustice done to blacks in the context of South African *apartheid* or a Latin American *favella*. And it is in the presence of sheer awfulness that the moral imperative of the natural law tradition is at its most persuasive – in simply articulating what is the case. In most other contexts moral ambiguity is the norm, and there is no alternative to living with conflict.

A conflict theory of Christian identity has to be eschatological; that is to say, the resolution of the ambiguous narrative of human history cannot reside in the establishment of a perfect kingdom of righteousness and peace by human agency on the earth. The mythology of the millennial rule of Christ resists translation into social engineering, even as it provokes dissatisfaction with injustice and deprivation in human affairs. Christianity is eschatological; but it is not for that reason dualist in its anthropology, nor Manichean in its depair of the flesh. Platonism, or what is popularly thought to be Platonism, is another matter. Though in the second century of the Christian era a decisive battle was waged with the world-denying philosophies of the Gnostics, the long-standing dialogue with Platonism, especially in neo-Platonic form, has frequently brought Christian theology to the point of domesticating an opposition between flesh and spirit, and the reservation of compensatory justice for the *post-mortem* life of the spirit.

Against such a thesis it has to be argued that the fundamental ritual of Chrisianity, baptismal initiation into the eucharistic community, is radically egalitarian in character. As they went down into the baptismal waters (it behoves the discreet and wary sprinklers of the northern hemisphere to remember) the baptised removed all their clothes, symbols of human status, and died with Christ, rising again in 'newness of life' to be reclothed with a plain white garment, and to be enthroned with Christ, participating in his kingly priesthood over the whole of creation. Such was the root metaphor of the *rite de passage*, and it could not be entirely forgotten even when re-aggregation into the structures of society returned the baptised to slavery, patriarchy, feudalism, or the class structure of capitalism. Even in a remarkably changed ritual context it remains plain that the characteristic moral content of baptism rests on the intrinsic worth of that humanity for which God is said to have condescended to take human flesh and to die. The 'myth' of Christianity is compatible with a range of detailed diagnoses of the fallen human condition; Christian doctrine has from the fourth century onwards amplified its anthropology from philosophical sources. Anti-collectivists are simply mistaken if they suppose that their relatively pessimistic view of human nature is in any strong sense legitimated or required by Christian doctrine. They are doubly mistaken if they hope thereby to blunt the edge of Christian moral ciritcism of institutionalised injustice to the unprotected.

Such injustices Christians themselves have long been ready to commit, as the baleful history of persecution of Jews and heretics makes plain. It is admittedly late in the day for Christians to discover that the profession of Christianity requires defence of the freedom of conscience. But it is a lesson learnt through the experience of irresolvable religious conflict, ineradicable within Christianity itself, and yet contributing to the realisation of the human good. For lack of anything better it may be an experiment worth considerable intellectual and practical effort to embrace ineradicable inter-religious and ideological conflict within the context of a modern, but consciously Chrisitan state. But to do so will require an effective and sophisticated analysis of the moral claims of minorities, both religious and secular; and to achieve that, I believe it will be necessary to retrieve theological and ethical resources which have been recklessly ignored in the present century.

Notes and References

1. The statistics are drawn from the *UK Christian Handbook 1987/88* ed. P. W. Brierley (London, 1988), and refer to the total community figures for 1985.
2. I have examined this history at greater length in 'Theological Study: The Nineteenth Century and After', in B. Hebblethwaite and S. Sutherland (eds), *The Philosophical Frontiers of Christian Theology* (Cambridge, 1982): 95–118, and 'The Study of Theology in University and School', in J. Barnett (ed.), *Theology at 16+* (London, 1984): 132–48.
3. An important exception is the essay of Professor D. M. Mackinnon, 'Theology as a Discipline of a Modern University', in T. Shanin (ed.), *The Rules of the Game* (London, 1972): 162–74.
4. See E. J. Sharpe, *Comparative Religion, A History* (London, 1975).
5. The Church of England set up in 1967 a commission to report on religious education in schools, whose background information and conclusions remain influential in modern discussion, *The Fourth R* (London, 1970).
6. N. Sykes, *The English Religious Tradition* (London, 1953).
7. Expounded with flair and originality by the Catholic theologian, Adrian Hastings, in *A History of English Christianity, 1920–1985* (London, 1986); see especially 644.
8. See the fruits of an ecumenical symposium held at Downside Abbey in 1963, J. Coulson (ed.), *Theology and the University* (London, 1964).
9. *Dignitatis Humanae,* 7 December 1965; English text in A. Flannery (ed.), *Vatican Council II* (rev. edn, Dublin, 1988): 799–812.
10. G. Kitson Clark, *The Kingdom of Free Men* (Cambridge, 1957): 134–55 referrring to a speech of Cardinal Ottaviani's reported in *Osservatore Romano* (4 March 1953); text: 210–13.

11. The principal agent here was Professor, later Bishop, I. T. Ramsey, Chairman of the Archbishops' Commission on Christian Doctrine which produced the Report *Subscription and Assent to the Thirty-Nine Articles* in 1968. See 'Subscription to Articles', in I. T. Ramsey, *One Being Sure in Religion* (London, 1963): 48–90.
12. *Christian Believing: The Nature of the Christian Faith and its Expression in Holy Scripture and Creeds* (London, 1976). Numerically their representation was by no means preponderant. But their influence was such that agreement on a common text with more conservative theologians (in the end, a mere 42 pages) was a matter of extreme difficulty.
13. From 1978 to the present there has been an unprecedented outpouring of publications on the nature of Anglicanism, especially the problem of authority in Anglicanism.
14. Bernice Martin, *A Sociology of Contemporary Cultural Change* (London, 1981).
15. See the discussion of Islam and religious education in E. Hulmes, *Commitment and Neutrality in Religious Education* (London, 1979).
16. Larry Sidentop, in the *Times Literary Supplement* (24–30 March 1989): 308.
17. A useful collection of essays from 1969 to the later 1970s is G. Gutierrez, *The Power of the Poor in History* (New York, 1983).
18. Christopher Rowland, *Radical Christianity* (Cambridge, 1988) gives a number of examples of the impact of millenarian doctrines on Christian theology prior to liberation theology.

6 The Church and the Government

Raymond Plant

The election of the Conservative government in 1979 commited to radical policies, particularly in relation to economic liberalisation, the freeing of markets, the diminution of the role of government and a more limited role for the welfare state occasioned major controversies with mainstream British churches which continue unabated. At the centre of the argument is first of all a dispute about the nature and degree of involvement by the churches in matters of public policy. Should the churches really have a view about social and economic policy or should they be more concerned, as a Conservative MP said in 1984, with putting more bottoms on pews? Is the Church's concern primarily with individual, personal salvation or does it have a central concern with people's material conditions and the public policies which have a rôle in producing and distributing those conditions?

To a great extent the publication of *Faith in the City*,[1] the result of the deliberations of a Working Party set up by the Archbishop of Canterbury to look at the Church's role in inner cities, was the catalyst for this dispute, but controversy has not been confined to the Anglican Church and the debate has broadened to cover the main areas of social and economic policy. The churches have been very critical of the government's economic policy, both in terms of its social effects and the kind of vision of human nature which this policy is supposed to embody. The response has not only come from the Anglican Church but also from the Roman Catholics, particularly from Archbishop Worlock in Liverpool who wrote *Better Together*[2] with David Sheppard, his Anglican counterpart, a book which is a biting indictment of the government's policies towards inner cities; from the Church of Scotland, particularly after Mrs Thatcher's address to its General Assembly when she was presented with a copy of *Just Sharing*[3] which is an attempt by the authors representing the Church and Nation Committee of the Church of Scotland to justify an approach to social policy more oriented to social justice and less to free-market capitalism; and from the Methodist Church where the

Chairman of the Methodist Conference used his speech to make a scathing attack on the Government's policy. However, in some respects, the response of the Anglican Church is perhaps the most significant mainly because it is the established Church which through its ceremonies, its role on state occasions, its representation in the House of Lords, and its position as the National Church plays, at least implicitly, a role in legitimising the state, as a civil religion. So to have the established Church so much at loggerheads with the government of the day is a rather disturbing phenomenon.

However, it is also very interesting that the dispute since 1979 and particularly in the aftermath of the debate about *Faith in the City*, reveals very important things on the one hand about the churches' view of theology and its political implications; on the other it also reveals features of the philosophy of the present government which might otherwise have been left inexplicit and unaddressed. It is doubtful whether any British Prime Minister since Gladstone has been so concerned to argue the moral basis of public policy as Mrs Thatcher and the controversy with the churches has to some extent elicited this moral defence of her policies. She has chosen, particularly in the speech to the General Assembly of the Church of Scotland, to carry the debate about public policy onto the moral high ground chosen by the churches and in this she has been followed by Ministers. Both the Home Secretary and the then Secretary of State for Education Mr Baker have sought to defend the government's record on grounds of moral principle and to criticise the churches for their inadequate response to what the government is doing, in speeches at the General Synod of the Church of England. Other advisers such as Professor Bryan Griffiths, Head of the Downing Street Policy Unit, and sympathisers with the government's cause such as Lord Harris of High Cross and Sir Fred Catherwood, have also sought to take the debate onto the churches' ground at various meetings held by the churches over the past few years and in their respective books and pamphlets. I want to concentrate on the issues which have emerged in this debate, which as I have said, has occasioned a debate about the fundamental principles behind public policy. The quality of the debate has improved enormously over the period in question and reveals very important features of the attitudes of the protagonists.

Perhaps I should say a word at first about why I believe the quality of the debate has improved. On the Conservative side when *Faith in the City* was first published, which as I have said was the catalyst for much of what has happened, the response was decidedly unsubtle. There were two immediate reactions. The first was that the Church has no business in pronouncing on political issues because its message is spiritual and transcendental, a point made in a speech by Mr John Butcher, now a junior minister, in a contribution which seemed to be representative of the views of many Conservatives. The second was the comment of a then senior minister, widely assumed to be Mr Norman Tebbit, that *Faith in the City* was 'Marxist theology'. This second comment was frankly absurd, for two reasons. It would be difficult to read *Faith in the City* as embodying much more than representative assumptions of post-war social democracy, or the central assumptions of what is sometimes called the 'Keynesian consensus'. No doubt the government and Mrs Thatcher in particular saw it as part of its mission at least to shake up if not to destroy that consensus, but that is little reason for branding the consensus, in so far as it existed from 1945, as Marxist. The second, deeper, reason to which we shall return, is that in one central respect *Faith in the City* is decidedly anti-Marxist, whether its authors realised it or not. Central to the theological chapter of the document is the claim that the production of wealth has to go hand in hand with its just distribution. This is a central tenet of social democracy, but it is also one which Marx trenchantly criticised in his discussion of the German Social Democratic Party's approach in his *The Critique of the Gotha Programme*. In this piece of invective Marx argued that it was impossible to secure a just distribution of wealth when the means of production are in private hands. It was impossible in Marx's view to separate off the issue of distribution from the nature of production. If the means of production are privately owned, then it was necessarily the case that the distribution of resources which occurred in the capitalist economy should be skewed in favour of the people who owned capital. In a sense there is nothing unjust about this on a Marxist view. Given the distribution of ownership, the distribution of the resources which the means of production created would broadly mirror the distribution of ownership and property rights in the economy and this could not, despite the illusion of social democrats, be changed by purely political means, a central assumption of social democrats from Lacily to Crosland. Hence, when *Faith in the City* argued that the production of wealth in a capitalist economy had to be linked to a politically acceptable just distribution of it, then it committed itself to a much more social democratic view than a Marxist one. However, as we shall see this issue of social justice does remain a central issue in the moral debate within the Church and between the churches and the government. This issue has been much more satisfactorily addressed in more recent debates.

The second argument, that the Christian message is otherwordly about personal salvation rather than social conditions and their reform, lacks a sense of history in that since the time of the early Fathers the Church's theologians have discussed at length the role of private property, the legitimacy of social and economic inequality, the relative responsibilities of the individual and the state in relation to the relief of poverty, the role of commerce and the rights and wrongs of Christian engagement in it, particularly in the light of the verse from Ecclesiasticus:

> A merchant shall hardly keep himself from doing wrong
> And a huckster shall not be freed from sin
> As a nail sticketh fast between the joining of the stones
> So doth sin stick close between the buying and selling.[4]

At a more general level Christian theologians from the earliest times have considered the relationship between the Christian faith and politics, coming to very different conclusions. Tertullian (160–220) took the otherworldly view seeing Christianity as a kind of counterculture to the prevailing Roman Empire, echoing St Peter that 'Christians were pilgrims in a foreign land':

> We are a body knit together as such by common religious profession by unity of discipline and by the bond of a common hope . . . Your citizenship, your magistracies, and the very name of your curia is the Church of Christ . . . You are an alien in this world, and a citizen of the City of Jerusalem that is above.[5]

On the other hand, Eusebius (264–340) provided a positive political theology which sought to make sense in theological terms of the Christian/State settlement which arrived with Constantine. In his thought, and in what was actually happening, as Duncan Forrester says, 'Christianity was already taking over the traditional role of a civil religion, sacralising power, legitimating the existing order of things and inculcating in the populace reverence for the authorities and obedience to orders'.[6]

Throughout its subsequent history Christianity has frequently played this role of a civil religion, providing an undergirding of legitimacy for the state and its accompanying social order. Of course, this was not uniform. For example, Augustine in *De Civitate Dei*[7] takes a different view because with the sack of Rome and the collapse of the Roman Empire Christianity as the civil religion of that empire in its late form has become vulnerable to that Empire's own collapse. If as Eusebius argued the Constantinian settlement was providential and Christianity was part of its legitimating role then Christianity was vulnerable with the collapse of the Empire. In Augustine's view there had to be a much more critical view of the relationship between Christianity and civil power and in order to theorise this he developed his idea of the two cities: *civitas dei* and *civitas terrena* with the latter being incomplete and concerned with balancing the interests of fallen creatures which had to be seen as provisional compared to *civitas dei* characterised by absolute justice and divine love. No human being could owe unqualified allegiance to the earthly city, but rather to *civitas dei* which knows no divisions between race, class, or state. In Aquinas too in *Summa Contra Gentiles* we find a theology of politics and the role of the Christian within the political community. In Aquinas's view the Christian does not 'belong to the political community with the whole of his being nor with all that is his'.[8]

Any sense of the history of Christian thought would soon disabuse one of the idea that political theology is some sort of modern invention. Throughout its history the Church has had to come to a view about its relationship to the prevailing principalities and powers. The Anglican Church as the national Church since the sixteenth century has frequently been involved in developing a political theology which would allow it to play the role of a civil religion, underpinning and legitimising the state whether in Hooker's *Laws of Ecclesiastical Polity*, in doctrines about the Divine Right of Kings or at a more mundane level in the way that its catechism played an important role in disseminating the idea of a civil religion through all the orders of society as Laslett and Schochet have shown.[9] This was particularly true in terms of providing a religious sanction for social hierachy. In case the reader should think that such ideas were part of 'the world we have lost' so remote as to be irrelevant now, it is interesting to consider the type of sermon which Flora Thompson heard in her village church on the Hampshire/Oxford border in the closing years of the nineteenth century and which she recorded in *Lark Rise to Candleford* published in 1945:

> Another subject was the social order as it then existed. God in his infinite wisdom had appointed a place for every man, woman and child on this earth and it was their bounden duty to remain

contentedly in their niches. A gentleman might seem to some of his listeners to have a pleasant easy life compared with theirs as field labourers; but he had duties and responsibilities which would far exceed their capabilities. He had to pay taxes, sit on the bench of magistrates, oversee his estates and keep up his position by entertaining. Could they do these things? No of course they could not; nor did he suppose that a gentleman could cut as straight a furrow or thatch a rick as expertly as they could.[10]

Flora Thompson does not say what text the preacher used but a good guess might be Ecclesiasticus 38: 24–34 which was used by Burke in *Reflections on the Revolution in France*[11] to make much the same point.

It is important to recognise that when Christian theological reflection is being used as a way of securing the power and legitimacy of prevailing ideas, and social and political institutions, it is relatively uncontroversial. However the rise of socialism and social democracy in the nineteenth century influenced the Church a good deal and the late nineteenth century saw the rise of Christian socialism, which within the Anglican Church was particularly associated with Scott Holland, Stewart Headlam, and Charles Gore who attempted to give the movement a theological base, particularly through his Christology and his writing on the Incarnation.[12] However, in the hands of Gore and Scott Holland Christian 'socialism' had more in common with social democracy than Marxist socialism. This might be expected, given the influence which the works of T. H. Green had on them – Green being the major intellectual progenitor of New or Social Liberalism.[13] Nevertheless this social democratic interpretation of Christian theology is very important partly because it did provide in the late nineteenth century a critique of classical liberalism and capitalist economics, and partly because in this century from 1945 onwards this kind of theology has come more and more to underpin the churches' stance on issues of public policy. It is not surprising therefore that the advent of a government in 1979 with the aim of destroying the 'social democratic consensus' has led to deep controversy within the Church and between the Church and the government, given the ways in which the churches had become intellectually and morally locked into that consensus.

The intellectual link between late-nineteenth-century Christian social democratic political theology and contemporary controversies can be seen if we look at the following passage from a report to the

Convocation of Canterbury in 1907 which bears a rather startling similarity to *Faith in the City*, as just one illustration of the way in which the Anglican Church has always contained a significant group of people who are hostile to *laissez-faire* capitalism because in their view it encourages what they see as a false form of individualism and neglects social justice:

> political economy thought it necessary to isolate the production and distribution of wealth; to deal with it as if no motive were to be admitted into this economic region except the selfish desire of the individual to enrich himself. Abstract laws of supply and demand . . . were supposed to rule out in the scientific treatment of commerce and industry all questions of justice and mercy to wage earners . . . it ministered undoubtedly to the common human tendency to regard commercial and economic dealings as outside the control of morality and religion . . . and the Christian Church allowed itself to be silenced by the terrors of supposed inexorable laws . . . The real end of industrial organisation is to combine efficient production with such distribution of the commonwealth.[14]

Compare this with what is said in *Faith in the City*:

> The creation of wealth must always go hand in hand with just distribution . . . There is a long Christian tradition, running back to the Old Testament Prophets and supported by influential schools of economic and political thought, which firmly rejects the amassing of wealth unless it is justly obtained and fairly distributed. If these provisos are not insisted upon the creation of wealth cannot be allowed to go unchallenged as a first principle of national policy.[15]

The essential challenge to the present government's social and economic policy is present in the same way in each of these passages: social justice or the just distribution of social resources is central to politics in the churches' view and it is this which legitimises the creation of wealth. In so far as the government rejects social justice it turns wealth creation from being an instrument of social benefit into one of private aggrandisement.

In the view of the government the churches critique of capitalism is misplaced, and that it has neglected to address issues of personal morality, particularly in relation to personal responsibility which in its view have as much a role in the causation of the problems of poverty with which the Church is rightly concerned as its misplaced panacea of social justice and greater social equality. In the view of the government inner city deprivation cannot be divorced from the dispositions of the poor and the role which public policy has had since 1945 in creating those dispositions, particularly in generating a sense of dependency and being trapped within welfare.

This is the debate which I want to explore: the churches' conviction that social justice must be at the heart of social policy and the government's conviction that the pursuit of social justice in the post-war world has created institutions which have in fact created dependency and that if the churches had a clearer view of social issues, rather than one which is locked into the assumptions of the Keynesian consensus, they would see that poverty is as much a cultural problem, to do with character and motivation, as it is with distributive justice.

The critique of social justice is central to the economic liberalism which the government has to a great degree espoused in its economic policy. The roots of the critique are to be found in the writings of theorists such as Hayek[16] and Friedman[17] but are echoed in Mrs Thatcher's *Let Our Children Grow Tall;*[18] in Lord Joseph's *Equality,*[19] *Stranded on the Middle Ground,*[20] and *Monetarism is Not Enough;*[21] in Nigel Lawson's *The State of the Market,*[22] *The Tide of Ideas from Attlee to Thatcher,*[23] and in *The New Conservatism.*[24] The critique as developed by Hayek is deep and wide ranging, but it is important to grasp its main lines.

Those who believe in social justice such as the authors of *Faith in the City* believe that public policy should be concerned with the just distribution of resources between individuals, and that this is a prime responsibility of government. The free market economy does not produce just results and there is therefore a need for the market as the wealth creating sector, powered by self-interest, to be constrained in the interests of social justice.

In the view of critics this approach makes a number of false moral assumptions and its political consequences are ruinous. The first assumption made is that it is possible to use criteria of social justice to criticise market outcomes and the inequalities to which they give rise. However, the defender of the market will argue that justice is an irrelevant issue here. Injustice can be caused only by intentional action. That is why we do not regard genetic handicaps or earthquakes as injustices; they are bad luck but not injustices since no one intentionally caused them. However, market outcomes are uninten-ded. They are the unintended result of millions of particular acts of buying and selling. While each of these individual actions may have been undertaken for intentional reasons, nevertheless the outcome of all this buying and selling is not intended by anyone. It is a product of human action, but not of human design. Given that injustice can arise only as the result of intentional action it follows that the outcomes of markets are not unjust, whatever the degree of inequality involved.

Secondly to have the basis of a critique of markets in terms of social justice, there have to be agreed, consensual criteria of justice if they are to guide public policy. However, these criteria are lacking. We can envisage distributing social resources according to various criteria: need, merit, desert, entitlement, etc. Using one rather than another of these criteria will produce different distributions of goods and services. If we believe that all of the criteria have a place, how are they to be weighted? For example, when does the claim of need take priority over entitlement, for example in relation to property rights? When the churches invoke social justice, as they do in *Faith in the City*, they do not go beyond the rhetoric of social justice in the view of critics, and, indeed, cannot go beyond it because once one tries to be more specific the problems indicated above become central and insoluble in a diverse, pluralistic society. It may be, as *Faith in the City* claims, that Old Testament Prophets had a concern with the just distribution of resources, but if this is true it is also revealing because in fact they lived in small homogeneous societies, with a very high degree of moral consensus which allowed them to use the rhetoric of justice in an unproblematic way. In a small, morally homogeneous society, we may have clear views about need and desert and the relative priority of one over the other; however, we are not in that position in modern western societies. The appeal to social justice assumes a degree of consensus about social values which is not available.

However, the consequences of believing in the 'mirage of social justice', to quote Hayek, are ruinous and go far beyond the moral problems involved in invoking the concept. First of all the essential ambiguity of the concept which has already been mentioned means that it cannot yield detailed rules to guide public policy, and that bureaucracies charged with distributing social resources in a just manner cannot avoid acting in arbitrary and discretionary ways just because their distributive function cannot be guided by clear rules given the inherent ambiguity and disputability of what social justice requires. This means that a government whose public policies were to be guided by social justice would entrench at the heart of its policy a necessarily arbitrary form of power and this is incompatible with the rule of law central to a liberal idea of the state.

Social justice also requires the appearance of a strong state. If we are concerned to distribute resources in a just manner, then clearly this cannot be done either by markets or by voluntary action. It cannot be done by markets otherwise there would be no point in criticising market outcomes in terms of social justice in the first place; it cannot be done by voluntary action which is inherently discretionary – people have to be able to choose who are to be the beneficiaries of their time, money and gifts, and given this voluntary action cannot achieve social justice which has to do with the rights of each citizen to a just share of social resources. Resources have to be administered by the state if social justice is to be achieved, and doing this will have a number of effects which the government believes will be adverse: intervention in the economy, very active regional policies, high levels of public expenditure as a percentage of GDP, the politicisation of more and more issues of resources in the economy and a general increase in regulation and the scope of government. All of these developments have adverse effects on the economy in the view of economic liberals and in so far as the post-war consensus involved a commitment to public policies of social justice it led to this increase in the role of government.

However, while government may have grown as an inexorable result of a concern with distributive politics, this very growth had the effect of weakening government in various ways. There is a range of issues here but one is worth particular mention. In the view of critics of social justice, given that there are no consensual criteria of justice to guide the politics of distribution, distributive politics becomes highly competitive with groups seeking to extract from government what they believe to be their appropriate distributive share, whether these resources are financial or subsidies or preferential legislation. Given that there is no agreed framework for distribution, social justice becomes a camouflage for the special pleading of interest groups and in the absence of criteria of justice, the government will usually meet the demands of the most powerful interests in society. Hence social justice, a value which is usually espoused as being in the interest of the worst off, actually leads to a very destructive form of politics, of morally unconstrained competition for social resources which favours the best organised and most powerful groups in society. This lies at the heart of the problems in the late 1970s in the view of many economic liberals within the

Conservative Party.

The government finds it difficult to understand the churches' attachment to ideas like social justice which bear with them the sorts of problems I have just described. In their view if the Church uses the idea of social justice because it is concerned with the poor, then it would be better advised to consider the role of the free market in a less prejudiced way as a means of enhancing the position of the worst off more effectively than the state regulation which follows directly from a concern with social justice. On the government's view there is a good deal of confusion about the nature and extent of poverty and while the churches may, in the title of Bishop Sheppard's book,[25] have a bias to the poor, we need to think more clearly about who the poor are and what are the best policies to remedy their condition.

The issue of poverty as one of moral concern has recently risen up the political agenda as the result of a speech by Mr John Moore the former Secretary of State for Social Services in which he criticised the relative view of poverty. The relative view of poverty links the idea of poverty to an idea of a normal or decent level of consumption relating to the values and expectations of a particular society. One is poor if one is cut off by one's standard of living from the sorts of activities and patterns of consumption and expenditure which are normal or typical in a particular society. Relative poverty thus links poverty to a rising standard of citizenship and is thus difficult to distinguish clearly from the idea of inequality. In the view of the government what matters to the poor is not in any sense the gap between themselves and the rest of society, that is to say the degree of inequality between them and other groups, but whether the poor on their own terms are getting better off on a year by year basis. Poverty as relative poverty, and thus as a form of inequality, requires direct state action to remedy and is just another way of talking about social justice in that the relatively poor fail to attain a status which is somehow regarded as the just status due to a citizen. However, poverty understood in this more absolute sense of the gradual improvement in the living standards of the poor in their own terms can be left much more to the market. The trickle-down or echelon-advance effect of the market may well bring with it increased inequality, but it will also improve the living standards of the poor more than state action will. The important thing is not to have government programmes to relieve dubious relative poverty, but rather to latch more and more of the poor onto the enterprise culture and the free market. Hence the bias to the poor in the view of the government does not, *pace* the churches, involve or entail a concern with social justice and greater equality. In emphasising these values as being central to social policy the churches have actually done the poor a disservice because these concerns have spawned a range of welfare policies, institutions and bureaucracies which have actually created dependency and made participation in the market economy less attractive to poor people.

The churches are right to stress the importance of values in social policy, but in the view of the government they have put their emphasis in the wrong place on social values such as social justice for which there is no consensus in a pluralistic society, while they have neglected to emphasise personal values such as independence and personal responsibility which are important as means to induce individuals to participate more in the dynamic economy which alone will mean that the bias to the poor properly understood can be realised. In this context Mrs Thatcher has shown more respect for the view of the Chief Rabbi whom she ennobled as Lord Jacobovits, just because in his response to *Faith in the City* he stressed the importance which his own community attached to matters of personal morality in relation to poverty rather than state-led programmes of social justice which are characteristic of *Faith in the City*. For example in the context of poverty among inner-city blacks he argues as follows:

> Let them give two or three hours extra schooling everyday to their children as we gave to ours; let them build up charitable endeavours, great federations of social welfare, as we did for our poor; let them instil in all negroes a feeling of shame for any crime committed by a negro . . . let them encourage ambition and excellence in every negro child, as Jewish parents encouraged in their children – and they will pull down the ghetto as surely as we demolished ours.[26]

In his view the work ethic is central to the Old Testament tradition and this ethic has to be encouraged by individual and community action, not by professionalised and bureaucratised state policy; only then in the words of the psalmist 'you shall eat the fruit of the labour of your hands; you shall be happy and it shall be well with you'.

Certainly the government has emphasised similar values of self-help and has stressed the importance of the family as a unit in providing a background to the development of more positive work-centred attitudes and again Lord Jacobovits endorses this point:

For when the family breaks down, the most essential conditions
for raising happy, law-abiding and creatively ambitious citizens are
frustrated . . . Through a dedication to hard work, self help and
the rebuilding of family life, the new ghettos can be transformed
as were the old and the resources of the nation can be shared by
all.[27]

Hence, at the end of the day, the dispute between the churches and
the government is fundamental. It has to do with the nature and role
of government, the nature of poverty and citizenship, the role or lack
of it of social justice and what the government sees as the churches'
failure to emphasise personal moral values at the expense of collective
ones. Central to this dispute is something very deep about the
understanding of the values of our own society. In its economic
liberal guise the government suggests that we do not have the moral
resources in terms of consensual agreement to constrain economic
outcomes and markets by values such as social justice. Markets are
in principle unprincipled and in these circumstances economic life
has to embody the subjective choices of consumers because there are
no agreed collective moral values which can countervail these.
However, when it comes to its own views about poverty and the role
of character and independence, that is to say in terms of values which
characterise personal and private life, they do believe that there is a
consensus about values. The churches are asserting that morality is a
seamless web, that if there are values which can guide public policy
as in relation to private life, then in principle there is no reason why
there cannot be collective moral values to guide distribution. It is
central to economic liberalism to resist this argument, but in so doing
defenders of the government's position have not come up with a
convincing account of why the moral situation is so difficult in these
cases.[28]

Notes and References

1. *Faith in the City* (London, 1985).
2. *Better Together* (2nd edn; London, 1989).
3. D. Forrester and D. Skane (eds), *Just Sharing* (London, 1988).
4. Ecclesiasticus, Chapter 6.
5. Quoted in D. B. Forrester, *Theology and Politics* (Oxford, 1988).
6. Forrester, *Theology and Politics*: 21; see Augustine *De Civitate Dei*

Book 6, Chapter 5.
7. *De Civitate Dei*, English trans. (London, 1972).
8. *Summa Theologicae* 2a 21 4. (London, 1929).
9. Peter Laslett, *The World We Have Lost* (London, 1965); G. Schochet, *Patriarchalism in Political Thought* (Oxford, 1975).
10. *Lark Rise to Candleford* (Oxford, 1945): 201.
11. *Reflections on the Revolution in France* (London, 1910): 46.
12. *Vide* D. Nicholls, 'Christianity and Politics', in Nicholls, *The Religion of the Incarnation: Anglican Essays in Commemoration of Lux Mundi* (Bristol, 1989); D. Nicholls, *Deity and Domination* (London, 1989); D. Nicholls and R. Williams, *Politics and Theological Identity* (London, 1984).
13. For further discussion, see A. Vincent and R. Plant, *Philosophy, Politics and Citizenship: The Life and Times of the British Idealists* (Oxford, 1984).
14. 'The Moral Witness of the Church on Economic Subjects', Appendix to C. Gore, *The New Theology and the Old Religion* (London, 1907).
15. *Faith in the City*: 53.
16. F. A. Hayek, *Law Legislation and Liberty*, vol. 2, *The Mirage of Social Justice* (London, 1976).
17. M. Friedman, *Capitalism and Freedom* (Chicago, 1962).
18. *Let Our Children Grow Tall* (London, 1977).
19. *Equality* (with J. Sumption) (London, 1979).
20. *Stranded on the Middle Ground* (London, 1976).
21. *Monetarism is Not Enough* (London, no date).
22. *The State of the Market* (London, 1989).
23. *The Tide of Ideas from Attlee to Thatcher* (London, 1988).
24. *The New Conservatism* (London, 1980).
25. *Bias to the Poor* (London, 1983).
26. *The Jewish Chronicle* (24 January 1986).
27. *The Jewish Chronicle* (24 January 1986).
28. For an attempt to reinstate the idea of social justice as a central objective of public policy see R. Plant, *Equality, Markets and the State* (London, 1984) and K. Hoover and R. Plant, *Conservative Capitalism in Britain and the United States: A Critical Appraisal* (London, 1988).

7 Theology, Philosophy and Politics

Stephen Grover

Popular attacks upon liberal theology usually contain two claims, similar in form but relating to different aspects of the theological enterprise. The first, addressing its credal content, sees scepticism about the historical accuracy of scripture and a tendency to water down the traditional doctrines of Christianity as driven by subservience to secular philosophy, rather than by anything internal to biblical and doctrinal scholarship. The second accuses the liberal theologians of substituting for the supernatural claims of their religion an attachment to contemporary political and ethical programmes which have no specifically Christian content. Thus A. J. Ayer's *Language, Truth and Logic*, published in 1936, has long been credited with generating amongst theologians, and also amongst philosophers of religion sympathetic to religious belief, a kind of liberal funk, in which the fear of being seen to be out of line with contemporary philosophical orthodoxy drove them to abandon the defence of traditional faith, and to set about re-interpreting the central doctrines of Christian theism so as to conform to Ayer's empiricist strictures on meaning and truth. Likewise, changing attitudes to ethical and political issues within the churches are thought to have their roots in a desperate desire to appear relevant to an intelligentsia increasingly disaffected with religion, rather than being generated by sincere attempts to relate the biblical message to present realities.

Like many popular accounts of goings-on within academic disciplines, this one misleads rather more than it informs. Given Ayer's later attitude, it would be surprising if *Language, Truth and Logic* was a major turning-point, or even something whose impact was long-lasting.[1] Just as post-modern theology has already been with us for a good few years (though not yet long enough for there to be much agreement on what exactly a post-modern theology might be),[2] and post-liberal theology for much longer,[3] so the roots of liberalism in theology lie a good deal further back than the publication of Ayer's Anglicised version of Viennese logical positivism. This last point has a degree of public recognition already. The furore which by now

130

traditionally greets each doctrinal utterance of David Jenkins, the Bishop of Durham, usually contains at least some reference to the fact, known to those with even the faintest grasp of the history of theology, that little is being said which has not been common coin since the middle of the nineteenth century. But the diversity of opinion within twentieth-century theology is not so widely known. No simple analysis can do justice to the complex influences from both within and outside the discipline over the last fifty years or so, and so no simple opposition between liberal and conservative can capture the present state of theology within the churches and universities.

This opposition of liberal and conservative was always something of a fiction, generated in large measure by reading onto the world of academic theology the disputes and disagreements which periodically break out within the churches over matters of ecclesiastical discipline and change, of which the current dispute in the Church of England over the ordination of women is only the latest example. Divisions over controversial ecclesiastical issues such as this do not match up with divisions over the methods of biblical scholarship or over the interpretation of doctrine, any more than they correspond with distinctions of churchmanship; it is difficult to tie up the theological rows over John Robinson's *Honest to God*[4] in the early 1960s, *The Myth of God Incarnate* collection, edited by John Hick,[5] in the late 1970s, and Don Cupitt's television series, *The Sea of Faith*[6] in the mid-1980s with other arguments over the modernisation of the liturgy, the future of the ministry or the relaxation of attitudes towards homosexuality and divorce amongst the clergy. But still, it is true that something rather new is going on in the world of philosophical theology, in which unrest at the general state of the discipline is heard from several different quarters, and in which unhappiness at a supposedly dominant liberal orthodoxy is achieving a voice. Philosophers who privately profess religious belief have tired of seeing theologians apparently under the sway of philosophical positions which they consider outmoded and false, and so have gone into the business of doctrinal formulation for themselves.[7] Meanwhile, many theologians and philosophers of religion have come to feel that the framework of the 'old liberalism' is insufficient to deal with the major problems of contemporary thinking about religion, and particularly the pressing problem of dialogue with the other faiths, and so they have borrowed extensively from contemporary philosophy in order to give an account of the nature of doctrine in which adherents of any one religious tradition can happily have their own cake whilst the adherents of all the others also get to eat theirs.[8] Any simple equation of conservatism in biblical interpretation with conservatism in social and political matters will not hold, as the example of David Sheppard, Anglican Bishop of Liverpool, makes clear. Sheppard and his Roman Catholic counterpart, Derek Worlock, are also evidence of another trend: alliances between the churches in social action no longer wait upon agreement in matters of doctrine and ecclesiastical organisation, just as unhappiness about change in these areas crosses political boundaries.

These various developments cannot be said to constitute any coherent challenge to the dominant tradition in theology, but, at most, evidence of its intellectual exhaustion. That it is somehow unsatisfactory is widely felt, but precisely how it is so, and how it is to be reformed, is not agreed upon. Of those whose main disagreement is with liberal theology's attitude to the Bible, many, no doubt influenced by the simplistic tale of liberal funk dismissed above, have claimed to find behind the conclusions of those contemporary scripture scholars who doubt the historical accuracy of much of the biblical material a subservience to outmoded philosophical orthodoxies.[9] This is the complaint levelled at 'liberal' biblical scholarship by people such as William Charlton in Britain, and by many of the practitioners of 'Christian philosophy' in the US. The sources of these poisonous philosophical preconceptions are variously identified; often it is Ayer, serving as the modern representative of a tradition in philosophy going back at least as far as Hume, in which all the supernatural elements of Christianity are judged unworthy of acceptance by any rational believer. Thus, biblical scholars who hold that certain miracle stories from the New Testament are later accretions, perhaps extending this kind of claim to the infancy and resurrection narratives as well, are accused of importing into their study of the text convictions about the possibility of such events which actually derive from crude empiricism.[10] Sometimes the philosophical villains behind contemporary biblical scholarship are not our home-grown British empiricists, but German idealists and phenomenologists, whose pessimism about the possibility of rational theology, and conviction that all interpretation moves within a hermeneutic circle, is held to have deceived critics into the belief that all that is recoverable from the text is the *kerygma* of the early Church.[11] But whatever the supposed origin of the corruption, what is denied is that the methods of biblical scholarship have their own integrity, and that the results which they have produced can therefore be regarded as relevant to the task of the theologian in the formulation of doctrine.

There is a deep irony here; Charlton claims that 'there are no events better attested in ancient history than the trial, death and resurrection of Christ',[12] and yet protests against scholars like Kasemann and Sanders for treating these attestations as they would any others from antiquity – with all the tools of literary and historical criticism which they have at their disposal. Scholars such as these do not reject biblical narratives simply because they report divine interventions, but rather because this is what the accepted methods of ancient-historical scholarship incline them to believe. For example, in any ancient document, a close correspondence between a prophecy and its fulfilment would provide reasonable grounds for believing that the prophecy postdates the events it predicts. If an ancient historian would take this attitude to prophecies in Babylonian religious texts, then he should do so to those of Judaism and Christianity. The only reason one could have for adopting a different attitude to the Old or New Testament would be an independent conviction, on this occasion presumably deriving from faith rather than philosophy, that the prophetic narrative was historically accurate. Yet this commonplace of historical scholarship is the kind of example which Charlton cites to show that Sanders is ruled not by evidence drawn from the texts but by dogmatic rationalism.[13] The accusation that faulty philosophy lies behind the conclusions of biblical scholars is meant to distract us from the fact that no arguments are actually being offered in favour of other and more 'conservative' readings of the Bible. Sadly, it is all too characteristic of those who intervene in biblical scholarship from outside that they will seize upon any development within the discipline which seems to offer hope for their own favoured cause, whilst disparaging the methodology of the discipline in general, and so one is often treated to the spectacle of those of fundamentalist orientation championing the work of individual scholars, whilst condemning the enterprise in which they are engaged.[14]

There is, of course, a more respectable version of the point which Charlton and others like him wish to make, which is that textual criticism, and the subsequent formulation of doctrine, must take place within some framework of beliefs, the content of which may be open to dispute. But this weaker claim will not do the work which Charlton and others require of it, which is to show that one, conservative, way of interpreting the texts and formulating doctrine is superior to all others. This more respectable point captures the grain of truth embedded in the legend surrounding *Language, Truth and Logic*: that philosophical theology, at least in the twentieth century, but perhaps since the beginning of the modern period in philosophy, has always been conducted within a framework which is set by prevailing philosophical orthodoxy. This point is an obvious one, but also important. Just as Ayer's book spawned a shoal of articles and books on theology and verification or falsification,[15] so contemporary theology takes its agenda from the dominant strains in epistemology, philosophy of science and philosophy of language.

Of the schools of thought active in Britain, it is the Wittgensteinians who see themselves as most obviously at odds with the liberal tradition supposedly generated in response to Ayer's rhetoric. For writers such as D. Z. Phillips, the Humean empiricist legacy has dominated theology and the philosophy of religion for too long, resting as it does upon a mistaken identification of theological statements with statements of empirical fact. Once this fundamental error is committed, it seems that the only way forward for theology is to abandon the traditional understanding of religious beliefs as having propositional content, and to replace this understanding with one in which they are regarded as disguised statements of moral intentions. This is the essence of Braithwaite's 'empiricist's view' of religious belief.[16] Phillips rejects this approach as a form of reductionism.[17] From the work of the later Wittgenstein, he extracts a view of language in which religious utterances and the forms of life in which they are embedded are subject only to their own tests of coherence, meaningfulness and truth.[18] Both natural theology and natural atheology thus turn out to rest upon philosophical error, a result which has irritated philosophers sympathetic to religion quite as much as it has infuriated those hostile to it.[19] Yet the fact that Wittgenstein has also proved a powerful inspiration to Don Cupitt in his most recent attempts to achieve a new understanding of religion[20] should make it clear that theologians invoking the name of Wittgenstein are not always obvious allies of those who wish to return to a more conservative approach in theology. Indeed, many have seen what Phillips and the other so-called 'Wittgensteinian fideists' are doing as simply continuing the liberal flight from traditional religion which subjugation to Humean empiricism first precipitated.[21]

Certainly, it is true that Phillips's understanding of 'genuine religion' is at odds with what most ordinary believers take themselves to be doing, for example when they pray. But it would be a mistake to see Phillips as someone who, like Cupitt, is proposing a *re-interpretation* of religious belief, for the essence of the Wittgensteinian position, as Phillips understands it, is that philosophy leaves everything as it is, and this can lend encouragement to those who wish to see at least the forms of religious practice preserved intact. In contrast to the mild series of reminders of actual usages of religious language which Phillips assembles, Cupitt is about the business of declaring much of traditional religiosity obsolete, and encouraging speculation into the new forms which it might take as we enter the post-modern age. In his work, the machinery of Wittgensteinian linguistic philosophy is used to emphasise the cultural dependence of all language, and hence of all thought, so as to free us of the notion that there stands outside our language some reality to which that language relates, and so 'the dissolution of Enlightenment and Modernist ideology gathers pace'.[22] Something very unWittgensteinian is going on here: for all Cupitt's protestations of the incoherence of the notion of a truth which is transcendent of our linguistic and cultural practices, it is clear that our coming to recognise this incoherence is supposed to have dramatic consequences for our view of ourselves and our place within the world, as if our most ordinary beliefs were all tainted with the poison of Cartesian rationalism.[23] The hand of Nietzsche is surely more apparent here than that of Wittgenstein – God is dead, and all metaphysics with Him, and we had better start looking for something more humble to serve as His replacement, namely our neighbours, to whom Christians should now turn in a secular humanist faith, much as environmentalists have turned to the earth as their own object of devotion.[24]

Cupitt, then, is an undisguised atheist, and operating altogether outside the limits of the older liberal tradition in theology. By contrast with him, the Bishop of Durham stands firmly within that school of Anglican thought in which the results of biblical criticism join with a modern distrust of superstition to produce a Christianity in which the historical events surrounding the life and death of Jesus of Nazareth gain their status as the climax of God's progressive Self-revelation to man by virtue of the effects which this revelation has upon the Christian believer, rather than by virtue of anything miraculous about those events themselves.[25] Jenkins's rejection of a God who works 'laser beam' miracles[26] falls short of the complete rejection of all metaphysics as superstition which characterises both the work of Cupitt and, though in a very different way, that of Wittgensteinians like Phillips. For all its scepticism about the historical accuracy of the biblical record and concentration upon the transformation of the individual, rather than upon the sacramental mystery of Christ's atoning death, the liberal tradition which Jenkins represents is still quite distinctively Christian. Traditionalists may cringe at the language in which Jenkins expresses his theology, but he is thoroughly conservative in his defence of the idea of God as a transcendent reality, in his claim that this reality is most fully revealed to us in the life, death and resurrection of Jesus, and in his attachment to the doctrine of the Trinity.[27] It is precisely the inability of the liberal tradition to deal with the problem of religious pluralism that has driven others besides Cupitt to emphasise the historical and cultural dependence of all human responses to what John Hick chooses to call 'the Real'.[28] But few of these have chosen to go as far as Cupitt, as this talk of the Real makes clear. For Hick, as for Cantwell Smith and Lindbeck, metaphysics is still clinging on, however tenuously. Description, even thought, concerning this transcendent realm of value must be contained within traditions and systems of concepts which are entirely of human making, so that talk of correspondence between particular human faiths and the Real is incoherent, but enough remains of the notion of some level of existence to which we are answerable, rather than vice versa, to ground judgements about the rightness or wrongness of particular ways in which we choose to live our lives.[29]

It is precisely an external standard of this kind, however dimly perceived, which Cupitt lacks. For him, all life-choices must reflect the discipline of 'the Void'[30] – Cupitt's term for what Hick would presumably have to call 'the Unreal', and a term carefully chosen to avoid any suggestion that there is some 'gap' left by the death of the God of traditional theism which might be filled by some new metaphysical principle. This lack generates the most fundamental of the many questions to which Cupitt's new understanding of religion gives rise: why should disciplining ourselves to the Void lead us towards devotion to our neighbours rather than destruction of them? It would seem that the only 'life-line' which is definitively ruled out by this discipline is that of old-time theistic religion; other than this descent into superstition, what else could be an incorrect response to the post-modern condition in which 'there isn't much reality around'?[31] Even if, as Cupitt argues, traditional metaphysical realism, when pressed to its logical conclusion, topples into nihilism,[32] this does not show that he has anything over the realist except the rather dubious advantage that he starts off in the condition in which the realist is bound to end up. This does not show that nihilism does not threaten to leave us without any standard by which to judge 'the appropriateness of all the various ways of life open to us, but only that the threat is inescapable.

Of course, Cupitt does not really believe that any way of life is as good as any other. The discipline of the Void is strict, for although 'Things have the value we give them; their value is a matter of how much we care about them',[33] it is clear that Cupitt thinks we should value others as we value ourselves, that we should care as much about women as we do about men, that we should preserve rather than poison the planet on which we live, and so on. What can ground these judgements if *all* life-outcomes are equally valid? However thinly conceptualised Hick's 'the Real' is, it at least gives him something to point to as a goal which we can fall short of, or as a level of existence which we can fail to attain.[34] A critique of some religion wholly from within could not give us reason to condemn it as antithetical to human flourishing, for the religion will itself define what flourishing consists in, and this is why the Wittgensteinans are right to say that philosophy leaves everything as it is, and why Cupitt cannot rest content with the sort of position which Phillips adopts. Cupitt does not want things left as they are, particularly in the social and political realm. But only if there is some independent standard by which to judge particular religious responses could we share Cupitt's conviction that appropriate responses will not be (what the liberal regards as) mean-spirited, manipulative, vicious or authoritarian.

Cupitt's 'new religious ethics', then, is not so new. Whatever the status of its metaphysical underpinning, the moral and political superstructure is essentially that of many of those whom he calls 'semi-realists' (John Robinson, and perhaps also Hick), and also of those who, like Jenkins, stand firmly in the liberal tradition which Cupitt so roundly condemns. Cupitt's choice of this democratic and humanitarian ethic, with its concern for human rights and the environment, cannot represent anything more than a personal preference, which he would doubtless like others to share, but which he can give no reason for sharing. Just because the Christian message retains some vestige of metaphysical truth for theologians like Robinson (and philosophers like Hick), the claim that the Christian (or 'Reality-centred') way of life is binding upon all men can be given some justification. But then the problem becomes the translation of that message into a programme of personal and social action. It is here that the second part of the popular attack on liberal theology comes into play – the accusation that the content of the pastoral, and more specifically political, theology which has predominated amongst theologians in recent years derives from the secular rather than the spiritual realm.

Now this accusation has, like its companion, a grain of truth. Particular views about the historical accuracy of the biblical record, about the making of Christian doctrine within the early church, about the philosophical status of theological statements, or about the standing of non-Christian religions, cannot coerce any particular view about the content of religious ethics, particularly where those ethics enter the political arena. The emphasis upon the historical and cultural dependence of all doctrinal formulation, typically used to open up a space in which the only absolute values are those of pluralism and toleration, falls far short of a theological justification for political liberalism. To read the Bible as dominated by a political concern for the poor and underprivileged, for example, is to exercise a choice which no amount of textual criticism can compel – there are other and equally responsible ways in which to combine study of the biblical material with analysis of 'the present pressures on and in our society'.[35] Certainly, the rich man is commanded to sell all he has and give the proceeds to the poor, as preparation for taking up the cross and following Christ (Luke 18: 22), but so also we are told that a man must hate his father and mother, his wife and his children, his brothers and sisters, and even his own life, if he is to become a disciple (Luke 14: 26). Those who find in Christ's teaching a condemnation of riches, but no condemnation of other worldly ties, read the New Testament with a selectivity which no amount of source- or form-criticism can justify, as do those who, like Mrs Thatcher, find in the gospels a defence of family values. The parable of the Good Samaritan will serve equally well as a model of private charitable giving or as a defence of public health provision, which of course means that it can serve properly as neither. If we take the text seriously, we can see it only as Christ intended it – as an answer to the question, 'Who is my neighbour?', and it might then serve as a condemnation of at least some forms of racial and religious prejudice. But this kind of approach is generally unrewarding; the proclamation of the imminence of the kingdom of God is not a social programme, nor capable of yielding such a programme. Secular concerns have to be read into the texts before they can be dragged out as 'Christian ethics'.

Interestingly, Cupitt recognises just this point, noting that before the nineteenth century, Christianity had little interest in liberal, humanitarian or democratic concerns; these have been imposed upon the historic structure of faith in such a way that many have now come to regard them as contained within it. Of course, nothing could be further from the truth for Cupitt: it is only when we have rid ourselves of God, whose exclusive claim to the role of creator of value made genuine humanitarianism impossible, that the error of thinking of Christianity as humanitarian can be converted into truth through the creation of liberal values *ex nihilo*.[36] Traditional Christianity is not politically and ethically liberal, but has to be made so. This indicates a strange similarity between Cupitt and Edward Norman, who is equally clear that the 'politicisation' of Christianity represents a radical departure from tradition.[37] They differ in that Cupitt celebrates this departure whilst Norman bemoans it. Cupitt wishes to retain the liberal ethical programme and dispense with Christian theology, Norman hopes for a return to a private theology of 'the ethereal' which leaves the political arena to the politicians; Cupitt does not want things left as they are, Norman longs for things to be as they used to be. Both are misguided. Christian theology, whether derived strictly from the Bible, or drawing also upon sources within the history of the Church, cannot determine any particular political theology, so Cupitt is certainly wrong to think that we have to take leave of God and become mere Jesus admirers if we are to produce a Christian ethics which is genuinely humanitarian. But so also is Norman mistaken in thinking that the fact that theology underdetermines social policy means that it is essentially concerned with 'the condition of the inward soul of man'.[38] All this fact implies is that there is no political programme which is wholly and exclusively Christian, a point which Norman would agree with, but which he fails to see applies as much to the politics of his 'depoliticised' Christianity as it does to the extremes of liberation theology.

In fact, Norman's position is a characteristically Lutheran one, and the tendency of conservative Anglicans to fall back upon this position, although perhaps odd, is widespread.[39] The essence of Lutheran political theology is the 'two kingdoms' theory, in which the autonomy of the temporal order is asserted: provided that the state does not intervene in the realm of the spiritual, the church has nothing to say to it, for the only proper realm of religion is the private and inward. In no sense is such a theology 'depoliticised', and the inclination to describe it as such is itself a reflection of a political stance which,

though permissible for a Christian, is not compulsory. The search for
a theology that is devoid of political content is futile, tending only to
lead to a kind of sacralising of the existing order more characteristic
of the imperial religion of Rome than of anything genuinely Christian.[40] But equally futile is the attempt to generate entirely from
within theology a 'Christian ethics' which is adequate to address the
political and social realities of the day. The complaint that the content
of Christianity is being 'drained away into the great pool of secular
idealism'[41] fails to realise that *any* detailed Christian attitude to
politics must borrow from outside. Norman himself borrows largely
from the now-popular set of ideas dubbed 'the politics of imperfection', and can thus be grouped with non-religious thinkers such as
Michael Oakeshott, Anthony Quinton, Roger Scruton and the former
Conservative Chancellor of the Exchequer, Nigel Lawson, all of
whom have appealed to human weakness and ignorance in order to
defend right-wing policies of various kinds.[42] But, as Ronald Preston
has argued,[43] those elements of the politics of imperfection which are
conformable with Christianity need not lead towards the political
right any more than towards the left. Reinhold Niebuhr, active on
the left all his life, is perhaps more preoccupied with the sinfulness
of human nature than any twentieth-century theologian save Karl
Barth, and Barth, of course, rejected the Lutheran theory of two
kingdoms in favour of a wholehearted defence of the claim that the
church must preach politics.[44] Neither Niebuhr nor Barth can be
described as 'liberal' theologians, and indeed it was the influence of
Barth in particular that drove the first 'reaction from liberalism' in
Britain in the 1930s.[45] Nor can the label of 'liberal' attach to Dietrich
Bonhoeffer, the Lutheran pastor executed by the Nazis for his part
in the plot to assassinate Hitler, and who now serves as a major
inspiration to those who find in Christianity a command to struggle
against manifest injustice and tyranny. More recently, Peter Hinchliff
has combined Norman's insistence that no political programme can
attract the wholehearted support of Christians, and his stress on the
sinfulness of man, with a strong defence of the need for the Church
to soil its hands with politics.[46]

    In none of these thinkers is there any tendency to allow secular
idealism to swamp the content of the Christian message, which
remains one of prophetic condemnation of all that is inimical to the
good news of Christ. The proclaiming of the true gospel cannot shy
away from the condemnation of false gospels, and the state therefore
invites condemnation whenever it aligns itself with the false against

the true. It did so in Nazi Germany, and does so in, for example, present-day South Africa, and in neither case just by intruding into the sphere of private spirituality. The commandment to render unto Caesar the things which are Caesar's is always qualified by the commandment to render unto God the things that are God's. As all things come from God, so all things must be rendered unto him.[47] The obligation to give back to God what God has given cannot be limited to the 'ethereal qualities of immortality' alone, and so no limit can be set in advance for the involvement of the Church in politics. But neither, as Norman rightly says, can any political programme contain the whole content of the Christian message. The prophetic condemnation of particular policies derives its force from considerations which lie outside social theory, and so any complete rendering of Christian belief in secular terms is indeed heretical. Cupitt is certainly guilty of this heresy, but there are few others who are as careless or unChristian as he.

Of course, what drives the call for the 'depoliticisation' of Christianity in Britain is a reasonable recognition that the state is not aligned with any false gospel comparable with Nazism or *apartheid* here. Often added to this is a desire to see the churches act as forces of social cohesion rather than criticism. But neither of these are strictly theological points: the former is a moral judgement which most share, and which is open only to moral debate; the latter is a piece of sociology. Nothing within Christian theology can show that one of the functions of faith is to maintain social stability rather than undermine it, for the psychological or sociological functions of faith are not themselves part of the content of the faith.[48] Equally, nothing within Christian theology can tell us whether monetarism is sound economic theory or not, though it surely can tell us that the poor, like lepers, prostitutes and tax-gatherers, should hold a special place in the hearts of Christians, just as they did for Christ himself. Because Britain now has few lepers, because clergymen generally feel rather awkward about prostitutes, and because tax-gatherers are now no more stigmatised than the tax-advisers which many of them become, it is not altogether surprising that the poor have become a focus of concern for the churches. This kind of religious commitment to the marginal elements of society is often separate and always separable from any particular attitude to scripture or to the doctrines of the Church, just as it is not reducible to an attachment to the framework of the post-war political consensus. Things are altogether more complicated than popular readings of the state of theology imply.

Accusations of subservience to prevailing orthodoxy, whether philosophical or ethical, do not stick – or at least, those making such
accusations should note one of the least difficult to interpret, though
most difficult to heed, of the sayings of Christ: 'He that is without
sin among you, let him cast the first stone' (John 8: 7).

Notes and References

1. Ayer, in conversation with Bryan Magee in the mid 1970s, said of Logical
   Positivism that 'I suppose the most important of the defects was that
   nearly all of it was false', B. Magee, *Men of Ideas* (London, 1978): 107.
2. See, for example, the discussion of the outlines of various postmodern
   theologies in N. Murphy and J. W. McClendon, Jr, 'Distinguishing
   Modern and Postmodern Theologies', *Modern Theology*, 5 (April 1989):
   191–214.
3. In Britain, the reaction from liberalism can be dated to the year
   before *Language, Truth and Logic* reached the bookshops, when Alan
   Richardson published *The Redemption of Modernism* (Skeffington,
   1935). The post-liberalism of the 1930s, which was powerfully influenced
   by Karl Barth, is discussed in Michael Ramsey's 'After Liberalism:
   Reflections on Four Decades' in R. H. Preston (ed.), *Theology and
   Change: Essays in Memory of Alan Richardson* (London, 1975).
4. London, 1963.
5. London, 1977.
6. London, 1984.
7. For example, T. V. Morris, *The Logic of God Incarnate* (Ithaca, NY,
   1986); W. Charlton, *Philosophy and Christian Belief* (London, 1988); T.
   V. Morris (ed.), *Philosophy and Christian Faith* (University of Notre
   Dame Press, 1988); R. G. Swinburne, *Forgiveness and Atonement*
   (Oxford, 1989).
8. For example, W. Cantwell Smith, *Faith and Belief* (Princeton, 1979); G.
   A. Lindbeck, *The Nature of Doctrine: Religion and Theology in a
   Postliberal Age* (London, 1984); J. Hick, *God and the Universe of Faiths*
   (London, 1973), *An Interpretation of Religion* (London, 1989).
9. The myths surrounding the fundamentalist assault on so-called 'liberal'
   biblical scholarship are most effectively exposed in John Barton's 1988
   Bampton Lectures, published as *People of the Book?* (London, 1988).
   Barton argues that 'aspects of Scripture to which fundamentalists
   insistently point can be better allies in the cause of a constructive non-
   conservative theory of Scripture than they are in what seems to so many
   their natural conservative habitat', *People of the Book?*: 3.
10. This is the substance of T. V. Morris's suspicions about modern biblical
    scholarship: 'If on the basis of some philosophical argument or, more
    commonly, rumors of such an argument, the biblical scholar comes to
    believe that one or other traditional doctrine is deeply flawed . . . he or

she may well be less inclined to acknowledge intimations or anticipations of the problematic formulation in the *authentic* sayings of Jesus or in the earliest witness of the church', *Philosophy and Christian Faith*: 5.

11. These are William Charlton's chosen sources for the view, which he attributes to 'a majority of professional scripture scholars', that biblical scholarship seeks 'to explain how, given that hardly any of the events recorded really happened, our documents could have come into being', *Philosophy and Christian Belief*: 89.

12. Charlton, *Philosophy and Christian Belief*: 92.

13. Charlton, *Philosophy and Christian Belief*: 93.

14. For example, those biblical conservatives who have rallied around the hermeneutically-inspired 'Bible as literature' movement; see Barton, *People of the Book?*: 64–5.

15. For example, R. B. Braithwaite's 1955 Eddington Memorial Lecture, 'An Empiricist's View of the Nature of Religious Belief', reprinted in B. G. Mitchell (ed.), *The Philosophy of Religion* (Oxford, 1971), a collection which also reproduces the famous 'University Discussion' between A. Flew, R. M. Hare and B. G. Mitchell, and contains other papers on related topics by I. M. Crombie and J. Hick.

16. See note 15 above.

17. D. Z. Phillips, *Religion Without Explanation* (Oxford, 1976): 140–5.

18. See, for example, D. Z. Phillips, *The Concept of Prayer* (London, 1965); Phillips (ed.), *Religion and Understanding* (Oxford, 1967); Phillips, *Faith After Foundationalism* (London, 1988).

19. For example, the religious sceptic Kai Nielson has devoted much space to attacks on the 'Wittgensteinian fideists' in *Contemporary Critiques of Religion* (London, 1971): 94ff., and in *An Introduction to the Philosophy of Religion* (London, 1982): 43ff. The Christian philosopher Richard Swinburne is equally critical of Phillips in *Faith and Reason* (Oxford, 1981): 137, 140n.

20. D. Cupitt, *Life Lines* (London, 1986); *The Long-Legged Fly* (London, 1987); *Radicals and the Future of the Church* (London, 1989).

21. See, for example, J. L. Mackie, *The Miracle of Theism* (Oxford, 1982): 217ff.; C. S. Evans, *Philosophy of Religion* (Leicester, 1985): 151ff.; J. Hick, *An Interpretation of Religion*: 198ff. Hick seems to me mistaken in thinking Phillips's position to be particularly close to that of Cupitt.

22. *Radicals and the Future of the Church*: 39.

23. Just how unWittgensteinian Cupitt's position is can be seen in remarks such as this, from *The New Christian Ethics* (London, 1988): 12: 'everything, including our own nature and our own desires, is constituted within language and is mutable and contingent. There is no bedrock and nothing is fixed, not my identity nor my sexuality nor my categories of thought, nothing' which contrasts sharply with Wittgenstein's position in, for example, *Philosophical Investigations* (Oxford, 1953): 217: 'If I have exhausted the justifications I have reached bedrock, and my spade is turned. Then I am inclined to say: "This is simply what I do"'.

24. *Radicals and the Future of the Church*: 137.

25. Jenkins's thought is represented most recently by three books: *God, Miracle and the Church of England* (London, 1987); *God, Jesus and Life*

in the Spirit (London, 1988); and *God, Politics and the Future* (London, 1988). In none of these does his theological position differ substantially from that of his 1966 Bampton lectures, published as *The Glory of Man* (London, 1967).

26. Jenkins disputes a particular interpretation of miracles as proofs of faith, preferring to regard them as 'gifts – to faith and for faith, but not public and objective pressures into faith', *God, Miracle and the Church of England*: 31.

27. See, for example, *God, Jesus and Life in the Spirit*: 25:

> God is. He is as he is in Jesus. So there is hope.
> God is. He is for us. So it is worth it.

According to Jenkins, the first of these 'mini-creeds' is about the doctrine of the Trinity and eschatology, and the second about the doctrine of the atonement and sanctification.

28. J. Hick, *An Interpretation of Religion* (London, 1989): 11.

29. Jenkins is emphatic on this point: 'Thus, any view one holds about one's favourite features of Jesus being somehow of general or universal significance becomes entirely subjective and, probably, entirely individualistic once one has decided on atheism and rejected Christian faith in God', *God, Politics and the Future*: 46.

30. *Radicals and the Future of the Church*: 141ff.

31. *Radicals and the Future of the Church*: 79.

32. *Radicals and the Future of the Church*: 159. The argument seems to be that, because any form of metaphysical realism must treat the truth of statements as a matter of their correspondence with independent reality, and because the only thing which could correspond with reality perfectly would be reality itself, the search for ever more accurate representations of reality is doomed to failure.

33. *Radicals and the Future of the Church*: 158.

34. Thus Hick finds within each of the world's religions a common soteriological strand, 'the transformation of human existence from self-centredness to Reality-centredness' (*An Interpretation of Religion*: 36). It is clear that this shift is finally justified only because there is a Reality on which human existence can be centred.

35. Jenkins, in *God, Politics and the Future*, Chapter 5, claims otherwise. For him, 'the threefold eschatological structure of the judgment of the kingdom, the building of the kingdom, and waiting for the kingdom' (60) make the preferential option for the poor obligatory.

36. *The New Christian Ethics*: 14–15.

37. E. R. Norman, *Christianity and the World Order* (Oxford, 1979).

38. Norman, *Christianity and the World Order*: 76.

39. This point is noted, and Norman's position criticised, in D. B. Forrester, *Theology and Politics* (Oxford, 1988): 44ff. For similar criticisms of Norman, see also R. H. Preston, *The Future of Christian Ethics* (London, 1987): 163ff. The oddity of Norman's Lutheran attitude to political theology lies in his combining it with a defence of the establishment of the Church of England, and here Norman is influenced by the 'Christendom'

tradition of Christian Sociology. Other exponents of this approach include David Martin, in *The Breaking of the Image: A Sociology of Christian Theory and Practice* (Oxford, 1980), and John Habgood, *Church and Nation in a Secular Age* (London, 1983), both of whose arguments for establishment rely on sociological considerations.

40. Forrester, *Theology and Politics*: 29ff.
41. Norman, *Christianity and the World Order*: 13.
42. M. Oakeshott, *Rationalism in Politics and Other Essays* (London, 1962); A. M. Quinton, *The Politics of Imperfection* (London, 1978); R. Scruton, *The Meaning of Conservatism* (Harmondsworth, 1980); N. Lawson, *The New Conservatism* (London: Centre for Policy Studies, 1980).
43. *The Future of Christian Ethics*: 145ff., 204ff.
44. See, for example, *Against the Stream* (London, 1954): 47 (quoted by Forrester, *Theology and Politics*: 49.).
45. See note 3 above.
46. P. Hinchliff, *Holiness and Politics* (London, 1982).
47. Hinchliff, *Holiness and Politics*: 4ff.
48. This is why an atheist such as Scruton, in *The Meaning of Conservatism*, can defend the establishment of religion entirely in secular and untheological terms, and why theologians need take no note of his arguments.

Part IV
Social Policy: Meritocracy and Responsibility

8 Needs, Entitlements and Obligations: Towards a New Consensus on Welfare Policy*
S. J. D. Green

The barrier to radical reform of social policy is not the pain it would cause the intended beneficiaries . . . but the pain it would cause the donors.[1]

Welfare policy, more than most other forms of public administration, is a poor, makeshift thing. It is vulnerable not only to the limitations of our collective resources, but also to the limitations of our common knowledge. As such, it is a branch of political activity susceptible to the cant of 'moralism', and to the sententious pursuit of nebulous political goals under the guise of humanitarian generosity.[2] But, at last, it has become possible – if not quite respectable – to say so. During the last decade, beginning in the United States, but now spreading across Western Europe, a new theoretical consensus has emerged amongst welfare analysts which has drawn considered opinion away from some of the vaguer invocations of political utopianism, and has concentrated critical attention upon the record – the mundane sociological record – of what forty years of state-sponsored welfarism have actually *done* for the poor and for the not-so-poor, in advanced societies. In the wake of this reappraisal, there are encouraging signs that welfare policy may yet mature into a branch of political activity and public administration that will be judged by its results, and not by its intentions, and still less by the self-justifications of those who earn their living from its provision. For the results of those four decades of effort, in this country as elsewhere, suggest, to those who would look at the evidence with open eyes, that an old theoretical orthodoxy about the provision of public welfare has finally hit the buffers.

That orthodoxy may be called the political theory of public transfer. No-one expressed the ideal underlying this theory more eloquently than R. H. Tawney. He argued for 'the pooling of surplus resources by means of taxation, and the use of the funds thus obtained to make accessible to all . . . the conditions of civilisation which, in the absence of such measures, can be enjoyed only by the rich'.[3] But, in his eloquence, Tawney assumed rather than established the validity of a synthetic doctrine composed of two, quite distinct, ethical imperatives. The first is wholly unobjectionable. It presumes, very simply, that the inevitable risks of life, the products of brute luck such as illness, injury, and other misfortune, as well as the inevitable burdens of human vulnerability, such as extreme youth and old age, though endured individually, are properly borne collectively. This proposition does not, of course, follow as a matter of logical necessity. It would be easy to *imagine* a society in which every adult person was capable of generating sufficient income in order to insure himself (and his dependents) against the impact of brute luck and human vulnerability, and in which each and every one of its exigencies, individually endured, could also be individually borne. But if it is easy to imagine such a society, it is not easy to envisage even the most advanced of the industrial nations actually developing to such a level of general prosperity in which this state of affairs could easily be brought about. It will remain, for the foreseeable future, a figment of the imagination.

The argument that, in matters of brute luck and human vulnerability, what is individually endured is, nevertheless, best borne collectively is – for all but doctrinaire socialists – essentially a pragmatic proposition. In every advanced society actually known to us, it is the case, and for the foreseeable future it will be the case that there will be many persons who, for many reasons, will be incapable of providing for themselves against the intrusions of brute luck and human vulnerability into their lives. They will be the victims of personal misfortune, and there will not be private insurance markets capable of dealing either with the problem of their misfortune, or with their capacity to make provisions for its eventuality. It is right and proper that public provisions should be made for their needs.[4] Such persons we may reasonably call 'the vulnerable'. Welfare policy should be directed towards their protection.[5] Exactly how that might be achieved is another matter.

But the political theory of public transfer has a second ethical component. This is the assertion that, in addition to protecting those who are, through no fault of their own, vulnerable to the sway of fortune, public policy should actively seek to promote a more general public good through the mechanism of fiscal transfer; that is, that public revenues should be devoted towards social policies specifically designed to promote a public good above and beyond the protection of the vulnerable persons through public means. This is the egalitarian temptation: the assertion that social policy should be directed to correct those inequalities of social welfare which free-market relations in the economy, and in society generally, inevitably generate. In the words of Anthony Crosland: '[S]ocial expenditure . . . can promote . . . social equality . . . in two ways: first, by removing the greater handicap which poorer families suffer as compared with richer, during sickness, old age and the period of heaviest family reponsibility, and secondly by creating standards of public health, education and housing which are comparable in scope and quality with the best available for private purchase.'[6] It is the confusion of these two conceptually distinct ideals into one apparently unified theory – the political theory of public transfer – which accounts for much of the present plight of welfare thinking. And it is the assertion that the first necessarily entails the second (which it does not), which explains so much of the crass moralism which has traditionally plagued this subject. For, if the first proposition is unobjectionable, the second is deeply flawed.

Those flaws may be analysed in terms of their perverse distributive consequences. Post-war advocates for the extension of publicly endowed welfare provision presumed that welfare policies directed to the pursuit of such apparently unambiguously desirable social goals as universal standards of health care, free public education, and comprehensive national insurance and pensions schemes, would necessarily benefit the poor more than the well-off, and therefore extend the boundaries of social equality in an otherwise inegalitarian society.[7] But it has been found, on detailed inspection, that these policies invariably have perverse distributive consequences. In this country, for instance, the middle classes gain more from free public education, especially from secondary and tertiary education, and benefit longer from comprehensive national insurance and pensions schemes than do the working classes.[8] Just how significant those perverse consequences are, and if indeed they are really perverse, is a matter for debate. It may be that in pursuit of these, otherwise desirable, social goals perverse distributive consequences are unavoidable in all but the most economically egalitarian of societies. It may be also that, in pursuit of these, apparently worthwhile, ends perverse distributive consequences are worth the price of their perversity. Or it may be not.[9] That question will not be broached here.

It will be ignored, not because it is of no importance (it clearly is), but because to concentrate too much on the distributive aspects of welfare policy is to make the same mistake, merely inverted, which so many of these 'welfarists' made: it is to neglect the perverse behavioural consequences of poorly conceived social policy. For what is truly wrong with so much 'transferist' social policy is not merely, or even most importantly, its perverse distributive consequences, but rather the perverse behavioural consequences it wreaks upon large sections of the population. That fault is rooted in social analysis which insists upon addressing only the distributive symptoms, and not the social causes of poverty and social distress. It emerges in social policies which, however generously inspired, often do more harm than good. It may be traced to the failure of an earlier generation of welfare analysts to distinguish between the protection of the vulnerable (which, ultimately, is reducible to matters of public transfer), and the amelioration of poverty and social distress (which, ultimately, is *not* reducible to matters of public transfer). To make that distinction is to avoid making a simple error of diagnosis: that the poor are poor solely because they lack income. And it is to avoid making an equally simple error in treatment: to insist that, this being so, it must be the case that to extend the eligibility of individuals to welfare services and to increase the 'generosity' of those services will be to diminish the absolute numbers, and the relative suffering, of the poor; in other words, to eliminate poverty and to reduce social inequality at one and the same time, and through the same fiscal mechanism. This diagnosis is incomplete at best, and simply wrong at worst. And the long-term consequences of the treatment it implies are sometimes disastrous for the patient. Not least for the ways in which it adversely affects his or her subsequent behaviour. It has led many poor people down the road to helpless dependency. It has created many more poor people than there might otherwise have been. It has lifted remarkably few – scandalously few – poor and deprived persons into the realms of independence and prosperity. It has not made society more 'equal'; nor has it made society any more 'generous' or 'humane'.

It is the mark of the new consensus in the welfare debate that protagonists from both sides of the political divide, and both sides of the Atlantic, have begun to recognise and appreciate the validity of some of these salutary truths. They have begun to understand, and to act upon their understanding of the fact that the poor are poor for very many different reasons, and that no single strategy either will, or conceivably could, attend successfully to the various problems of individual poverty and social distress. They have accepted that, whilst for some of the poor welfare policies constitute an essential form of public support, for others what is needed is not so much an extension of the welfare system as its replacement. And they have conceded that for a growing minority of the young poor, especially, in North America and increasingly in Western Europe, the cure to this particular form of illness lies less in the superficial treatment of individual deprivations and more in general attention to a profound problem of social pathology. In so doing, they have learned to sever the spurious link between the 'war on poverty' and the pursuit of social equality, and to insist that the intelligent exercise of the first almost certainly rules out the specious – transferist – pursuit of the second.[10] But they are not 'ungenerous' or 'inhumane' people.[11] They are, in Charles Murray's words, 'generous people', who have 'stopped kidding themselves'.[12]

Many fallacies surrounded the 'transferist' understanding of the 'poor' in advanced societies. None, perhaps, is more misleading, and ultimately more pernicious, than the lazy assumption of their homogeneity. Paradoxically, that assumption is *more* easily made now than it was a century ago. The old division of the poor into 'deserving' and 'undeserving' has fallen foul of modern sensibilities.[13] Unfortunatley nothing has taken its place. Ironically, as social research has banished the concept of personal responsibility from the respectable canons of sociological explanation, so it has – paradoxically – diminished rather than increased our capacity to understand why so many people in otherwise wealthy societies are, and remain, poor. The only way to enhance that understanding is to learn, once again as it were, to distinguish between persons within the ranks of the designated 'poor'; not, of course, so crudely as to distinguish only between the 'deserving' and the 'undeserving', but nevertheless to distinguish sociologically between the continuously poor and the continually poor; also between the poor in and of stable families; between the poor in and of displaced, or one-parent families; and (if necessary), between the socially integrated and the socially alienated poor in our society.

It is important to be clear what is meant by these distinctions. To distinguish between the poor, that is to distinguish between the causes and the consequences of poverty for *different types of poor people*, is not to blame the victims of poverty. On the contrary. It is the only way in which to begin the difficult and complex process of targeting different kinds of support to different kinds of poor people. Again, it is important to be clear what is meant by 'targeting' in this respect. Welfare targeting, to date, has amounted to no more than a more elaborate method of channelling cash benefits to the poor in such a way, by means-testing, as to avert unnecessary fiscal waste, and with the effect of eliminating at least some of the perverse distributive consequences of universal benefit programmes. The merits of this idea are, however, less clear-cut than current (official) fashion allows. Financial targeting, even if it is successful, can also have perverse behavioural consequences. It may encourage the poor to restrict their income, so as to remain eligible. It can stimulate fraud. It does increase administrative costs. Worst of all, it highlights the alleged distinction between the truly needy and the properly self-sufficient in such a way as to reaffirm the implicit assumption that welfare policy is, and must be, only about providing for those who cannot provide for themselves.[14]

But welfare policy is not just about providing for those who cannot provide for themselves. It is, or it should be, additionally about enabling as many people as possible to provide for themselves and for their dependents by maintaining – for themselves – an independent income and an independent existence, on the basis of regular employment. It is, or should be, as much about the preservation of common values through public policies as about the alleviation of common distress through fiscal mechanisms. By matching common values with common sense, welfare policy can avoid the temptations of 'moralism'. It can come to terms with the fact that it is entirely possible that the extension of personal eligibility and an increased 'generosity' of welfare benefits will, for some of the poor, only exacerbate the problem of dependency.[15] It can be aware that, for others, the provision of publicly-supported employment opportunities *in itself* will do little to diminish the problem of voluntary non-participation in the labour-force.[16] In short, it must learn to appreciate that to approach the problem of poverty successfully, it is necessary not only to target persons, and not merely to target resources, but also to target particular kinds of help – particular policies – to particular types of persons. This is called the policy of 'divide and conquer'.[17]

The idea is scarcely remarkable. What is remarkable is the degree of intelligent support it now commands across traditional political boundaries, at least amongst those who analyse these problems, rather than those who remain content to derive moralistic self-satisfaction from their rhetorical exploitation. Those, and there are now many of them on both sides of the Atlantic, who have brought themselves to acknowledge that just throwing more money at the problem of poverty might actually make it worse *in some respects*, and that just 'providing more jobs' will not necessarily substantially reduce the number of permanently unemployed persons *amongst certain sections of the poor*, have gone a long way in beginning to understand how complex the problem of poverty in advanced societies actually is, and just how little an uninformed 'generosity' can do to solve or even to assuage it; indeed, how much it might do to make the problem worse. Armed with that knowledge, they have begun to approach the problems of poverty and social distress in a rather different way and proposed solutions which display a new sophistication and a new realism in the consideration of these problems.

The most important of these approaches is disaggregation. At one level, disaggregation is no more than common sense. It is a way of acknowledging that a working adult at the head of a two-parent family is poor because he or she simply does not earn enough money to prevent himself or herself, and his or her family, from being poor; but that a non-working adult in a one-parent family may be poor, and his or her children may be poor, because he or she, given his or her special family circumstances, is either unable or unwilling to secure permanent employment, and that a non-working youth, with no dependents, may be poor because he or she prefers not to work at all.[18] The poverty of the first is essentially a matter of deficiency of performance in the labour market. The poverty of the second may be related to that deficiency, but it is integrally connected with deficiencies of family structure. The poverty of the third may be related to both performance in the labour market and family structure, but it is also connected with much wider questions of character and culture. That kind of analytical differentiation between poor persons often offends the welfare lobby.[19] So be it. For unless government is prepared to differentiate between certain forms of poverty, at least insofar as it constructs and administers those incentives and disincentives that inevitably constitute any form of welfare policy, then, equally inevitably, it risks the possibility of encouraging and stimulating the creation of more dependent persons and the creation of more poverty. Social security cheques which enable young people to abandon the pursuit of socially necessary skills, or to delay to search for work, are not charity. They are forms of deception. Fiscal incentives which actually induce teenage girls to bear children for which their father will (almost certainly) accept no responsibility are neither generous nor caring. They are cruel and inconsiderate.[20]

A generous society will care for people at the moments of their personal catastrophes. But it will not pursue social policies that will actively encourage some of the least fortunate in society to turn their lives into one long personal catastrophe. That is why disaggregation matters. And that is why categorical differentiation of poor persons must *not* be deprived of a moral content. The moral content of categorical differentiation is a guide to the different types of welfare policy which are appropriate for the needs of different types of poor people. In other words, categorical differentiation implies different entitlements and different obligations for different types of poor people. Of course, nothing is more likely, *a priori*, to offend traditional liberal sensibilities than that.[21] Yet, on closer inspection, what may appear to be a transgression of the fundamental rights of citizenship amounts to no more than a proper acknowledgement by society of the different needs and the different capabilities of different people. For instance, there may be a strong case for providing income support to working adults at the head of two-parent families, especially if, as is invariably the case, their poverty is continual rather than continuous, but little or no case for providing the same income support, *per se*, for welfare mothers and adolescent delinquents.[22] For, whilst there is every reason to encourage people in work to stay in work, and those caring for their families, as families, to continue to do so, and whilst there is every reason for society to support them and their families, and (within bounds) to provide them with additional income in order to do so, there is no reason for society to provide teenage mothers with additional income to bear more children, or to furnish delinquent adolescents with additional income in order not to work. This may sound harsh. But the fact remains that, in most western countries at the moment, there is 'little aid, incentive or pressure for single parents to work'.[23] Or, indeed, for adolescents who prefer the leisure option.[24]

The road away from welfare policies which actually provoke perverse behavioural consequences can only begin with a proper recognition of these facts. In so doing, it will also recognise the perverse implications of so much 'means tested' welfare, especially for those who are obeying society's rules, and who are trying to claw their way out of poverty. It must learn to help people when they are down, perahps by providing working families with short-term family support, reduced only *gradually* as their independent incomes increase; and, at the same time, it must have the courage to remove support from those who would do best without it. For instance, there may be, as David Ellwood insists, a strong case for terminating welfare payments to welfare mothers after a period of time (he suggests eighteen to twenty-six months) and insisting that they take work. If public authorities could guarantee that work, there would be a very strong case.[25] At the very least it is essential to distinguish between the mother and the child. The child will always be deserving of support – particularly by his or her father if traceable. The mother will not always be so deserving.

But nowhere is the problem of desert and responsibility more striking than in the case of the adolescent poor. In the United States, tens of thousands of the young especially have plunged into what is now widely, if somewhat unrigorously, called an 'underclass'.[26] The word has yet to become common currency in this country. But we should not be complacent. There is every reason to believe that the problem will be with us soon. Anyone who walks the streets of Central London with his or her eyes open should be aware that, in certain parts of urban Britain, the problem is with us already. It is a problem which is easily, if glibly, traced to the inefficiencies of the Youth Training Scheme and its local programmes. More important, it is a problem which is not going to be solved by any number of Youth Training Schemes. This not to question the value of compulsory training schemes. Nor is it to belittle the value of training. If it does nothing else, youth training can impart certain very basic skills, such as punctuality, concentration and minimal efficiency, to trainees.[27] At its best, it can give young people a grounding in more complex skills. But the evidence is not particularly convincing. Both in this country and in the United States most public-sponsored 'trainees' of this sort seem to go from training, past menial jobs, and back into welfare shortly afterwards.[28]

To appreciate this melancholy tale is also to acknowledge the profound limits of any welfare policy which attempts only to treat the symptoms of poverty, and only *some* of the symptoms of poverty (i.e., income deprivation) at that. Nowhere is that failure more poignant than amongst the adolescent poor. No section of the poor – in theory – is, or should be, more amenable to cultural and behavioural stimuli, and incentives that could drag many of its erstwhile victims out of the culture of poverty. But, if so, it is mere wishful thinking to extol the virtues of 'training' amongst the unskilled and socially alienated adolescent population. The damage has been done long before that. Just as in the United States, British schools produce a frighteningly large number of unskilled persons. And just as in the United States, British cities are increasingly becoming places where, for a large section of the population, the acquisition of socially usable skills has all but lost its traditional appeal. For this section of society welfare policy will never be more than a sop to the consciences of the donors unless it begins (and ends) with a determined effort to break down not only the physical realities, but also the ethical culture of the ghettoes. There are two ways of doing this: first, to encourage the introduction of business and professional life, and their clientele, into erstwhile deprived areas, and not merely as a means of affording new employment opportunities to the poor through the 'trickle effect', but also with the explicit purpose of breaking down the social exclusivity and cultural homogeneity of poor ghettoes; and secondly, by reinforcing the proper role of schools as an avenue out of deprivation. This may require the use of (apparently) crude methods to induce the children of the poor to remain within the educational system and to derive material benefit from it. That may mean the use of personal rewards (i.e., paying them to stay), and obvious incentives, such as the provision of technical and vocational education.[29] It must mean the abandonment of the simple-minded idea that a diluted version of liberal education constitutes equal opportunities for all.

It would also be to launch a 'war on poverty' that would neither blame nor deceive the victim, but equip him or her with some of the means to render himself or herself less of a victim in and of society. For in a free society, and in a competitive free society especially, some will inevitably do better than others. They will have the skills and the luck (natural and historical) to produce more of what others want, and to gain more of society's rewards than others. This is the price we pay for a free society. Because we are aware that under these conditions of freedom some, through the natural processes of human vulnerability, will fare badly, and others, through brute luck (natural and historical) will also fare badly, we consider it right that, collectively, we should bear some of the burdens of their individual vulnerability and misfortune. And it is right that we should do so. But it is also right that we should encourage as many of our future citizens as we possibly can to make – independently – what they can of what their skills and reasonable good fortune has given them, or could give them. To do that we *must* make demands of them that they will, in turn, make demands of themselves. Not to do so is to let them down. The new theoretical consensus has taught us that

S. J. D. Green

159

much at least. It is time that theory was put into practice.

Notes and References

* I would like to thank the editor and Professor Nathan Glazer for their extremely helpful comments on an earlier version of this chapter.
1. Charles Murray, *Losing Ground: American Social Policy, 1950–1980* (New York, 1984): 236.
2. By 'moralism', I mean that form of special pleading which is as far removed from practical reason as it would be possible to be.
3. R. H. Tawney, *Equality* (London, 1964): 122.
4. For this argument, see Nicholas Barr, *The Economics Of The Welfare State* (London, 1987) Chapter 5.
5. On which, see Robert E. Goodin, *Protecting The Vulnerable: A Reanalysis of Our Social Responsibilities* (Chicago, 1985) especially Chapters 5 and 6.
6. C. A. R. Crosland, *The Future of Socialism* (London, 1956): 579.
7. See, for instance, T. H. Marshall, *Social Policy* (London, 3rd edn, 1970) Chapter 12; P. Townsend, *Sociology and Social Policy* (London, 1975): 28ff.; as for the United States, see J. Tobin, 'On Limiting The Domain of Inequality', *Journal of Law and Economics*, 13 (1970): 263–77.
8. The *locus classicus* of this argument is Julian Le Grand, *The Strategy of Equality: Redistribution and The Social Services* (London, 1982) especially Chapters 3 and 4.
9. For a balanced view of this problem, see Robert E. Goodin and Julian Le Grand, *et al.*, *Not Only The Poor: The Middle Classes And The Welfare State* (London, 1987) Chapter 10.
10. The protagonists are too numerous to list; I take the publication of David T. Ellwood, *Poor Support: Poverty in The American Family* (New York, 1988) to be axiomatic of the new consensus, in that it shows just how far an intelligent political liberal has come to meet some of the most important criticisms of welfare policy, and of the assumptions of welfarism, made by neo-conservative and neo-liberal critics of the system and its ethical justifications; at a more theoretical level, Robert E. Goodin, *Reasons For Welfare* (Princeton, 1988) shows how far a political radical is willing to defend a 'minimal' welfare state against *both* conservative and socialist criticisms, but it also shows how little an intelligent 'welfarist' is prepared to defend his argument in terms of 'social equality'.
11. And it is at least arguable that, knowingly or not, they are much closer to the views expressed by William Beveridge in his famous report, *Social Insurance And Allied Services* (London, 1942) especially 7–9.
12. Murray, *Losing Ground*: 236.
13. The best historical account of this concept may be found in Gertrude Himmelfarb, *The Idea of Poverty: England In The Early Industrial Age*

(London, 1984) especially Chapter 14.

14. For a balanced discussion of the relative merits of 'universal' and 'means-tested' social programmes, see Nathan Glazer, *The Limits of Social Policy* (Cambridge, Mass., 1988) Chapter 10.

15. See the classic 'Harold and Phyllis' example in Murray, *Losing Ground*: 156–64.

16. On this, see especially the remarks of Lawrence M. Mead, 'The New Welfare Debate', *Commentary*, 85 (March 1988): 47–8.

17. The phrase is Mary Jo Bane's.

18. It is not assumed that all, or even a majority of, non-working youths are voluntarily unemployed; nor is it assumed that none of them are; the problem of these, especially amongst the inner-city young who now prefer to work in the illegitimate economy is another question.

19. For a truly hysterical response, see Fred Block, Richard A. Cloward, Barbara Ehrenreich and Frances Fox Piven, *The Mean Season: The Attack On The Welfare State* (New York, 1987) *passim*.

20. The debate on *exactly* what is the relationship between welfare incentives and single-parent families is controversial, and confusing, even for the USA, where the data is most extensive; for a summary of the state of the argument and the evidence from US sources, see Daniel Patrick Moynihan, *Family and Nation* (New York, 1987): 216–18.

21. See, for instance, the remarks of Ralf Dahrendorf, *The Modern Social Conflict: An Essay on The Politics of Liberty* (London, 1988): 33–4.

22. Exactly what *form* of income support is another matter. The case against negative income taxes as means of poor support was generally thought to have been established in the 'Negative Income Tax' experiment carried out under the Office For Equal Opportunities, in New Jersey and Pennsylvania, between 1968 and 1972; for a summary of the results, see Murray, *Losing Ground*: 148–53. The case for *short-term* support, and income and family related support, may be greater.

23. David Whitman, 'The Return Of The New Dealers', *The Public Interest*, 94 (Winter 1989): 109; the citation is from Ellwood, *Poor Support*: 180.

24. In the United Kingdom, school-leavers are now required to enlist on Youth Training Programmes in order to receive Social Security payments. But these programmes are short-lived. Too often, they succeed only in postponing the problem.

25. For this argument, see Ellwood, *Poor Support*: 176–85.

26. The most scholarly study of this phenomenon is William Julius Wilson, *The Truly Disadvantaged: The Inner City, The Underclass and Public Policy* (Chicago, 1987) especially Chapters 2, 3 and 4.

27. On the general argument that welfare must be accompanied by work, the best case is provided in Lawrence M. Mead, *Beyond Entitlement: The Social Obligations of Citizenship* (New York, 1986) Chapters 4 and 5.

28. Mead, 'The New Welfare Debate', p. 48.

29. For a number of genuinely provocative ideas on this question, see Murray, *Losing Ground*: 223–7.

9 Education: From Boyle to Baker
Adrian Wooldridge

> Our chance to influence the world for good, our chance to raise
> our standard of life, our chance to de-barbarise our society, all
> these depend upon our making an explosion: an explosion of wrath
> against the present inadequate education that the children of our
> country are getting.[1]

In 1963 no right-thinking politician or pundit would have dissented
from this judgement: Noel Annan was doing little more than
expressing a commonplace thought with uncommon eloquence. The
British establishment (political as well as cerebral) subscribed to a
progressive consensus which had been invented between the wars
(mainly by R. H. Tawney) and revised in the 1950s (notably by Tony
Crosland). It wanted to abolish the 11-plus, to expand higher
education, and to liberalise teaching; and it regarded education not
only as a good in itself but also as a powerful instrument of social
reform and public enlightenment.

This consensus rested on three assumptions. The first was that
increased educational inputs would lead to improved educational
outputs. More expenditure on teachers and textbooks would produce
a better educated workforce; and compensatory expenditure on
disadvantaged pupils would create a more equal population. The
second was that educational expenditure would reap economic
rewards. Educational expansion and economic growth would become
mutually supporting, with higher expenditure on education fuelling
higher growth and higher growth financing higher expenditure on
education. The third was that the abolition of the 11-plus would
diminish class antagonisms. Educated in common schools, workers
and managers would imbibe a common culture, sink their traditional
differences and work together for the common good. The establishment repeated a litany of criticisms of selection: that it reinforced
social class divisions and discriminated in favour of middle-class
children; that it was at once inaccurate and ruthless; and that it
consigned the majority of children to inferior schooling. Hypnotised
by these ideas, they conducted a holy war against what they regarded

as the great blight of British education: selective schooling.[2]

Anyone who questioned the progressive establishment – who argued that increased expenditure would not necessarily lead to improved results; who pointed out that grammar schools had provided unique opportunities for able working-class children; who argued that comprehensives in middle-class areas would be rather different from comprehensives in working-class areas; or who wondered why egalitarians so often sent their own children to independent schools – was dismissed as a decrepit educational Powellite.[3]

This progressive consensus appealed strongly to one of the country's most important political constituencies – the burgeoning new class of public service workers. The enormous post-war expansion of the state, of local government, and of the service sector produced a new class of sub-professionals – social workers, polytechnic lecturers, local government officers and the like – who had a vested interest in an educational explosion and little time for public-sector restraint or free-market economics. Both their sense of self-worth and their instinct for self-advancement converted them to the cause of egalitarianism, to the culture of the 'people', and to the politics of interest groups.

THE FAILURE OF THE PROGRESSIVE CONSENSUS

Throughout the 1960s and early 1970s the three sociological assumptions upon which the progressive consensus depended were tested in practice – and dramatically discredited.

Increased expenditure did not necessarily lead to improved results. In his authoritative study of educational opportunity in the United States, James Coleman demonstrated that differences in expenditure between schools were almost unrelated to differences in academic performance. Achievement depended on the student's family background rather than on the quality of the school.[4] He noted that only one feature of the school made a major difference to pupil performance: its ethos. Ironically, the comprehensive revolution destroyed a group of schools which had developed a highly successful ethos.

The expansion of higher education did not produce a more productive labour force. (It is tempting to say that the only self-sustaining growth it created was a self-sustaining growth in the supply of educators.) The investment was used to democratise liberal education rather than to galvanise vocational training. Arts departments flourished while engineering departments languished. Motivated by a combination of financial pressure and academic snobbery, the new universities and polytechnics emphasised low-cost arts subjects at the expense of high-cost science subjects; and they found no lack of arts-trained students and arts-trained academics to fill their courses. Polytechnics (or 'artytechnics' as they might almost be called) often insisted on providing courses in art history and music. One of the largest philosophy departments in the country is in a polytechnic. The result was a further supply of arts graduates hungry for niches in the academic-administrative complex and contemptuous of business and technology.

The abolition of the 11-plus has not produced a more mobile or a more united society. The comprehensives have dramatically failed to live up to the ideals of their supporters. They have done little, if anything, to promote social mobility or break down class distinctions; and they have failed to tap the pool of talent wasted in the secondary moderns. Selection had extracted able working-class children from their localities, providing them with an ethos in which education was valued, effort expected and achievement rewarded. Neighbourhood comprehensives, on the other hand, failed to have a dramatic impact on their pupils, allowing the able children of uneducated parents to absorb the values of their neighbourhoods, put little faith in education, and leave school for unskilled jobs. The able but recalcitrant working-class child fell further down the comprehensive school than the grammar school; and, in large schools in mixed neighbourhoods, working-class children, regardless of their ability, gathered together in the lower forms, alienated from their schools and unable to fulfill their potential.[5]

The failure of local comprehensive schools is hardly surprising. Compelled to select their pupils on the basis of family residence rather than individual aptitudes, they have become bastions of inequality: selection by class has replaced selection by merit. Middle-class pupils inevitably attend middle-class comprehensives, with capable staff, excellent facilities, and an encouraging atmosphere; working-class children are consigned to working-class comprehensives with limited opportunities and innumerable social problems: Holland Park is not Risinghill. Indeed, it seems that the abolition of the 11-plus has destroyed a unique mechanism of social mobility. With the grammar schools abolished the pre-eminence of the public schools is secure. In 1979 64 per cent of Oxbridge open awards went to pupils from independent schools. The quest for equality has rigidified class divisions.

The comprehensive system also failed to promote more purely educational ends. The public is increasingly convinced that the established system has failed to promote productivity or inculcate politeness – and it has no shortage of evidence to support its pessimism. Forty per cent of children leave school with no qualifications, their education wasted and their prospects negligible. Inner-city schools have disturbingly high levels of truancy and violence: an alienated population treats free education not as an opportunity to be seized but as an obligation to be resisted. Our educational problems are dramatically demonstrated in comparisons with other advanced nations. Here 82 per cent of children leave school at 16 as compared with 4 per cent in Japan and about 10 per cent in Germany and the United States. In 1980 50 per cent of German children left schools for apprenticeships compared with 14 per cent of British children.[6] British children in the lower half of the ability range are as much as two years behind their German counterparts in mathematical skills. Standards in mathematics are plummeting. Between 1964 and 1981 – the era of comprehensive reorganisation – English children fell from 3rd to 22nd place in an international league table of academic performance.[7]

The failure of radical education reform was not peculiar to Britain. In the United States, where President Johnson's declaration in 1964 of 'unconditional war on poverty' had led to a plethora of legislation, government programmes, social science literature and educational innovation, radical failure was even more dramatic. Despite lavish Federal expenditure on compensatory education for the disadvantaged – and in particular for ethnic minorities – the inter-generational poverty cycle remained unbroken. In 1966 James S. Coleman's report on *Equality of Educational Opportunity*, which had been commissioned on the assumption that differences in the average school performance of blacks and whites were largely due to inequalities in educational resources and that more expenditure on black pupils would lead to improved black performances, demonstrated that variations in the performance of pupils had very little to do with variations in the resources of schools: the explanation of educational inequality lay not so much in the quality of schools or teachers as in the home backgrounds and characteristics of fellow pupils.[8] Other evaluations of 'Head Start programmes', such as the Westinghouse Report on pre-school education, began to multiply evidence that they made no substantial long-term impact on children's intellectual and social development.[9] In 1972 Christopher Jencks's classic study, *Inequality*, acknowledged the demise of educational optimism, arguing on the basis of a mass of evidence that educational reform could do little to solve social inequalities. He insisted that school reform could do little to bring about significant social changes outside the schools; equal educational opportunity could do little to alter life-chances. The social position of a child's parents, combined with the cultural and psychological characteristics of his home, did more to influence his educational achievement than either his IQ or the quality of his schooling. The characteristics of a school's *alumni* depended almost exclusively on the characteristics of its recruits; increased expenditure or reformed policies mattered little. Given the role of chance in determining an individual's income, educational reformers needed to concentrate not on altering schools but instead on reducing the rewards for competitive success and the costs of failure in the community at large.[10]

European developments tended to confirm such scepticism. During the 1950s and 1960s a vast expansion of educational institutions, together with a professed commitment to equal opportunity and upward mobility, had failed to alter the social composition of the élite. The life-chances of children continued to be determined by their class and home backgrounds, with middle-class children seizing the expanded opportunities and working-class children ignoring them. Not surprisingly, the high optimism of the mid-1960s was replaced by profound pessimism in the early 1970s. By 1972, it seemed that 'the essential fact of twentieth century educational history is that egalitarian policies have failed'.[11]

Scepticism about egalitarianism coincided with mounting scepticism about more extravagant forms of progressive education. Based on a belief in children's ability to educate themselves, and sceptical about the claims of adult authority, progressive schooling led to a number of experiments which appalled the conservative public and which even gave radical fellow-travellers pause for doubt. In both Britain and America policy-makers were heavily influenced by a 'back-to-basics' movement, which argued for rote learning, examinations, school discipline; the ethos of effort and the classification of children by merit was once again a popular reforming movement.

The collapse of this consensus about education was reinforced by the collapse of a wider consensus about the welfare state. The public provision of social services has recently attracted penetrating criticism.

The left demonstrated that the welfare state has done little to produce equality. The middle classes do remarkably well out of free public services in general, and out of free educational services in particular.[12] The right pointed out that the unchecked expansion of welfare expenditure may well overload the administration, overburden the economy, and multiply the problems it was designed to alleviate.[13] Declining faith in the effectiveness of the welfare state coincided with a political and intellectual crisis for the Left. The radical intelligentsia, with its obsession with gender, race and sexual orientation, and its determination to politicise the personal, transformed the socialist creed into a vehicle for special interests and a fashion for bohemian misfits; middle-class trendies polluted the moral legacy of working-class autodidacts. The Trade Unions have undermined Labour's claim to ethical purity. Like all producer monopolies, they prospered at the expense of consumers in general and the unemployed in particular. One man's pay rise was another man's price rise; one man's job security was another man's UB40.

THE ANTI-PROGRESSIVE BACKLASH

The progressive consensus consequently began to run into sustained intellectual opposition in the late 1960s and 1970s. Disillusioned by the impact of social reforms, and sceptical about liberal faith in the elasticity of human nature, a small but influential group of intellectuals in Britain and America began to rethink educational policy. Educators, disgusted with the impact of progressive education on the quality of teaching, called for a return to more traditional 'standards'; neo-conservative intellectuals, distressed by what they took to be a subversion of liberalism from within, emphasised the merits of equality of opportunity over equality of outcome; psychologists, reacting against the environmentalist orthodoxy, began to re-examine the theory behind IQ testing; biologists, sceptical about the unqualified sociological explanations popular in the universities, suggested alternative biological explanations; and philosophers began to question the merits of equality.

This reaction found its most forceful expression in the *Black Papers*, a series of polemical pamphlets initiated by two English literature dons, Brian Cox and A. E. Dyson. Originally intended to combat radical student interference with academic traditions, the *Black Papers* soon widened their scope to deal with the 'general crisis in education'.[14] They attracted numerous well-known and articulate contributors, including academics, politicians, schoolteachers, and writers.[15] These contributors differed widely in their intellectual and political commitments – some were dyed-in-the-wool Tories, some were habitual Labour voters disillusioned with Labour's educational policies, and some continued to regard themselves as socialists – but all disliked student protests, levelling politics, and permissive ethics; regarded the 1960s as a 'hideous decade', in which 'ill-thought-out notions of spontaneity, self-realisation and equality' had invaded and subverted education;[16] and insisted on the virtues of high culture, reasoned argument, and disciplined learning.

They reserved their most aggressive polemic for left-wing students and progressive teachers. Student militants they regarded as vandals in 'the temple of culture',[17] financed by the state to subvert traditional civilisation, and they blamed their existence on over-ambitious university expansion. Kingsley Amis put the point bluntly: 'the universities today are full of students who do not understand what study is about, and who are painfully bewildered by the whole business and purpose of university life; more has meant worse'.[18] They also ascribed student unrest to lack of discipline in the schools. Progressive educational thought, ossified into dogma and applied uncritically, had produced a generation of ignorant, ill-disciplined and selfish adolescents. Deprived of adult guidance, let loose in non-structured schools, with no rules, no discipline, no school uniform, no homework, no morning assembly, no rituals, no team games, no Houses, no form classes, no set subjects, and no timetables, and encouraged simply to discover and express their 'true personalities', children inevitably became soft-minded and self-centred victims of the pop and television culture. The vacuum left by lack of instruction was filled by a mass culture which conditioned children to accept life as trivial, violence as normal, authority as contemptible, reason as irrelevant, and self-gratification as admirable.[19]

By mixing educational arguments with more general criticisms of permissive morals, the *Black Papers* built up a composite picture of educational decline and social decay: tension in the home, as Spock-inspired methods of child-rearing undermined family discipline; anarchy in the infant and junior schools, with permissive teachers preferring hedonism to work-discipline and self-discovery to instruction; declining standards of teaching and behaviour in the senior schools; and student unrest and government interference in the universities, as over-rapid expansion led to the recruitment of unsuitable students and academics.[20]

Not surprisingly, the *Black Paper* writers repeatedly called for a return to the traditional virtues of intellectual rigour and academic learning. Convinced that the essential duty of the teacher was to expound the 'great achievements of past civilisation',[21] they hoped that instruction would again replace experiment at the heart of the school syllabus. Education should introduce the child to high culture, furnish him with information, and force him to reason; and the inescapable accompaniment of success was discipline and hard work. Self-improvement rather than self-expression was the touchstone of educational achievement. 'What education exists to do', A. E. Dyson argued, 'is to inform, train, extend and enrich the "self", to offer knowledge, insight, ideals and discipline far beyond the self-regarding sterilities of our pop-culture world'.[22]

The *Black Paper* writers argued that a successful educational system would inevitably employ the well-tried mechanisms of competition, examination, and streaming. Competition stimulated individual effort, narrowed the gap between capacity and performance, and promoted higher standards and aspirations; it also prepared children to take part in the relentless adult struggle for limited resources.[23] Examinations provided a fixed standard for measuring educational achievement, preventing students from distorting their results by currying favour and protecting teachers from the temptations of sex-appeal, pseudo-friendship, and mute appeals from weakness.[24] 'All life depends upon passing exams', Cox insisted. 'If you fail at football, they drop you to the reserves. If you fail in business, you go bankrupt. If you fail in politics, you are forced to resign (or, in some countries, get shot). Exams measure people against standards distilled from human traditions and achievements, not against inclinations spun lazily out of the "self".'[25] Finally, streaming increased educational efficiency and instilled realistic attitudes in children. 'Society is inevitably hierarchical', Richard Lynn argued. 'Streaming teaches children this fact of life and that if they wish to do well in the hierarchy they must use their intelligence and work hard.'.[26]

Perhaps to the surprise of their contributors, the *Black Papers* attracted a great deal of public attention, with the first two selling 80,000 copies. Unlike most writings on education, they were readable and engaging; and they sounded a tub-thumping, almost revivalist, tone calculated to appeal to the prejudices of the conservative public. A free copy was sent to every MP, leading to a number of parliamentary questions. Thousands of teachers purchased them.

Universities and colleges of education held 'teach-ins' on them, publicising their argument even as they anathematised them. Huge radio, television, and newspaper coverage carried their arguments, duly sensationalised with stories of violence and educational decline, to an audience peripherally concerned with education but permanently willing to be outraged. *Black Paper* contributors were overwhelmed with invitations to speak at parents' meetings and political debates.[27] Mr Short, Labour Secretary of State for Education, provided the *Black Papers* with welcome publicity when he unblushingly described the publication of the first of the series as 'marking one of the blackest days for education in the past century'.

The impact of the *Black Papers* was consequently considerable. They broke the fashionable progressive consensus on education, initiated a reappraisal of radical assumptions, and demonstrated the existence of a coherent alternative philosophy. They transformed the anti-progressive campaign, linking isolated battles against the destruction of grammar schools into a national movement and inspiring parents and teachers, who had hitherto endured the progressive revolution with anything from impotent rage to uneasy resignation, with a renewed sense of purpose. 'In the late 1960s', Cox and Boyson recalled, 'it seemed that the educational revolution in the United Kingdom would wreak its havoc with little or no opposition. The retreat from teaching and structure, the flight from high culture to pop culture, the move to non-selective education, still advanced on all sides and even influenced the programme of political parties'.[28] Organised by the *Black Paper* group, opposition to this leftward drift began to influence policy. 'In the 1970s', Cox and Boyson gloated, 'we are witnessing a slow return to common sense, to formal teaching, to a renewed awareness that the child's happiness and personal fulfillment depend on a secure environment under the control of adults'.[29]

The *Black Paper* case was reinforced by two well-publicised incidents in 1976 – the inquiry into the breakdown of discipline in the William Tyndale Junior and Infants Schools and the publication of Neville Bennett's findings on educational standards.

Between 1974 and 1976 William Tyndale was controlled by committed progressive teachers. They expounded a 'democratic, egalitarian and non-sexist philosophy', rejected 'arbitrary standards of attainment and behaviour', and encouraged children to 'make their own decisions about their learning and lives'. They granted their pupils a wide degree of freedom, allowing them to decide not only what they should learn but also whether and when they should learn. When teaching they 'sought to diminish role-difference between them and their children, to a point where each could be seen to have something of value to offer the other on an equal level'.[30] Several teachers and numerous parents objected to such progressive mumbo-jumbo, and the school rapidly fell apart. Parents withdrew their children; the Inner London Education Authority tried to inspect; newspapers printed sensational headlines; seven teachers went on strike, and then set up their own school, claiming to be victims of political harassment. A public inquiry, conducted by Robin Auld QC and widely reported in the press, took on something of the form of a national inquest on progressive teaching. It concluded that, by the time Terry Ellis had completed two terms as Headmaster, the school was in 'complete turmoil'; with the teaching organisation ruined, the quality and content of instruction low, and school discipline undermined.[31] Children defied their teachers, swore openly at teachers and staff, and fought among themselves.[32] Instead of becoming 'self-motivated' by freedom, they were often bored and listless. After the novelty of being able to do largely as they liked had worn off, some became discontented with the lack of pattern to their days, and indicated that they wanted to be taught again.[33]

Neville Bennett's report on primary school teaching, *Teaching Styles and Pupil Progress* (1976),[34] reinforced doubts about progressive orthodoxy. Based on a comparative study of 37 teachers whose methods ranged from the highly formal to the extremely informal, the report concluded that pupils who were taught formally showed superior progress in the basic subjects, were no worse in imaginative story writing, and were less prone to make grammatical errors. In the course of a single school year the formally-taught children shot ahead by three to four months in reading age, by three to four months in English, and by four to five months in mathematics. Anxious children in particular suffered in informal classrooms, working less, gossiping and gazing into space more and misbehaving more than they did in formal settings. The more formal the teaching, then, the more time pupils spent in working on the subject-matter at hand; and the more time they spent working on a subject, the more they improved at it. The key to improving teaching of basic skills lay, in general, in a clear structuring of activities within a cognitively-oriented curriculum – or, more succinctly, in traditional rather than progressive methods.

Stimulated by revelations about the excesses and inadequacies of informal teaching, and goaded and organised by *Black Paper* polemicists, public opinion began to turn against progressive education. Press comment throughout 1976 reflected widespread anxiety about educational standards and pupil discipline. Children's standards of performance in school work – and particularly in the 'three Rs' – were said to have declined. The curriculum – or so the argument went – paid too little attention to the basic skills of reading, writing and arithmetic, and was overcrowded with 'fringe' subjects. Teachers lacked adequate skills, and did not know how to discipline children or to instil in them a concern for hard work or good manners; all too often they were the victims of soft-minded dislike for traditional virtues or, more sinisterly, the exponents of social subversion and political revolution. Above all, the educational system was out of touch with the need to win economic survival in a competitive world.

Sensing this widespread anxiety about educational innovation, the Labour Government threw its weight behind a more conservative policy. It ceased to flirt with radical theories about abolishing examinations and encouraging self-expression and talked instead of standards, rewards and economic efficiency. In his speech on 18 October 1976 in Ruskin College, Oxford, Prime Minister James Callaghan asserted some trenchant commonplaces on the importance of preserving standards of achievement and preparing children for a productive role in industry and commerce. Gathering his '*Black Paper* cloak around him',[35] he sympathised with the unease felt by parents and teachers about the new informal methods of teaching.

Even as the Callaghan administration retreated from the progressive consensus, it was being outmanoeuvred on the right. The boldest attempt to rethink educational policy came from the advocates of the free-market right, hitherto regarded as antediluvian eccentrics. Free marketeers argued that our public education was a disaster. State schools were failing to teach the skills which Britain needs if it is to remain a competitive nation. Wherever they looked in the educational world free marketeers saw monsters. The National Union of Teachers was a conspiracy against the public. Teacher Training Colleges, which had the misfortune of recruiting many of their staff in the 1960s, were indoctrinating future teachers with Marxist dogma and counter-cultural mumbo-jumbo. The *lumpen intelligentsia* was entrenched in the educational system, denouncing industry and stirring up social conflict. In particular, professional anti-racists were exacerbating the problems they claimed to oppose. Motivated by a combination of self-interest and self-righteousness, they were busy institutionalising racial divisions and inflaming racial antagonisms.

The radical right had no doubts about the cause of the public sector's poor performance. Local Education Authorities were in fact Local Education Monopolies – closed corporations with captive customers and no incentives to improve their services. They pointed out that the low standards in the public sector contrast sharply with the high standards in the private sector. Independent schools, which educated about 6 per cent of British children, won about 16 per cent of all O-level passes, 25 per cent of A-level passes and 50 per cent of grade A A-level passes.

To them the solution to Britain's educational problems was simple: privatisation. The public sector needed to be subjected to the market disciplines which have made the private sector so successful. One much vaunted way of doing this was through an educational voucher. Under this scheme educational fees were to be paid not to the schools but to the parents: state grants would become family vouchers. Parents would be free to spend their vouchers at the school of their choice. Good schools would prosper, poor schools would go under, and the educational service would constantly improve. The voucher scheme has never been implemented in practice. Instead, the Conservatives relied on a more subtle idea: the internal market. This puts a price on every child's head (essentially turning him or her into a voucher) and makes schools' incomes dependent on attracting children.

Even more disturbingly for the Left, IQ testing gradually came back into fashion. The revival of interest in mental measurement was triggered off by Arthur Jensen's article 'How much can we boost IQ and scholastic achievement?', published in the *Harvard Educational Review* in 1969. Jensen's argument was directed against 'compensatory education' – a scheme intended to increase the IQ scores of deprived children by providing them with improved pre-school education. Despite 'unprecedented support from Federal funds' and 'theoretical sanction from social scientists', compensatory education had failed to narrow the gap between 'minority' and 'majority' pupils.[36] Jensen argued that this failure was not accidental – a consequence of too little money or inefficient teaching – but fundamental and inescapable. The premise upon which the scheme was based – that poor academic performance stemmed mainly from economic deprivation and social discrmination – was simply false.

In supporting this case, Jensen revived all the standard claims of IQ testers. He suggested that 'the most important fact about intelligence is that we can measure it',[37] dismissing claims that tests were inaccurate or culturally-loaded. He claimed that 'intelligence fully meets the usual scientific criteria for being regarded as an aspect of objective reality, just as much as do atoms, genes, and electromagnetic fields' and insisted that it was a 'biological reality and not just a figment of social convention'.[38] Against the environmentalist orthodoxy, he argued at length that differences in intellectual capacity were partly the result of genetic factors which conformed to the same polygenic principles involved in the inheritance of physical characteristics.[39]

Another American psychologist, Richard Herrnstein, reinforced the case for intelligence-testing in a long article in a semi-popular magazine, *The Atlantic*, published in September 1971. Like Jensen, he insisted that the informed consensus was that intelligence was highly heritable: about 80 per cent of the variation in IQ in the population derived from the genes.[40] He also suggested that the substantial correlation between IQ and social class – the upper class scored about 30 IQ points above the lower class – resulted not from the cultural bias of the tests but from the success with which desirable occupations recruited able employees. Compelled to select people capable of performing complex intellectual operations, and confronted with a large number of candidates, the professions naturally filled up with individuals with high IQs.[41]

Both Jensen and Herrnstein provoked widespread discussion in England as well as in the United States. In particular, Hans Eysenck took the opportunity to defend and publicise the hereditarian argument. In *Race, Intelligence and Education* (1971) he praised Jensen, lambasted his critics, and expounded hereditarian orthodoxy. Jensen was an honest scientist hounded by dogmatists. His so-called 'heresy' was 'nothing but purest orthodoxy', agreed upon by specialists and confirmed by the evidence.[42] The caricature of his argument, against which most criticisms were directed, was 'a nonsense, an analogy, an extravagance, a farrago, a mare's nest, an amphigouri' – the invention of polemicists who failed to understand his text.[43] Convinced that individuals differed widely in their innate abilities, he denounced comprehensive education and praised the tripartite system as socially just and educationally efficient. He felt that current educational reforms were a step backwards – a flight from sense into fantasy. He was particularly incensed by the left-wing campaign against intelligence tests.[44] The main impact of tests had been to promote the interests of able working-class children at the expense of dull middle-class children; their removal would make it 'less likely that bright children who are socially disadvantaged will obtain an education suited to their natural capacities while dull children with social advantages will receive an education which they cannot properly appreciate'.[45] He concluded acidly that 'the conscious cultivation of a mediocrity, in which the bright, the original, the innovators, the geniuses are held back in order to spare the mediocre the spectacle of outstanding success is to me an abomination'.[46]

By a felicitous combination of accident and design the new hereditarians also commanded a vast popular audience for their ideas. Every major news magazine discussed Jensen's arguments in some detail.[47] A thorough account in the *New York Times Magazine*[48] – 'Jensenism, *n*. Or the theory that IQ is largely determined by the genes' – provoked more letters to the editor than any article it had ever published.[49] The British media followed the American example, and Eysenck, Burt, Hammerton, C. P. Snow and Nathaniel Weyl all gave vigorous support to the hereditarian position. The revival of interest in IQ testing was undoubtedly a highly successful exercise in intellectual revisionism. Directed against two shibboleths of the 1960s – egalitarianism and environmentalism – masterminded by a small and embattled group of academics, and greeted with intense hostility, the revival nevertheless commanded some public support and political sympathy. It appealed to a public alienated by university radicals, an intelligentsia weary of sociological clichés and millennial prophecies, and a political class worried by public spending and popular morality.

Another argument came to the fore as the progressive consensus disintegrated: the argument for educational selection. An influential group of academics argued that selective schools were quite simply more *effective* than non-selective schools. The quality of schools, they insisted, depends not on their material resources but on their educational *ethos*; and selective schools are much better at promoting a successful educational ethos than non-selective schools.

They gave four main reasons for this. First, selective schools pursue clear goals. They establish firm objectives, elaborate appropriate methods, and impose necessary incentives. If they fail to meet their objectives, they can quickly modify their collective behaviour. Non-selective schools pursue vague aims, adopt haphazard measures, and impose inappropriate or confusing incentives. Because they are unclear about their goals, they are unable to evaluate their performance and slow to change their methods. Secondly, selective schools impose their corporate identity upon their pupils. They demand that pupils identify with their school rather than their peer group – for example that they wear school uniforms rather than casual clothes. They mould their personalities so that they internalise the norms not of adolescent but of adult society. Selection is essential to their institutional power: pupils attend selective schools out of choice rather than accident and are frightened of losing their place. More important than fear is ambition. Schoolteachers can point to illustrious alumni, telling pupils that, if only they persevere, they too will be successful. This gives them enormous power to influence behaviour. For in general it seems that the capacity of a school to change life-chances and reorient values depends on the power of its charter – on the type of social position which it is chartered to offer its clients at the end of their school careers. Selective schools have strong charters, non-selective schools have weak ones.[50] Thirdly, selective schools are necessarily competitive schools. They distribute personal status according to academic achievement. They channel adolescent competitiveness (which might so easily be expressed, as it is in the United States, in pursuing athletic honours or social popularity)[51] into the quest for academic excellence. Under the pressure of competition, children perform as nearly as possible to their full potentials. They work with teachers rather than against them; they concentrate on their lessons; and they work in the evenings and at weekends. Inspired by the reputations of their institutions, and motivated by the rivalry of their classmates, they do much of their teachers' work for them. Finally, selective schools teach pupils with similar abilities and aspirations. Teachers are not in danger of alienating the able, by proceeding too slowly, or the dull, by proceeding too quickly. Pupils are confronted by demanding but manageable courses, conscious that failure reflects a lack of will rather than an absence of ability.

THE FIRST THATCHER DECADE

This intellectual revolution, which began in the late 1960s and gathered force throughout the 1970s, has enabled the Conservative Party to capture the initiative from the Labour Party, which had hitherto enjoyed a near-monopoly of educational innovation. (The major innovations of the six decades between 1918 and 1979 – secondary education for all, the raising of the school leaving age, the abolition of the 11-plus, the expansion of higher education – were either inspired or implemented by the Left.) But the counter-revolution took some time to get under way: educational reform was low on the Thatcherite agenda.

The first two Thatcher administrations did little to displace the progressive consensus. Mark Carlisle, Mrs Thatcher's first education secretary, distrusted the radical agenda (and was duly dismissed in the autumn of 1981). The Education Act of 1980 introduced the Assisted Places Scheme (subsidies for children to leave the public for the private sector) and made it easier for parents to send their children across administrative boundaries. But the first measure neatly sidestepped the explosive problem of selection in the public sector and the second had little practical impact. Sir Keith (now Lord) Joseph, Carlisle's successor, was certainly no wet. The guru of Thatcherism, he felt that the educational establishment was deeply implicated in Britain's decline. Educationalists were hostile to the disciplines of competition and productivity, preaching anti-industrial values and steering their talented pupils into academia and administration. He wanted to change the ethos of intellectual life: to increase the status of business and enterprise; to break down the restrictive practices which had cocooned educationalists and administrators; and to turn education into an instrument of market-driven regeneration. But Joseph was a diffident figure, as lacking in political cunning as he was brimful of ideas. The Education Act 1986 was a messy piece of legislation, the creation of inchoate back-bench resentments rather than coordinated national policy. When Joseph resigned in 1986, driven out by teacher strikes and middle-class discontent, it seemed as if the educational establishment had triumphed.

The triumph was illusory. His successor, Kenneth Baker, hitherto a Heathman rather than a Thatcherite, succeeded brilliantly in implementing the radical agenda. His reforms were a judicious mix of centralisation and de-centralisation: of *dirigisme* and *laissez-faire*. As sensitive to political realities as he was indifferent to ideological niceties, he happily drew his inspiration from both Bonapartism and free-market liberalism.

Baker the Bonapartist introduced a national curriculum reinforced by a sequence of national examinations: for the first time in British history both the curriculum and its assessment will be nationalised. Baker the de-centraliser began to set schools free from both central and local control. Heads and school governors will take over responsibility for managing their own financial affairs; the new City Technology Colleges will be outside Education Authority control, funded partly by the government and partly by private industry; and selected schools will be encouraged to opt out of Local Educational Authority control and turn themselves into grant-maintained schools, funded directly by the Department of Education and Science. Baker the free-marketeer began the introduction of an internal market into education. Schools will be financed according to the number of pupils on their rolls: the more pupils, the more cash. In effect, each child becomes an educational voucher: 'think of each pupil as a bag of cash', a Department of Education official once explained to educationalists.[52] Schools will have a self-evident incentive to perform well and attract pupils. At the same time open enrollment will free parents to move their children from bad schools to good.

Baker's scheme is not such an ideological mish-mash as his tidy-minded critics might imagine. The state establishes a framework of standards (as it does with the currency); schools compete to deliver high-quality services; and consumers shop around between schools for the best service.

The Act will introduce a much-needed element of competition into the state sector: and competition will eventually lead to the re-introduction of selection. Local educational monopolies will be broken up and suppliers of educational services will be forced to compete for customers. The most prominent feature of the educational system in the immediate future will be competition between schools for pupils. But in the longer term this will be matched by an equally vigorous competition between pupils for schools. Some local authority schools will perform much better than others. Having established reputations for high-quality teaching, they will attract large numbers of applicants. Despite the incentive to increase their incomes by increasing their enrolment they will be forced to be selective: good schools cannot remain good schools if they are filled to overflowing. Grant-maintained schools, which may well become hugely popular, will be allowed to recruit their pupils from outside their local catchment area – that is, to select them on the basis of their intellectual abilities rather than their place of birth. And if City Technology Colleges are as successful as their prototypes, the American magnet schools, they will be vastly over-subscribed. All this will make the widespread re-introduction of some sort of selection unavoidable. The main problem for successful schools will not be *whether* to select but *how* to select. But the reforms will not simply reintroduce the binary divide between grammar schools and secondary moderns. Instead, it will introduce a complex and elastic hierarchy, which will be much more difficult to challenge than the traditional selective system.

In introducing his programme Kenneth Baker skilfully exploited popular distaste for the progressive establishment. He argued that the educational establishment had failed to promote productivity or inculcate politeness – and he has had no shortage of evidence to support its conviction. Forty per cent of children, as we have already noted, leave school with no qualifications, their education wasted and their prospects negligible. Significantly, Kenneth Clarke has tried to push through a similar set of health service reforms – a combination of central control of standards, market-oriented funding and de-centralised control – by similar political means, and has failed to win popular support. The educational establishment is a much softer target than the medical establishment.

Baker tempered populist criticism of educational failure with judicious compromises with the educational establishment. Instead of rejecting progressive education lock, stock, and barrel (as many of his traditionalist colleagues demanded)[53] he hitched it to his reforming programme.[54] Progressive educationalists were always inspired by a mixture of common sense and utopian idealism. If they railed against industrial society, they also realised that education must engage the interests of pupils. Baker accepted the core of sense in progressivism – that education must engage children's interests or, as Shakespeare put it 'No profit grows, where is no pleasure ta'en/In brief, Sir, study what you most affect' – but rejected its utopian socialism; in effect, child-centred education has been given a pro-industrial twist.

In doing this, he found a powerful ally in Lord Young, who skilfully dressed John Dewey in Thatcherite clothing. While he was Chairman of the Manpower Services Commission, Young argued that the academic tradition had had a disastrous impact on the British economy. Mesmerised by the ideal of learning for learning's sake, and contemptuous of technical skills and vocational training, educationalists had failed to value practical intelligence and entrepreneurial initiative. The result has been all too predictable: the multiplication of pseudo-academic courses and the alienation of the bulk of the school population. The curriculum needed to be at once more practical and vocational, capable of equipping the entire workforce – not just a gilded élite – with personal discipline and technical skills.[55] Lord Young's Technical and Vocational Initiative, which tried to give practical substance to these ideas, received applause from some sections of the progressive establishment:

Young people of all abilities appreciate a more applied and vocational slant to their studies . . . Many respond well to courses which break the conventional timetable mould, allowing whole days or half-days to be spent on project work or work experience.[56]

The Conservatives have also presided over a *rapprochement* between education and business. Both the anti-education lobby (which influenced both the business community and the Conservative party) and the anti-business lobby (which held sway in the teacher training colleges and some local authorities) have been muzzled.[57] The CBI is delighted with recent educational reforms:

Since 1979 this Government has met most if not all of the demands which business might reasonably have made with respect to the educational system. Eight years ago, few would have predicted that so many of the changes business has long sought would be on the statute books or part of publicly-announced Government targets: a new curriculum with a greater emphasis on 'core' subjects, a technical vocational education initiative, work experience for every pupil during their school career, placements in business for 10 per cent of teachers each year, increased business representation on boards of governors, and delegation of financial and managerial responsibility for schools to the local level.[58]

This *rapprochement* has required a loosening of the Department of Education and Science's control over educational policy-making. Both the Department of Trade and Industry and the Department of Employment have been given a significant say in education. The DTI funded the 'micros in schools' project, intended to put a computer in every school in the nation. Its Industry Education Unit pump-primes key initiatives and monitors links between schools and companies. The Department of Employment, through its Manpower Services Commission, organised a Technical and Vocational Training Initiative, intended to encourage practical and technical skills, and funds 'city compacts' – job promises from local employers for local school-leavers.

The immediate reason for this was practical. The DES has little control over what local authorities do with education grants. In order to prevent money which it had earmarked for computer studies being spent on home economics – or still worse gender studies – the government funnelled it through the DTI, which is much better placed to keep track of it. But this initiative had the effect of challenging producer interests, which had hitherto held sway at the DES. (Harold Wilson once dismissed it as little more than a posting box between the local authorities and the teachers' unions.)[59] Significantly, the DES has rethought its traditional assumptions and distanced itself from the producer lobby. Shaken-up by competition from the DTI and the Department of Employment, re-educated by Sir Keith (now Lord) Joseph, and re-invigorated by Mr Kenneth Baker, it has launched its own pro-business initiatives. The Further Education Unit, for example, is formally attached to the DES but spiritually part of the DTI.

To reinforce this administrative change the Conservatives have ushered businessmen into schools and schoolteachers as well as schoolchildren into businesses. Some 35,000 places on the governing bodies of schools and colleges have been reserved for businessmen. (At the same time local financial management will force heads to become more business-like in their management of schools.) Ten per cent of schoolteachers every year have to spend some time in local businesses. All schoolchildren are sent on work experience.

Baker has been helped in his pro-business revolution by a convenient combination of economic recession and demographic trends. The economic recession of the early 1980s persuaded many educationalists to form closer links with local industries: the alternative was permanent unemployment for many of their charges. The demographic downturn of the late 1980s and early 1990s – the number of 16- and 17-year-olds will soon fall by a quarter, from 1.7 million in 1986 to 1.25 million in 1994 – has confronted businessmen with the prospect of severe shortages of labour and skills.

Encouraged by the success of the Education Reform Act, the Conservative Party is busy rethinking higher education. Once again three themes dominate their arguments: the importance of science and technology; the virtues of business; and the value of market mechanisms. They have courted the polytechnics, setting them free from local authority control and improving their funding and status. They have encouraged businessmen to sit on the boards of higher education institutions. Once again combining *dirigisme* with *laissez-faire*, they have also explored ways of using a combination of state control and market mechanisms to make higher education at once more efficient, more useful, and – a point which infuriates the Labour Party as much as it confuses the educational establishment – more accessible.

The White Paper inelegantly entitled *Meeting the Challenge* (April 1987) argued that the state should have more control over the use of its funds – in effect, that having paid the piper it should have a say in his choice of tunes. The taxpayers' financial contributions should be regarded not as a 'grant', but as a 'contract', with payments closely linked to specific services. The government also urged the universities to become more business-like in their man-management, replacing a trade-union-dominated with a flexible salary structure, sensitive to local labour costs and capable of attracting the best people in the national and international market place. More recently, the government has begun to rethink student grants. In its White Paper *Top-up Loans for Students* (November 1988) it suggests that, far from opening opportunity to the disadvantaged, the system of universal grants had subsidised the privileged and placed a rigid limit to the number of places in higher education. Top-up loans, with grants targeted specifically to the disadvantaged, will enable student numbers to vary with demand.

Despite their Bonapartist overtones, these reforms are intended to engineer a radical change in relationship between the state and the universities. The government no longer wants to be a monopoly supplier of university funds. Instead, it hopes to be a customer – and only one customer among many – for the services of higher educational institutions. Its main welfare function will be to enable others – notably students – to purchase educational services. Once it becomes a customer and enabler (so the argument runs), *dirigisme* will give way to *laissez-faire*. Higher educational institutions will come to see themselves as independent contractors – autonomous, flexible and competitive – earning income from a wide range of customers, including central government, which will distribute research funds to the most attractive bidders, and individual students, who will henceforth carry fee income with them.[60] An institutional income will depend on its capacity to attract students and research contracts; and this capacity in turn will depend on its flexibility, efficiency, and *panache*.

Central to these reforms is a rejection of one of the most cherished tenets of the 1960s: that higher public expenditure on education leads to increased economic growth. Instead, some policy-makers seem to suggest that the best way to make education an instrument of economic growth is not to increase but to *reduce* public expenditure – a doctrine which fits in well with the Thatcher government's determination to restrain public expenditure. High public expenditure (so the argument goes) had insulated education from the market place. Showered with money from the public purse, universities became the playgrounds of self-indulgent and inward-looking cliques rather than the engine rooms of a post-industrial economy. Conversely, lower public expenditure would force universities to rely on private sponsorship and make them more responsive to the needs of business.

As anyone who reads the *Times Higher Education Supplement* or listens to debates in the House of Lords will realise, it would be fanciful to pretend that the New Right has swept all before it. The progressive lobby remains firmly entrenched in the educational establishment, contemptuous of commercial values and adept at defending vested interests. Headmasters, school inspectors and professors of education are increasingly recruited from the 1960s generation: though some have rethought their values many more have not. Colleges of education continue to treat business with suspicion and traditional values with derision.[61] Dave Spart is still alive and well on the university campuses: all too often academic seminars proceed on the assumption that capitalism is an excuse for exploitation and a guarantee of racial and sexual discrimination. The Education Reform Act is a mixed bag: in part a measure of the influence of the New Right, in part a testimony to the continuing influence of the old-fashioned educational establishment.

A formidable list of obstacles, practical as much as ideological, still obstruct a successful educational policy. The most obvious of these is the low pay of some members of the teaching profession. Partly because the teaching unions are wedded to an inequitable system of national wage bargaining and partly because the Treasury finds teachers an easy target for wage restraints, the market rate has not been offered for teachers who live in areas of the country where house prices are high or who possess academic skills for which demand is intense. The mounting shortage of high-quality teachers, particularly in subjects central to the national curriculum such as mathematics, science and modern languages, is threatening to undermine the Education Reform Act.[62]

The attitudes of some spokesmen only compound this problem. Unlike the business community, the Conservative Party is still willing to listen to the anti-education lobby. Right-wing think-tanks – the Adam Smith Institute, the Social Affairs Unit and the Hillsgate group in particular – continue to churn out pamphlets about producer monopolies and subversive teachers. Back-benchers can still make political capital, while scare stories about reds and gays in the classrooms continue to raise Conservative hackles.

The low pay and status of science teachers is already undermining the government's attempt to train more scientists. Too many science graduates are either refusing to enter the teaching profession or leave it as soon as they can. In 1985 not one Cambridge physics graduate chose schoolteaching as a career. In 1986 a quarter of mathematics teachers and a third of physics teachers lacked appropriate qualifications. Not surprisingly, poor teaching puts students off the sciences; and those who persevere can command such high salaries in industry that they have to be somewhat perverse to go back into teaching. Despite unprecedented general unemployment industry is starved of skilled manpower. Ten per cent of CBI firms claim that their expansion is being restrained by a shortage of skilled labour.

The poverty of science teaching frustrates otherwise admirable government initiatives. In 1985 the government made £143 million available to pay for 4,000 extra places in engineering and technology at both universities and polytechnics – but at the same time there were already 1,100 unfilled places in science and technology (including 408 places in engineering and computing). Unless the supply of schoolchildren with science educations is improved – that is, unless school science teaching is improved – initiatives in tertiary education will fail.

So far, reforms have done too little to revamp vocational education, which remains an international embarrassment. The government's enthusiasm for inner-city technology colleges is certainly encouraging. These colleges are envisioned as both selective and vocational, sifting inner-city populations for talented children and directing them into wealth-creating disciplines. Ideally, they will provide both a spur and an example to the rest of the educational system. Policy is undoubtedly moving in the right direction: but, as the pace of international competition increases, it may well be too little too late. Three hundred Technical Schools failed to galvanise the educational system in the 1940s. Why should twenty – or 120 – Technology Colleges succeed in galvanising it in the 1990s? In 1988 only 30 per cent of British workers had held apprenticeships, compared with 60 per cent of German workers. Between 1978 and 1988 the number of adolescents gaining engineering qualifications increased by 60 per cent in France, by 35 per cent in West Germany, and *fell* by 30 per cent in the United Kingdom.[63]

The universities are disoriented and demoralised. Their budgets are shrinking rapidly – they lost 10 per cent of their funding between

1981 and 1986 and will lose another 10 per cent over the next five years. The government's attempt to reform universities through financial restraint has met with little success: its victims have tended to be valuable innovations rather than entrenched abuses. The early retirement scheme has done more to subsidise the flight of the able – and particularly able scientists – than to remove the tenured incompetent. For their part, the universities have done little to deal with the problems which make them such easy victims of government hostility; notoriously unproductive and incompetent academics keep their posts while productive and able graduate students are forced into other professions – or to the United States.

The national curriculum is still too egalitarian, based on the assumption that children do not differ widely in their intellectual capacities. Despite its right-wing credentials, it accepts and extends the egalitarian orthodoxy of the 1960s. It does something, but far too little, to recognise differences in innate abilities. Yet children differ enormously in their innate abilities. In a random class of 10-year-olds the most able may have a mental age of 15 and the least able a mental age of 5. A national syllabus will inevitably be too easy for the able and too difficult for the dull. The able will coast through school without being stretched and the dull will be discouraged – and may well be permanently alienated. 'You can't teach a calf the violin', remarks the house-master in Kipling's *Stalky and Company*, 'and, if you try, the creature's apt to kick out'. The educational system needs not one sequence of national examinations but several sequences, designed to cater for children with different abilities and different occupational destinations: a national curriculum needs to be supported by streaming or selection.

The most serious criticism of these initiatives is that they are doing too little too late. Britain's main competitors, which have a long tradition of gearing their educational systems to their economic needs, are still adapting more quickly. As we noted above, in Britain 82 per cent of children leave school at 16 as compared with 4 per cent in Japan and about 10 per cent in Germany and the United States; and 40 per cent of British school leavers have no qualifications whatsoever. In 1980 50 per cent of German children left schools for apprenticeships as compared with 14 per cent of British children. The complaint of the former Chairman of the Manpower Services Commission (Bryan Nicholson) that Britain's workforce is a 'bunch of thickies' reflects more than simple prejudice. Non-academic German children are successfully channelled into vocational training and industrial employment whereas non-academic British children are given debased academic educations and then consigned to the dole. Britain has singularly failed to come to terms with the problem of training non-academic children. For a country which is heavily dependent on trade – and which can compete with the Pacific Basin only on added quality rather than on price – this is a disturbing situation. British education may at last be strolling in the right direction. But Britain's main rivals, having started further down the track, are not strolling but sprinting.

The last ten years have witnessed a radical rethinking of educational policy. The progressive opinions of R. H. Tawney and Tony Crosland, though retaining some influence, have ceased to be hegemonic. With some of its major tenets discredited by social science and denigrated by both politicans and the public, and with its commitment to child-centred education given a pro-industrial emphasis, the progressive lobby has lost the intellectual initiative to the New Right. Recent educational policy has been based on three propositions which would have been regarded as at best eccentric and at worst repugnant in 1963: the value of competition; the virtues of business; and the merits of differentiation. Underlying these tenets is a vigorous hostility to equality in its many guises, particularly to equality and ability as a tenet about human nature and equality of reward as a goal of social policy. Such arguments will always be bitterly contested. But at the very least they have broken the mould of educational thinking, replacing comfortable orthodoxies with uncomfortable controversies.

Notes and References

1. Noel Annan, *The Guardian* (19 February 1963).
2. The literature based on these assumptions is immense. For a representative sample see Harold Silver (ed.), *Equal Opportunity in Education* (London, 1973): 108–259.
3. 'Education. The Backlash Starts', *The Observer* (23 March 1969).
4. James S. Coleman *et al.*, *Equality of Educational Opportunity* (US Government Printing Office, Washington DC, 1966).
5. J. W. B. Douglas *et al.*, *All Our Future* (London, 1968) especially 5, 28, 60, 65; Julienne Ford, *Social Class and the Comprehensive School* (London, 1969) especially 32–45.
6. Michael Sanderson, *Educational Opportunity and Social Change in England* (London, 1987): 122–7.
7. Sanderson, *Educational Opportunity*: 134–5.

8. James S. Coleman *et al.*, *Equality of Educational Opportunity* (New York, 1966). Cf. Frederick Mosteller and Daniel P. Moynihan, *On Equality of Educational Opportunity* (New York, 1972). For an account on the disillusionment felt by those who had taken part in the war on poverty see Moynihan, *Maximum Feasible Misunderstanding: Community Action in the War on Poverty* (New York, 1969).

9. V. G. Cicirelli *et al.*, 'The Impact of Head Start on Children's Cognitive and Affective Development', Westinghouse Learning Corporation (Washington DC, 1969) (the Westinghouse Report).

10. Christopher Jencks (and Marshall Smith, Henry Acland, Mary Jo Bane, David Cohen, Herbert Gintis, Barbara Heyns, Stephen Michelson), *Inequality: A Reassessment of the Effect of Family on Schooling in America* (New York, 1972).

11. A. H. Halsey (ed.), Department of Education and Science, *Educational Priority*, vol. 1, *Problems and Policies* (London, 1972): 6. Cf. Halsey, 'Sociology and the Equality Debate', *Oxford Review of Education*, 1 (Oxford, 1975): 9–26.

12. This was one of the main themes of post-war sociology. For convenient summaries of the literature see, Julian Le Grand, *The Strategy of Equality: Redistribution and the Social Services* (London, 1982) and Robert E. Goodin and Julian Le Grand, *Not Only the Poor: The Middle Classes and the Welfare State* (London, 1987).

13. See, for example, Charles Murray, *Losing Ground: American Social Policy, 1950–1980* (New York, 1984) and Nathan Glazer, *The Limits of Social Policy* (Cambridge, Mass., 1988).

14. C. B. Cox and A. E. Dyson, 'Introduction', in Cox and Dyson (eds), *The Black Papers on Education* (London, 1971): 9. Revised version of first three *Black Papers*, published in March 1969, October 1969 and November 1970, collected under one cover and furnished with a new introduction.

15. For example, Cyril Burt, Jacques Barzun, G. H. Bantock, Bryan Wilson, H. J. Eysenck, Max Beloff, Edward Norman, Kingsley Amis, Iris Murdoch, Rhodes Boyson, Angus Maude, Robert Conquest.

16. C. B. Cox and Rhodes Boyson, 'Background' in Cox and Boyson (eds), *Black Paper 1977* (London, 1977): 13.

17. A. E. Dyson, 'Culture and Anarchy. 1869–1969', *The Critical Quarterly* (1969).

18. Amis, 'Pernicious Participation', *The Black Papers on Education* (1971): 172.

19. See, for example, Cox and Dyson, 'Introduction', in Cox and Dyson (eds), *The Black Papers on Education*: 17–21; C. M. Johnson, 'Freedom in Junior Schools', in Cox and Dyson (eds), *The Black Papers on Education*: 100; A. E. Dyson, 'The Sleep of Reason', ibid.: 84–6.

20. 'Education; The Backlash Starts', *The Observer* (23 March 1969).

21. Cox and Dyson (eds), *The Black Papers on Education* (1971): 17.

22. Dyson, 'The Sleep of Reason', in Cox and Dyson (eds), *The Black Papers on Education*: 85.

23. Richard Lynn, 'Competition and Cooperation', in Cox and Boyson (eds), *Black Paper 1977*: 108–10.

24. Cox, 'In Praise of Examination', in Cox and Dyson (eds), *The Black Papers on Education*: 71–4.
25. Cox, 'In Praise of Examination': 76.
26. Richard Lynn, 'Streaming: Standards or Equality' in Cox and Dyson (eds), *The Black Papers on Education*: 82.
27. Cox and Dyson (eds), *The Black Papers on Education*: 10–13.
28. Cox and Boyson, 'Letter to MPs and Parents', *Black Paper 1975*: 3.
29. Cox and Boyson, 'Background', *Black Paper 1977*: 13.
30. Terry Ellis, Jackie McWhirter, Dorothy McDolgan and Brian Haddow, *William Tyndale; The Teacher's Story* (1976).
31. Robin Auld QC, *William Tyndale Junior and Infants Schools Public Inquiry* (July 1976): 274, para. 838.
32. Auld, *William Tyndale*: 79, para 253.
33. Auld, *William Tyndale*: 78, para 252.
34. Neville Bennett, *Teaching Styles and Pupil Progress* (London, 1976).
35. *The Times Education Supplement* (10 October 1976): 1.
36. Arthur R. Jensen, 'How Much Can We Boost IQ and Scholastic Achievement', *Harvard Educational Review*, 39 (1969): 2–3.
37. Jensen, 'How Much Can We Boost IQ': 5 and 8.
38. Jensen, 'How Much Can We Boost IQ': 19.
39. Jensen, 'How Much Can We Boost IQ': 32–3.
40. Richard Herrnstein, 'I.Q.,', *The Atlantic*, 228 (1971): 56, 58.
41. Herrnstein, 'I.Q.': 50–1.
42. Eysenck, *Race, Intelligence and Education* (London, 1971): 140.
43. Eysenck, *Race, Intelligence*: 145.
44. Eysenck, 'The Rise of the Mediocracy' in *Psychology is About People* (London, 1972): 160–99.
45. Eysenck, 'The Rise of the Mediocracy': 165.
46. Eysenck, 'The Rise of the Mediocracy': 19. See also Jeffrey Gray, 'Why Should Society Reward Intelligence?' *The Times* (8 September 1972).
47. See, for example, M. Hunt, 'The intelligent man's guide to intelligence', *Playboy*, 18 (February 1971): 94–6, 106, 191–4.
48. L. Edson, *New York Times Magazine* (31 August 1969): 10–11. For discussions see 21 and 28 September issues.
49. Jensen, *Genetics and Education* (London, 1972): 14.
50. John W. Meyer, 'The Charter: Conditions of Diffuse Socialisation in Schools', in W. Richard Scott, *Social Processes and Social Structures: An Introduction to Sociology* (New York, 1970) especially 565, 568, 572.
51. James S. Coleman, *The Adolescent Society: The Social Life of the Teenager and its Impact on Education* (New York, 1961): 318.
52. Quoted in Ken Jones, *Right Turn: The Conservative Revolution in Education* (London, 1989): 22.
53. For an amusing account of progressive education run wild see Jonathan Miller, 'Led Astray', in Brian Inglis (ed.), *John Bull's Schooldays* (London, 1961): 101–4.
54. For a careful mixture of John Dewey and Corelli Barnett see 'Secretary of State's Speech to the Society of Education Officers, 27 January 1989': 4–5.

55. David Young, *Knowing How and Knowing That: A Philosophy of the Vocational* (the Haldane Memorial Lecture, London, 1984). Viscount Haldane would have sympathised with Young's modernising instincts, if not with his free-market methods.
56. Quoted in Ken Jones, *Right Turn*: 110.
57. Sir Adrian Cadbury *et al.*, *Building a Stronger Partnership Between Business and Secondary Education: The Report of the CBI Business/Education Task Force* (London, 1988): 11–12.
58. Cadbury, *Building a Stronger Partnership*: 26–7.
59. Quoted in Peter Hennessy, *Whitehall* (London, 1989): 425.
60. Robert Jackson, 'The Higher Education Funding Debate: Some Conclusions Drawn', paper delivered to a Centre for Policy Studies Conference (9 May 1989): 10.
61. Dawn Gill and Les Levidow (eds), *Anti-Racist Science Teaching* (London, 1987).
62. This is the subject of a terse memorandum from Kenneth Baker to the Cabinet. See *The Sunday Telegraph* (30 July 1989).
63. Cadbury *et al.*, *Building a Stronger Partnership*: 30.

Part V
Economic Revival: Some Theoretical Premises

10 Ideology and Pragmatism in Economic Thatcherism

Patrick Minford

Ideology is often contrasted with pragmatism. But of course no policy was ever made, however 'pragmatic', without ideology, that is a set of informing ideas on causes and effects. For example, the policies of the Heath/Wilson/Callaghan Governments of the 1970s were all based on the ideology of corporatism, a corpus of thinking that others in this volume have defined and criticised. Yet proponents of these policies have often defended themselves as being more pragmatic and less ideological than their Thatcherite successors in the 1980s.

Whatever the intended meaning of this claim, it is clear that 'pragmatic' is a pro-word and 'ideological' is an anti-word. Yet if we were to counter-attack a self-styled pragmatist with the words, 'You mean that you have undertaken your actions with no thought or idea of their consequences', he would deny the charge vigorously; 'idea' is a pro-word, 'thoughtless action' an anti-phrase. Stripped of their rhetorical armour, all policies consist of

(a)   a theoretical framework for understanding events
(b)   a broad strategy for the implementation of change
(c)   tactics for detailed implementation.

The more effective policies are, the closer the correspondence between these elements; thus the tactics support the strategy, which is, according to the theory, most likely to succeed in its aims. Policies 'come apart' when this correspondence becomes remote – for example, if in the political battle for implementation too much is given away. Policies do not 'get off the ground' if any one part of the correspondent chain is omitted – most obviously if there are no tactics for practical implementation, but no less probably if there is poor theory behind them.

We could perhaps use these notions, without great abuse of language, to rank policies along a (non-rhetorical) spectrum from ideological to pragmatic. A set for example with poor or limited theory would be relatively pragmatic, one with good theory but poor tactics would be relatively ideological. Effective policies would be at the centre of this spectrum.

I have described Mrs Thatcher's economic programme and its results to date in two recent papers.[1] To review here the conclusions of those pieces, I argued that the programme could be divided into three main parts: the conquest of inflation, the promotion of efficiency, and the defeat of unemployment. These parts were pursued in a 'step-by-step' manner: they occurred largely in the chronological order above, and within each different components were adopted in a piecemeal, often experimental way. These tactics I compared to those of an entrepreneur introducing new products; the successful political entrepreneur sells a series of new political products in a competitive marketplace, and by that particular market test Mrs Thatcher's products have obviously done quite well. In spite of repeated mid-term vagaries in the polls, the trend in public opinion and the efforts of Labour to mimic the products suggest solid long-term success. I suggested finally that behind these tactics and strategy lay a vision of what a properly functioning economy and society might look like. What I did not do in these papers was draw out the ideology underlying strategy, tactics and vision. This is the focus of my efforts here.

THE LIBERAL TRADITION IN ECONOMIC THOUGHT

The economic thought on which Thatcherism draws is rich and extensive. The problem in defining the Thatcher ideology is not in finding it but in circumscribing it. The liberal classical tradition in economics has its source in David Hume, it flows through Adam Smith and the first flowering of supply-side economics leading to the dismantling of taxes and tariffs after the Napoleonic Wars, and became the dominant stream of thought in the early twentieth century (the Cambridge of Pigou, while the Continent was ruled by Austrian economics), only to be submerged post-war by the Keynesian revolution. Then came the Monetarist Counter-Revolution led by Milton Friedman, which incorporated the lessons of Keynes, and the liberal tradition was swept back into the mainstream as 'the neo-classical Synthesis', an amalgam of the classical model for the long term and the Keynesian model for the short.

For a time (the late 1960 early 1970s) peace ruled in economics.

Friedman and his critics, like James Tobin, came together and declared that the economy worked in this amalgamated way; empirical research would establish whether it was closer to the original classical or Keynesian concepts, but somewhere in this middle ground it would be.[2] This left a potential role for interventionist policies, notably to stabilise the economy over the business cycle, to ensure competition, and to provide 'public goods'. Controversy rumbled on over the details and how far empirically such policies did good, given the practical difficulties of implementation; but in principle it was agreed they could be useful. Monetarists or liberals battled over the details with Keynesians or corporatists, but within this set of ground rules.

This consensus was shattered by the international experience of the 1970s, nowhere more so than in Britain. Inflation soared, apparently uncontrollably; interventionism, invoked in increasing amounts to deal with inflation, appeared to spread like a weed into all corners of economic life. Public spending grew rapidly as a percentage of national income. Public opinion tired of the complacency of the mainstream economists, but most of all of the Keynesians within it. The monetarists declared empirical victory.

But matters went further still. Liberal economics was given a true shot in the arm by these events. Friedrich Hayek, always suspicious of models anyway from his Austrian viewpoint, reasserted the importance of political economy and the need to preserve the naturally-evolved institutions (such as the common law) which permit free contracting. James Buchanan and Gordon Tullock's public choice theory (that government should be analysed as the actions of self-interested politicians and civil servants rather than as those of a disinterested ruler)[3] was widely adopted. William Baumol[4] came up with the idea of 'contestability' from game theory; this made it possible to dispense with actual competition, provided potential entry (contestability) existed – and usually it was government regulation or protection that prevented it.

Perhaps most importantly of all, the idea of 'rational expectations' (where people are assumed to make efficient use of available information) gained widespread currency and empirical success as an ingredient in the newer monetarist models of the economy. This idea attacked the very citadel of interventionism – irrational expectations being the prime reason for controlling or even banning markets, their 'instability' being seen as a threat to the whole system.[5]

Once one has embraced rational expectations, one is irresistibly drawn into uprating the importance of supply-side economics, the long-standing study of how much market interventions and other 'distortions' of the free market price reduce the efficiency of the economy. For under rational expectations, the economy moves with all deliberate speed to the equilibrium where everyone is doing the best they can subject to these distortions. Hence except for brief periods of five years or less the economy's performance can only be affected by these and other underlying factors and not at all by the business cycle (if it exists), or monetary and fiscal policy – those matters overwhelmingly stressed in the earlier post-war economics. Supply-side economics too, then, has boomed in the new environment.

THE THATCHER GOVERNMENT'S INTELLECTUAL JOURNEY

With all this intellectual ferment going on around them, it would be surprising if Mrs Thatcher and her chief allies, notably Sir Keith (now Lord) Joseph, had not found that their thinking too was evolving not merely under the pressure of events but also in response to the shifting of ideas within the liberal tradition itself. There is not an area of policy that over the past decade has remained untouched by Thatcherism. One could trace this intellectual evolution in every one of them. Let me just do so in three – inflation, tax cuts and the supply side, and unemployment.

Inflation and Monetarism

Inflation was the main topic tackled in opposition prior to 1979. The ideas were heavily influenced by Friedman. There would be a bonfire of controls and the growth of money would be controlled within a gradually falling range ('gradualism'). Even then, however, there were additions with which Friedman disagreed – notably there was also to be a gradual reduction of the budget deficit and if necessary this would be achieved by raising taxes. This element arose from the originally Keynesian concern with the government's need to finance itself long term; too much issue of bonds (needed to finance the deficit without printing money) would give rise to an unsustainable interest burden.

Little attention was paid to which monetary aggregate would be controlled; it was assumed, again after Friedman, that it did not matter much – you chose on empirical grounds, stuck with it, and the others would behave more or less in line. What Friedman laid much stress on was that money should be controlled by fixing the growth of the monetary base (M0) and not by setting interest rates. However this was never accepted by the government (and least of all by the Bank of England); there was much debate in 1981 about it, eventually settled by the compromise of the 'indicator system' whereby the Bank would fix interest rates but move them rapidly and flexibly to achieve smooth growth within the target range.

So the start was already an ideologically mixed bag, though heavily influenced by Friedman's monetarism. It then changed steadily and not merely (as is often supposed) because of the famous overshooting of M3 targets in 1980–1.

First, in the budget of 1980 Sir Geoffrey Howe introduced the Medium Term Financial Strategy, the MTFS, which set out targets not just for that year but also for the succeeding five, a total innovation in policy anywhere. The idea came from rational expectations; the object was to establish by nailing the government's colours to the mast the seriousness with which these counter-inflation targets would be observed, thus to influence inflationary expectations and ease the fall in inflation with less cost in unemployment.

Second, by 1981 it became apparent that policy was much tighter than planned under gradualism, because the monetary target chosen was obviously misleading – it had overshot and yet as Lord Joseph remarked in a Cambridge debate 'we certainly achieved a massive squeeze'. There was now a deliberate loosening aimed at reducing sterling in particular that had sharply strengthened under the M3 regime. M0 was upgraded internally as a target while M3 was retained publicly.

This switch of targets – associated particularly with (now Sir) Alan Walters, who arrived as Mrs Thatcher's personal economic adviser at the start of 1981 – showed that the original Friedman set-up needed re-thinking; the model in which money measures did not matter was wrong, and the reason lay in the very decontrol that the government had introduced, in banking and foreign exchange. The Friedman model assumed tight bank controls on bank reserve ratios of cash to deposits and on the banks' powers to pay deposit interest; these controls were no more in Britain and we had a new monetary system on our hands, one much closer to the free banking systems of some past eras.

Third, probably earlier, it was realised that gradualism had in practice been replaced by a Hayek or Rational Expectations school sharp shock treatment. And it had worked, with inflation dropping sharply too, to 5 per cent by the end of 1982 from heights of over 20 per cent in 1980.

By 1983 monetary conditions had been stabilised, the budget deficit was well under control, and inflation was set to be held in a range of 3–5 per cent for the next five years. The policy thinking had settled too, in a rather different mould from its starting point. It was and still is a rational expectations framework in which four principles seem to rule:

1. The PSBR must be kept down to sustain market confidence. In a rational expectations world, the government's financing needs in the future must be able to be met without printing money, or people will expect future inflation.
2. M0 is a reliable indicator of monetary conditions; other money measures, which include deregulated deposits, are not because they reflect the market-wide competition for savings and not for money.
3. Rapid movements in the exchange rate may contain monetary signals, and will in general not be permitted, unless M0 confirms systematically after the event that they should.
4. In controlling monetary conditions what matters is that interest rates be moved *symmetrically* as dictated by targets (without political intervention for example to hold interest rates down) and that market participants can understand the system's *signals* in forming their expectations. Monetary Base control continues to be rejected in favour of a system using M0 as the key monetary indicator to guide interest rate changes.

Monetary policy is still by no means perfect, as the turbulent experiences of 1988 and 1989 show. In 1988 too much emphasis was given to holding down the pound against the DM, partly in a misjudged attempt to enter the European Monetary System by the back door; money was consequently loosened excessively. In early 1989 we are correcting that mistake with a policy that is extremely, possibly excessively, tight. The implementation of the principles set out above was poor, and it must be hoped that after this unintended volatility in the monetary tiller, it can once again be lashed to a stable course.

Tax Cuts and the Supply Side

The objective of cutting taxes by curbing public expenditure has always been at the heart of Mrs Thatcher's manifestos – if only once honest money permitted, that is once budget deficits were on their downward track as above. The objective was put off *sine die* in the early 1980s; in fact taxes were put up in the 1981 budget, but this was because of the deficit. Since that crisis passed, we have had more or less regular doses of 'cautious tax cuts' each budget time.

There are two basic reasons in the liberal tradition for tax cuts. The first is a mixture of political libertarianism and welfare economics: people should spend their own money, government should not spend it for them. People spend better than the government because they know better what they want, and they enjoy more liberty in so doing.

The second is to do with supply. Tax cuts give people better incentives to work, consequently not only is their welfare higher because they have a choice less distorted by taxation, but also they may work harder and if they do, the tax cuts to some extent pay for themselves as people pay more tax on their extra hours – clearly a highly attractive property, as the major constraint on tax cuts, that of government poverty, is eased.

This latter point is made by the famous Laffer curve, named after Arthur Laffer, an economist influential with the Reagan administration. The Laffer curve illustrates the revenues obtained as you raise the tax rate; at a zero rate, zero revenue of course, but zero revenue also obtains at a 100 per cent rate, since clearly no-one will work for nothing at all (zero may also obtain at lower rates than this). In between revenue will be positive, rising until the maximum revenue point is reached, then falling back. This is theoretically indisputable, but most tax rates are in a middling range where the empirical question arises of how flat the Laffer curve is, and whether it slopes up or down.

The government's theoretical rationale for tax cuts has shifted between these arguments in a way that has mirrored the economics profession's own empirical work on the Laffer curve. Initially, little was made of the supply argument; the emphasis was on returning money to the people as soon as honest money would permit. Tax cuts were the milk and honey waiting in the post-inflationary promised land. This approach was diametrically opposed to the Reagan administration's and that of the economists, including Friedman, who advised it; however it did ensure that monetary policy was not compromised by the budget deficit, a problem that the Reagan administration could finesse for a while given their strong financial starting point but in time caused them severe difficulties.

By 1986, remarkable evidence was beginning to appear of Laffer curve effects. Top tax rates have a low yield in revenue because they apply to only the top slices of income, and these rates were cut both by Reagan and Thatcher Governments early on. Extraordinarily, the revenues from people in these top brackets grew after the tax cuts faster than average revenues in other brackets — apparently showing that these rates were beyond the peak of the curve, and cutting them more than paid for itself. Econometric work by Lawrence Lindsey on US taxpayer data,[6] recently in Liverpool on UK worker data[7] and most recently of all by Ian Walker in Keele[8] also on UK workers is supporting the idea that these supply effects are in truth the reason for these remarkable results. A UK study, commissioned by the last Labour government at great cost from Chuck Brown in Stirling, reported low supply effects of tax cuts;[9] but these other studies explain away his results and suggest that the reason he gets them is that unionised workers with no choice of their hours are dominating his sample. Higher earners, typically non-unionised, who have a real choice of hours, and also non-union workers generally, show high supply responses.

Under the influence of this work the government has shifted to a more aggressive approach to tax cuts based on the supply argument. This was apparent in the 1988 budget which dramatically cut the top rate to 40 per cent and set a target for the standard rate of 20 per cent.

Similar tendencies to give greater credence to supply-side arguments have been apparent in related areas of policy for increasing efficiency in the British economy. This increasing confidence can similarly be put down to emerging evidence of supply improvements – better industrial relations, rising productivity growth, better profitability. For all the undoubted leftish bias among British academics, the emerging evidence has to their credit been recognised by them as well as by the government. The supply side is now all the rage.

What does all this show from the viewpoint of the history of ideas? Simply that empirical evidence – and even its highly sophisticated sister, econometrics – plays a crucial part in the development of ideas, of the manner and confidence in which they are held, and finally of their application by governments. Some in the liberal tradition – notably the Austrians – have scoffed at this type of evidence. Better they argue to stick to good principles and the economy will be well behaved in a way that econometrics cannot pick up. The limits of evidence are clear in the comparison of well-managed and poorly-managed economies over long periods of time. This attitude is not widespread for better or worse in the Anglo-Saxon part of that tradition as this episode shows.

Unemployment

Mrs Thatcher's 1979 administration had no special theory of unemployment. Unemployment was a symptom of the economy's general malfunctioning; both high inflation and lack of efficiency, from taxation, intervention and over-mighty unions, were at its root. Once restore a thriving enterprise economy free of inflation, and unemployment would return to the low rates of the 1960s or at least the low of early 1974.

In this view the government was following the general consensus of the time. Though the idea of the 'natural rate' of unemployment was well accepted among monetarists at least at the time, there was no work suggesting that it had risen sharply above that sort of range. Rather it seemed quite possible that once inflationary expectations had truly been broken, policy would no longer need to be so deflationary; if in addition productivity growth could increase above the lamentable performance (about 1 per cent p.a.) of the mid-1970s then higher growth too could bring down unemployment. Besides monetarists like Friedman taking this line, the models (Liverpool's included) all incorporated a relationship between growth and unemployment known as 'Okun's Law' after Arthur Okun; this had similar implications.

There had been some work in the mid-1960s done by Herbert Grubel and his co-workers[10] showing a relationship between unemployment benefit and unemployment. This was later shown to be quite a weak one and fell from view. However, work on the UK inter-war period by Daniel Benjamin and Levis Kochin demonstrated a much stronger effect of benefits in a period of mass unemployment.[11] Benefits acted they found rather like a permanent pension; they drew particular attention to the 'OXO' system whereby people shared a job, drawing benefits in the days they were not working.

I was particularly impressed with this work and when the Liverpool unemployment equation began, like all other 'models', to break down in 1980, I began work of my own to establish what the UK natural rate might be and how factors like benefits, unions and taxes might affect it, both directly and indirectly through wages and productivity. This could be called a special supply-side theory of unemployment.[12] The implication of this work is that by 1980 already, unbeknown to us all, the natural rate had reached over 3 million; the Thatcher squeeze and restoration of market discipline had the result of ending the massive overmanning of British industry that was concealing this true unemployment. Hence, suddenly as it were, the actual unemployment rate leapt up to meet and then because of the squeeze to surpass the natural rate.

Though this work was ruthlessly attacked and belittled by the Keynesian and Whitehall establishment, it – and work following it along the same lines, notably by Steven Nickell and Richard Layard[13] – has gradually become the basis of government policy, largely because of the failure of alternative analyses. Plainly unemployment was in the mid-1980s being held up by some forces quite other than inflation or lack of growth; inflation was down to a moderate 5 per cent or less and productivity with profitability had surged. Yet unemployment was stuck on its plateau of over 3 million.

The first overt actions by the government to implement this analysis came with the reviews by Norman Fowler of the benefit system. This in the end produced little change other than a tidying up and a smoothing of the sharp edges of the 'poverty trap'; but it proved highly educational to ministers, and laid the basis for a much tougher approach to unemployment fraud and benefit criteria. Around the same time David (now Lord) Young announced the crucial Restart programme, which revived the Beveridge worktest among other more politically palatable things like jobclubs. It is no coincidence that the month after this went national in July 1986, unemployment started falling – and has never stopped falling since.

This account of unemployment theory and its adoption by the Thatcher Government shows again that – with a lag that was unfortunate but understandable – the government followed theoretical and empirical developments as they occurred. Again what started out close to the standard monetarist paradigm developed well beyond it, drawing on much broader strands in the liberal tradition as well as on the tricks of modern econometrics.

CONCLUSION

This chapter is in no sense a full or proper intellectual history of Mrs Thatcher's administrations' thought. What I have tried to do is to sketch the main intellectual influences on key strands in the government's programme and draw out the nature of the intellectual path followed by the government, in order to illuminate the question of ideology versus pragmatism with which we began. What emerges is a picture of a government very much in touch with the work of economists and others trying to develop and apply the liberal tradition – itself more a broad stream than a single channel of thought. Within that stream it has selected those currents that suited its very British needs of political entrepreneurship on the tactical and strategic side. When those with whose approach it felt comfortable produced relevant thinking or evidence, the government has generally in time taken note and made some mid-course adjustments, if at times (as *par excellence* on unemployment) a little dangerously late in the day. This strikes me as on the whole within tolerable distance of the optimal mid-point between ideology and pragmatism we described above – perhaps about as close as one is ever likely to get in politics.

Notes and References

1. P. Minford, 'Mrs. Thatcher's Reform Programme – Past, Present and Future', in Robert Skidelsky (ed.), *Thatcherism* (London, 1988): 93–106; P. Minford and K. Matthews, 'Mrs. Thatcher's Economic Policies 1979–86', *Economic Policy* (1987), autumn special issue on *The New Conservative Revolution*.
2. See, for example, M. Friedman, 'The Role of Monetary Policy', *American Economic Review*, 58 (1968): 1–17.
3. E.g., J. M. Buchanan and G. Tullock, *The Calculus of Consent* (Ann Arbor, Michigan, 1962).
4. W. Baumol, 'Contestable Markets: An Uprising in the Theory of Industrial Structure', *American Economic Review*, 72 (1982): 1–15.
5. For an early example of this mode of thought see R. E. Lucas, Jr., 'Some International Evidence on Output in Inflation Trade-Offs', *American Economic Review*, 68 (1973): 326–34.
6. L. Lindsey, 'Individual Taxpayers' Response to Tax Cuts 1982–1984: With Implications for the Revenue-Maximizing Tax Rates', National Bureau for Economic Research (December 1986) (mimeo).
7. P. Minford and P. Ashton, 'The Poverty Trap and the Laffer Curve – What Can the GHS Tell Us?', CEPR discussion paper, 275 (1988).

8. Unpublished oral communication.
9. C. V. Brown, E. J. Levin, P. J. Rosa, R. J. Raffell and D. T. Ulph, *Taxation and Family Labour Supply: Final Report of H.M. Treasury Project* (London, 1987).
10. D. Maki and A. Spindler, 'The Effect of Unemployment Compensation on the Rate of Unemployment in Great Britain', *Oxford Economic Papers*, 27 (1975): 440–54.
11. D. Benjamin and L. Kochin, 'Searching for an Explanation of Unemployment in Interwar Britain', *Journal of Political Economy*, 87 (1979): 441–70.
12. Published eventually in articles and in P. Minford, D. Davies, M. Peel and A. Sprague, *Unemployment: Cause and Cure* (London, 1983).
13. R. Layard and S. Nickell, 'The Causes of British Unemployment', *National Institute Economic Review*, 3 (February 1985): 62–85.

11 The Collapse of Corporate State Keynesianism

Martin Holmes

By the end of the 1970s Britain's mixed economy had long since come to resemble a corporate state, jointly administered by the government of the day and the trade union leaders. The intellectual rationale for such an economy was derived from Keynesianism, although Keynes himself would have found repellent subsequent high levels of inflation. Nevertheless it surely owed its justification to Keynesian notions of government intervention, demand management, and full employment planning through an enlarged public sector. To be sure there had been dry runs for what was later to be called Thatcherism – the 1958 resignation of the Treasury team, the Selsdon period 1970–1, and Denis Healey's reluctant IMF-inspired monetarism – but the overwhelming majority of consensus politicans, civil servants and academic economists all expected the Keynesian corporate state to survive any return to free-market-based economic theory. The celebrated appeal for a change of strategy by the 364 economists, who after the 1981 budget urged a reflationary policy, was testimony to the expectation of a re-emergence of Keynesian macroeconomic management. Instead what has proved so remarkable about the economic changes introduced since 1979 has been the total intellectual collapse of the corporate state and the notions of governmental regulation which had sustained it.

The reason for such a collapse lies partly in the purely political determination of the Thatcher governments not to U-turn or abandon the economic strategy.[1] This political will had to be sustained at Cabinet level as the 'wets' of the first term, 1979–83, sought to alter economic policy from within. And the electoral pressure for a U-turn was greater in 1980–1 when the Conservatives trailed Labour (and the Alliance at times) than it had been in 1970–1. Few commentators thought the government could resist the strictly political disaster of three million unemployed. But political will alone did not enable the government to persevere. Equally important was the

intellectual critique of the failures of the corporate state which both
sustained government policy and provided a coherent framework of
economic revisionism to challenge many of the myths of 1945–79.
Without a sustained intellectual basis the tough decisions taken by
the government in its first term – primarily the 1981 budget –
would have been more difficult to justify.[2] One by one the notions
underpinning the desirability and permanence of the corporate state
soon evaporated.

The first myth was that government regulation of demand management could guarantee full employment. In reality unemployment had
risen, albeit unevenly in the 40 years which preceded 1979. At each
stage of the Keynesian reflationary cycle more jobs would be
destroyed by the adverse effects of inflation than were created by the
initial artificial surge in demand. It was Harold Wilson who saw (but
did not act upon the idea) that 'inflation is the mother and father of
unemployment'.[3] Moreover 'full' employment in the 1950s and 1960s
turned out to have been full overmanning in nationalised industries
and an expanded public sector. By the 1970s, Bacon and Ellis had
demonstrated the progressive weakening of the productive private
sector and the debilitating effects of penal taxation.[4] Britain's rate of
growth, which had sunk to the lowest in Europe by 1970, reflected
chronic overmanning and restrictive practices. In short the causes of
Britain's unemployment – up to and including the 1980s – were
not amenable to Keynesian demand management. Poor industrial
relations, the monopoly power of unions to price members out of
jobs, the burden on employers of the National Insurance Contribution
and National Insurance Surcharge, the welfare state disincentives to
take available jobs, the restrictions of the Planning Acts, the anti-
enterprise mentality of Labour local authorities, but most of all the
damaging effects of inflation, contributed to supply-side failures to
increase employment.

These factors, rather than any lack of aggregate demand, produced
a thirty-year crisis of rising unemployment. Although after 1979
James Callaghan repudiated any of Mrs Thatcher's policies which
bore a resemblance to his own, he accurately summed up the long-
term failure of Keynesianism at the 1976 Labour party conference,
arguing that

> We used to think that you could spend your way out of a
> recession and increase employment by cutting taxes and boosting
> Government spending. I tell you in all candour that that option no

longer exists, and that insofar as it ever did exist, it only worked on each occasion since the war by injecting a bigger dose of inflation into the economy, followed by a higher level of unemployment as the next step. Higher inflation followed by higher unemployment. We have just escaped from the highest rate of inflation this country has known; we have not yet escaped from the consequences: high unemployment. That is the history of the last twenty years.[5]

Consequently for the trade unions, as intimate partners in the corporate state, the pursuit of demand management enabled them to abdicate responsibility for the necessary function of trading wage increases with employment opportunities. If unemployment was caused by raising the price of labour beyond market levels the unions could simply ask the government to reflate the economy in the vain belief that they could escape the economic consequences of inevitably higher unemployment. This evasion of responsibility was predicted with amazing prescience as the inevitable consequence of Keynesian policies by Jacob Viner in a review of Keynes's *General Theory* soon after its publication: 'In a world organized in accordance with Keynes' specification there would be a constant race between the printing press and the business agents of the trade unions, with the problem of unemployment largely solved if the printing press could maintain a constant lead.'[6]

Whatever criticism of the Thatcher government is deserved in terms of its slowness to remove supply-side causes of unemployment, the post-1979 period would have seen far higher unemployment if a Heath-style U-turn had been performed. Furthermore it may be claimed that the Thatcher Government has provided a signal service of demonstrating to the electorate the limits of government in providing employment. In 1983 the promises of the Labour Party to spend their way to full employment and in 1987 to 'create' one million new jobs were regarded with suspicion by uncommitted voters. Indeed the fall in unemployment since mid-1986 would indicate the capacity of a free market economy to generate jobs without a Keynesian stimulus or bogus overmanning.

The second myth of the corporate state era was that inflation was caused by trade union wage demands rather than by governments. Certainly on more than one occasion the government would intensify its exhortation to wage restraint while simultaneously reflating the economy. Thus Britain's worst inflation, generated by the Heath Government, was accompanied by the most comprehensive peacetime

wage and price controls since the 1348 Statute of Labourers.[7]
Conveniently, governments sought to deflect public criticism onto
the trade unions. Flowing from this view was the belief that only
incomes policy could restrain inflation and that without it there would
be anarchy, chaos, a free-for-all and spiralling prices. Regulation and
restriction were thus the order of the day covering, in either
'voluntary' or statutory form, wages, prices, rents, profits, and
dividends. All governments since 1945 tried some variation of this
policy to disguise the inflationary aspects of Keynesian reflation. Pay
pauses, guiding lights, norms, severe restraints, percentage targets,
flat rate increases, tripartite agreements, Social Contracts – all were
introduced usually after the rate of inflation had started to accelerate.
The introduction of such policies allowed each government, but
particularly those in the 1970s, to present itself as politically dedicated
to defeating inflation while economically unwilling to tackle its causes.
Not surprisingly the Heath Government and its Labour successor
presided over levels of inflation that peaked at 27 per cent while
blaming anyone – unions, management, and retailers – but themselves. For nearly forty years the view that the inflationary effects of
Keynesian economics could be suppressed by wage and price controls
mesmerised not only the politicians but the economic establishment.
The voices who questioned the intellectual basis of such policies –
for example Alan Walters in 1972 – were few and far between.[8] Of
course the more honest Keynesians had by the end of the 1970s
admitted that incomes policies could not control inflation. Instead
the rationale shifted to preserving employment, a tacit admission of
the job-destructive potential of monopoly labour power. But this
half-shift from the incomes policy panacea was no substitute for
tackling those very abuses of trade union monopoly power which
threatened employment in the first place. In seeking to blame the
unions for the inflation that Keynesian policies had caused, the
politicians of the corporatist era failed to chide the unions for the
unemployment that their monopoly bargaining position delivered.
This dual delusion permitted both inflation and unemployment to
rise without any real attempt to tackle the cause rather than the
symptoms.

   The final intellectual collapse of the incomes policy myth occurred
when the Thatcher Government jettisoned the corporate state and
sought to re-establish the government's sole responsibility for maintaining a sound currency. However, instead of the inflationary
explosion which had been predicted in the absence of incomes policy,

inflation fell from 22 per cent to 4 per cent in the three years up to 1983. The re-establishment of the centrality of monetary policy, the refusal to reflate when unemployment topped three million, and the reductions in (and eventual elimination of) the Public Sector Borrowing Requirement all disproved the corporate state theory that only union cooperation with incomes policy could maintain stable prices. So completely had the incomes policy approach been discredited that the Labour opposition refrained from suggesting it during the temporary increases in inflation in 1985 and 1988–9.[9] Interest rate discipline had indeed replaced beer and sandwiches.[10]

The third myth of the corporate state era, which was directly derived from the first two, argued that industrial peace could be guaranteed only by the involvement of the trade unions in the economic policy process. Without union cooperation with the government of the day, so the theory ran, strikes and disruption would ensue, threatening inflation and industrial chaos. The electorate was encouraged to believe that the parties should be judged by how they could 'work with' the unions. The appearance of the trade union leaders at repeated Downing Street meetings seemed to have become institutionalised. As late as 1978, the Callaghan Government was hoping that its close relations with the union leaders could be used to electoral advantage in contrast to Mrs Thatcher's intended confrontation.[11] In reality the myth of trade union corporate state cooperation had the opposite results. The more that governments cooperated with the unions the greater was the level of industrial disruption. Harold Wilson's 1960s corporatism ended in the 1969–70 dirty jobs strike; in 1973–4 during the three-day week and miners' strike Heath's tripartite corporatism ended in the grotesque chaos of a Conservative Government being scuttled from office by the National Union of Mineworkers at the end of its worst election campaign; and the Social Contract dissolved into the Winter of Discontent in 1978–9 when public sector workers paralysed many social services with highly unpopular strike action.

Such a pattern was not an unhappy coincidence. Rather it flowed directly from the internal contradictions of the corporate state. For the more that each government would cooperate and conciliate the unions, the more likely that its will to resist strike action would decline. The greater each conciliation, the more apparent it became that industrial action would succeed. With the exceptions of the 1949 dock strike, 1971 Post Office strike, and 1976 firemen's strike, industrial battles were repeatedly won by the unions. A perverse political language developed whereby an industrial victory for a union would be described as compromise, conciliation, a negotiated settlement or a victory for common sense. Mr Heath even went so far as saying after defeat at the hands of the miners in 1972 that there were no winners and losers in industrial disputes![12] But each settlement to avert industrial disruption only made strike action more attractive to union leaders and working days lost through strikes rose steadily. Moreover, the economic logic of Keynesian reflation coupled with incomes policy restraints was an open invitation to restore collective bargaining once the inflationary effects ate into take-home pay. As well as the political determination of Joe Gormley to exploit the miners' bargaining potential in the wake of the 1973 oil crisis, it was Heath's dash for growth (wrongly blamed on Tony Barber) which led to the crisis of February 1974. Similarly Healey's wildly inflationary 1978 budget was as responsible for the Winter of Discontent as the National Union of Public Employees pickets.

Since 1979 the government's handling of the unions has been based on different principles from which have emerged wholly beneficial consequences. Industrial relations have been greatly improved by abandoning and rejecting the corporatist model of government–union collaboration. Certainly the reform of trade union law, especially the pre-strike ballot requirements, has enhanced industrial relations by transferring power from union leaders to their members. These changes, although carried out cautiously over two parliaments, unlike the ill-fated 1971 Industrial Relations Act, have redressed the imbalance of power by which union leaders, often motivated by political considerations, could marshall their members as a First World War general could marshall his infantry. But legal changes alone have been supplementary to the main reform since 1979 – the determination of the government to win industrial victories when faced with a series of set-piece strikes. The paradox of the Thatcherite approach is that a tough line when faced with strike action – civil servants, steelworkers, NHS ancillary workers and most spectacularly the NUM – has led to a diminution of industrial disputes with working days lost by strike action down to their lowest level for fifty years. Each successful government refusal to surrender to, or compromise with, public sector strike action has sent a clear message that striking will be unsuccessful.[13] Once the private sector, which historically has taken its lead on such matters from the government, sought to copy the uncompromising tough line, the union leaders realised that strikes had to be reserved as the weapon of last – not first – resort. Moreover the pre-1979 pattern of employers' climbdowns, disguised as a compromise, has been replaced by a truthful language of industrial victory and market-related pay bargaining. Thus, the government's industrial victories led in turn to those in the private sector in the *Stockport Messenger* and Wapping disputes. Picketing, which seemingly had a devastating effect in the 1970s, has been rendered a much less potent weapon in the 1980s. The symbolic triumph of Arthur Scargill's flying pickets at Saltley Gate in 1972 when the effectiveness of picketing forced the Heath Government to capitulate contrasted clearly with Orgreave in 1984, when picketing was unable to halt the movement of coal.

It would be too crude, however, to regard the overthrow of trade union corporatist power as simply the result of government assaults on a beseiged and politically enfeebled trade union movement. As well as the robust approach to industrial disputes, exemplified by the 359–day battle against Scargillism, the government has encouraged, and benefited from, the emergence of the 'new unionism'. Many unions have found themselves at home in a market environment and have relished participating in the overall reinvigoration of the economy. More individual trade unionists than ever before now vote Conservative and the absence of 'class' solidarity with Scargillism meant that the steelworkers, railwaymen and lorry drivers failed to heed the calls of union leaders to refuse to move coal. More significantly in the longer term has been the emergence of Roy Lynk's Union of Democratic Mineworkers and Eric Hammond's Electrical, Electronic, Telecommunications and Plumbing Unions, both prospering outside the TUC. Along with the Royal College of Nurses and the Professional Association of Teachers, these unions now constitute a numerically important and politically significant alternative new unionism. Given the winds of change blowing through the Engineers Union, who is to say where this process will end? No-strike agreements and binding arbitration have proved popular with workers who long since questioned the validity of class-based industrial conflict. Indeed it may be argued that the corporate state encouraged class-based anti-enterprise sentiments among trade unionists by implicitly suggesting that the interests of government and workers were in such conflict that a political process of negotiated bargaining between the two was desirable. The decline of class-based trade unionism in the 1980s is another consequence of the dismantling of corporatist political economy.

Just as important has been the growth of single-industry unionism

which has replaced the chaotic craft union system where up to twenty
or so different unions could be represented in one industry –
each competing against the other in demarcation disputes and by
'leapfrogging' wage claims. The new unionism has swept away such
backwardness. All the EETPU's and many other unions' new
arrangements are single-union. Fewer and fewer employers are now
prepared to sign deals with more than one union, thus removing
duplication, hassle and the potentiality for inter-union strife.[14]
Moreover the popularity of ballots, which affect many aspects of
trade union decision-making, have entrenched the principles of
consultation and democratic accountability which existed in name
only before the 1980, 1982 and 1984 legal reforms. As a consequence,
Britain's workforce has changed. Workers who own shares in industry
now outnumber trade unionists for the first time; many trade unionists
own shares in privatised industries; 67 per cent of households are
owner-occupied; and credit cards and consumer borrowing are not
just for the salaried professional classes. All these factors make it
less likely that workers regularly balloted by their unions will wish to
resort to damaging strike action. The new unionism is rooted in the
democratic support of individuals who are unlikely to be impressed
either by the Labour Party's hostility to Mrs Thatcher's reforms or
Arthur Scargill's calls for increased revolutionary consciousness to
overthrow capitalism. The success of the new unionism is due entirely
to events since 1979; it could never have emerged in the corporate
state atmosphere of hostility to private enterprise and antipathy to
internal trade union democracy.

The fourth myth of the corporate state era postulated that the
mixed economy, encompassing a large and growing public sector,
was both economically desirable and politically inevitable as a
consequence of consensus. The mixed economy was regarded as
the outcome of a *political* decision-making process of permanent
negotiation between government, unions and (to maintain a balance
of sorts) the employers. Thus the National Economic Development
Council, the National Plan, Nationalised Industry White Papers,
Enterprise Boards, Industry Acts, the Industrial Reorganisation
Corporation, and Social Contracts all sought to restrict or downgrade
the importance of the market economic process. The market's
invisible hand was replaced by an all-too-visible political process
of horse-trading, exhortation, and corporatist intervention. Every
incomes policy operated in this way, yet the economic damage caused
by the mixed economy was all too apparent. In the ever-growing

number of nationalised industries, market disciplines were scorned with damaging effects – for example, when the Heath Government scrapped financial targets and froze prices. Government decrees artificially to hold down the price of stamps were rescinded only after it transpired that the Post Office had already had stamps printed with the 'wrong' price on them. In other nationalised industries price controls destroyed financial targets, undermined the functions of management, and led directly to chronic deficits, many of which were inherited by the Thatcher Government. By the mid-1970s the process of nationalisation itself developed a momentum that Herbert Morrison would not have contemplated.

As well as formal planned nationalisation, governments resorted to *de facto* nationalisation caused by the fear of large scale, politically embarrassing redundancies.[15] In this way the 1974–9 Labour administration took into public ownership both British Leyland and Chrysler despite the fact that both companies were direct commercial rivals. Governments also sought by planning agreements, the National Enterprise Board, and restrictive regional policy to regulate industry in opposition to market forces.[16] Not surprisingly corporate profitability was low, economic growth stunted and by the end of the 1970s the self-employed sector had declined by 100,000 over the decade. Since 1979 the revival of both the manufacturing and service industries has pushed rates of economic growth to their post-war peak, raised profitability, encouraged an investment boom, and witnessed an increase of one million in the number of self-employed who now comprise 10 per cent of the workforce for the first time since the 1920s. The removal of corporate state direct government controls on industry released an entrepreneurial activity which had hitherto lain smothered. Vitally important to this process was the 1979 removal of exchange controls and the encouragement of both inward and outward capital investment. Indeed, British companies were acquiring capital assets overseas at such a rate that the process of asset liquidation associated with the First and Second World Wars was for the first time in reverse; by 1989, Britain had overtaken Japan in capital investment in the United States.

This transformation, along with the achievement of a balanced budget, and substantial income and corporate tax cuts, has reversed the process of comparative economic decline so familiar after 1945. Moreover, as Geoffrey Maynard has argued, the economic success of the decade as a whole has put into perspective the difficult years of disinflation 1979–81 on which critics have disproportionately dwelled.[17] Short of the return to power of a Labour government – which cannot be discounted while the Conservative General Election vote is static at 43 per cent – the intellectual foundations of corporate state Keynesianism have entirely collapsed as the beneficial consequences of a market-oriented economy have thrown into sharper relief the failures of 1945–79.

Notes and References

1. Notwithstanding the increases in inflation in 1985 and 1988–9 – the latter largely caused by the unwise policy of seeking to shadow the £ to the DM up to Spring 1988. The 1988 and 1989 budgets, by contrast, built up a substantial fiscal surplus.
2. See Alan Walters, *Britain's Economic Renaissance* (Oxford, 1986): 86–91 for an insider's account.
3. Harold Wilson, *Final Term* (London, 1979).
4. Robert Bacon and Walter Ellis, *Britain's Economic Problem: Too Few Producers* (London, 1976). The Heath government, for example, increased the number of civil servants by 90,000 in three years.
5. Reproduced in James Callaghan, *Time and Chance* (London, 1987).
6. *Quarterly Journal of Economics*, 51 (1936): 147–67.
7. For a detailed view of this period see Martin Holmes, *Political Pressure and Economic Policy: British Government 1970–4* (London, 1982).
8. See, for example, S. Brittain and P. Lilley, *The Delusion of Incomes Policy* (London, 1977).
9. The Labour Party did however urge the use of credit controls during 1989, demonstrating a lack of confidence in purely market solutions.
10. For the Chancellor's own intellectual overview of this process see N. Lawson, 'The State of the Market', IEA occasional paper, 80 (1988).
11. See Martin Holmes, *The Labour Government 1974–9: Political Aims and Economic Reality* (London, 1985).
12. Television broadcast reported in *The Times* (28 February 1972).
13. See Martin Holmes, *The First Thatcher Government: Contemporary Conservatism and Economic Change* (London, 1985) Chapter 6.
14. For a detailed account of these developments, see P. Bassett, *Strike Free* (London, 1986).
15. For a good account of this process, see John Redwood and John Hatch, *Controlling Public Industries* (Oxford, 1982).
16. See John Redwood, *Going for Broke . . . Gambling with Taxpayers' Money* (Oxford, 1984).
17. Geoffrey Maynard, *The Economy Under Mrs. Thatcher* (Oxford, 1988).

12 Popular Capitalism and World Politics

John Redwood*

In April 1976 I wrote that the government needed to make a new start in its approach to the nationalised industries.[1] I concluded that equity capital had to be issued to investors outside the government in order to create new disciplines for the businesses. Although the conclusions were hedged with a certain caution, necessary as the advice was being tendered tongue in cheek to a Labour Government, they evoked considerable disquiet and a strong counter-attack from one of the doyens of conventional economic thinking, Professor Lipton.[2] Sufficient controversy was provoked for the *Investors Chronicle* to ask me to write a series of articles probing the disappointing performance of the nationalised industries further. The first panoramic article of 7 January 1977 concluded 'to cut costs, improve services, and make investment steadily and profitably, live within your means, and make a success of your business needs the spur of competition, where you are judged by your bank manager and shareholders'. The following articles tried to expose the ways in which government intervention and ownership made successful business management in the interests of the customers and the shareholders impossible.

When I wrote these pieces I had no idea just how far the ideas would carry and whether it would be possible to persuade serious politicians that the time was ready for radical change. I did not envisage during the 1970s that the movement for industrial reform in the United Kingdom would become the pioneer of a worldwide movement which would transform radically the relationships between government, industry and commerce. Yet that process happened in the short space of ten years.

In the mid-1970s it was axiomatic in British debate that there were central industries in any economy that required nationalised ownership in order to deliver social obligations, to regulate them, to look after the social good and protect their employees. Professor Lipton put the case quite eloquently and implied in his refutation of my work that all the arguments I could produce in favour of competition and markets had been dealt with summarily years before in the academic literature. Professor Pryke had written a book attempting to demonstrate that in the 1950s and 1960s nationalisation had produced excellent results, both financially and for customers.[3] He was to be converted fairly early on in the debate into one of the strongest protagonists of denationalisation when his studies of the nationalised industries in the 1970s revealed a very different perform- ance.[4] His conversion was most welcome and was the first sign that the academic mood might be on the move.

It was also accepted in the Treasury that the nationalised industries had to remain nationalised and under firm control, because they were likely to remain unsuccessful loss-makers where it was vital that the custodians of the nation's purse strings had a substantial 'influence' over their conduct.[5] This was one of the most difficult parts of the orthodoxy to challenge as I had every sympathy with the Treasury's aim of reducing the claim on public resources represented by the nationalised industries, but I also felt that there needed to be a mechanism for giving the nationalised industries greater freedom in order to demonstrate their entrepreneurial abilities. The end result was obvious: they had to be denationalised. Getting there from the state of the debate in the mid-1970s was never likely to be easy, and it is one of the most remarkable phenomena of the Thatcher years that the impossible became possible within a relatively short time.[6]

Throughout the 1970s and the early 1980s the argument raged over how far a future Conservative government, or the new Conservative administration, could go in forcing change within the nationalised sector. The early view of the party was that it could not go too far. It would be possible to introduce new management, to set objectives to reduce subsidy, and to try to instil a more commercial approach. It would not be possible to do very much by way of denationalisation. After all, Edward Heath's government had tried to do so, only to end up nationalising substantially more than it sold following the collapse of Rolls Royce and the limp towards the public sector of the British motor industry.

The means by which the idea gained favour owed a lot to chance and to circumstance. Firstly, there was a precedent for sales of public assets as the Labour Government, under duress from the International Monetary Fund, had sold some of its shareholding in British Petro- leum. This precedent was important in political terms, as it provided ministers thinking of privatisation with a ready reply at the dispatch box should Labour, as they always did, challenge the underlying principle. Secondly, there was the dire necessity of the Treasury to raise more money to try to narrow the huge gap between state revenues and state spending. In the early years of the Thatcher administration there was little success in curbing public spending. The first year was disastrous, as the full cost of the public sector pay awards came through, a combination of the promises to honour the Clegg Review recommendations to increase relative pay in the public sector and of the high rate of inflation inherited from the out-going Labour administration. Taxes did have to be put up, and were put up, but the gap was still large. The idea of turning to asset and share sales to deal with some small portion of that gap was naturally attractive to the Treasury.

The second pressure which helped came from the belief spreading amongst the nationalised industry chairmen and directors themselves that maybe life in the private sector would offer a more exciting alternative. I used to run seminars for the nationalised industry chairmen's group over several years. The early ones were very constrained by the conventional approach to public sector industrial economics. The routine agendas covered Treasury capital controls and financing limits, rate of return objectives, investment appraisals and the corporate plans. It was all based upon a response of the nationalised industries to a very bureaucratic system of regulation and control. It was difficult trying to nudge the agenda towards the real business issues. What were the customers thinking of the product and the service? How could innovation be encouraged? How could assets be renewed whilst cashflow improved? How could boards of directors gain enough commercial freedom to make a success of their task? These were the type of issues I wished to see on the agenda which proved obstinately difficult to address.

As the years advanced, some people within the chairmen's group and amongst their advisers began to see the logic of turning their attention away from trying to reform the Byzantine control system to thinking of a way of escaping from the prison of public provision. The impossible become possible with a growing interplay between those in the industries who came to favour a private answer and those ministers who had the courage to see that, given backing from the industry, there might be political mileage in denationalisation. It is all credit to David Howell and Nigel Lawson at Energy, to Norman Fowler at Transport and to Keith Joseph at Industry that relatively early on in the life of the government decisions were taken to step up the pace of disposal.

The first year, 1979–80, saw the predictable sale of British Petroleum shares in order to raise ready money and small sales from the National Enterprise Board. The second year saw the honouring of the pledge to sell shares in British Aerospace, one of only two manifesto commitments. This was the result of the hard fought parliamentary battles against the nationalisation of the shipyards and the aerospace industry in the 1974–9 Parliament. There were also further asset sales from the National Enterprise Board.

In 1981–2 the government started to tackle the privatisation of companies other than those nationalised by the immediately preceding administration. Two businesses came close to volunteering themselves, Amersham International and Cable & Wireless. Both have been most successful privatisations and the managers have never looked back following their grant of freedom. The third major sale that year was the most remarkable of all. When Norman Fowler announced that he was interested in selling the National Freight Consortium, a road transport business, the managers and employees clubbed together in order to buy it for themselves. Their story has become a model for the world in how to handle an employee and management buyout, transforming attitudes, taking the business from retreat to growth and making all the employees substantial sums of money into the bargain. National Freight was a most welcome lucky break and the charismatic leadership of its chairman was important in winning many of the arguments about the social acceptability of privatisation. Lorry drivers who had worried for their jobs and seen their business in decline became highly motivated, better paid and through their share stakes started to build capital savings of their own. The purchaser of a £1 share six years ago now owns a share worth £100.[7] In 1982–3 Associated British Ports and Britoil followed into the private sector; Britoil's sale was led by its chairman who was a keen advocate of being free of Treasury controls as he wished to invest overseas.

The critical decision was taken by Keith Joseph towards the end of the first Thatcher administration to prepare British Telecom for sale. This represented a quantum leap forward in the government's understanding of how far privatisation could go. It took the policy into a core monopoly public sector business. It challenged the assumption that nationalisation has a divine right to control the commanding heights of the economy. It also began to establish the idea that some competitive forces and deregulation could do much more for jobs and prosperity and innovation in a core sector of the economy than a nationalised monopoly.

This painstaking progress seemed fraught with difficulty at the time. It was always fragile. The opposition threatened to renationalise anything that the government sold. Journalists felt it would be a temporary phase, with a Labour administration taking over in 1983 or 1984 and reversing the process back to the natural condition of nationalisation and government intervention. It was going to take time for the newly privatised industries to establish their track records and show that they were benefiting from the process. Whilst the principle of the National Freight Corporation sale to its employees was widely welcomed and was most difficult to oppose, it took two or three years before it was possible to demonstrate that the profits, investment and morale all improved as a result of the process.

The election victory of 1983 was crucial in two ways. Firstly, it demonstrated to the commentators and the public that some of the changes put through need not be temporary. Secondly, it gave the government the much needed opportunity to take privatisation on from being a matter of selling a few businesses where particular political pledges had been made or where a few unusual chairmen were happy to see their businesses transferred to the private sector, into a mass movement recruiting millions of new shareholders and challenging most parts of the public sector estate. The years 1983–7 saw privatisation move from being a minority taste into becoming a mass movement. It also saw its translation from being a series of policies designed in the UK to deal with what seemed very particular problems[8] into a worldwide phenomenon where many could see the attractions of radical restructuring of their own state enterprise sectors.[9]

The period 1983–7 was still dogged by controversy. The opposition tried to maintain the pressure, threatening renationalisation of many of the crucial industries, and trying to keep up the idea that somehow privatisation was against the natural grain of life. 'Normality' would return after a 1987 or 1988 opposition victory. The British Telecom sale was strongly contested, with trade unions keen to try to block it. In order to handle such a large sale of assets the government needed to bring in new types of shareholder. The City was very nervous, believing that it was too large to be done. A three-pronged strategy was developed, with a tranche of shares being sold in overseas markets, a second tranche being sold to the conventional United Kingdom institutions through the usual market mechanisms, and a large new third tranche being sold direct to the public through a mass advertising campaign. This third tranche included a direct appeal to the employees of British Telecom over the heads of their trade unions which was extremely successful. The combination of free shares and half price shares attracted employees, despite the union opposition to any employee shareholdings. The newly privatised British Telecom started life with large numbers of employee shareholders. This formula was followed for the subsequent sales of Gas and Steel and will be pursued for Water and Electricity.

The rhetoric and the intentions shifted as privatisation grew to maturity. In the early days it was seen as a way of raising money and of shedding the peripheral part of the public estate where there was no clear rationale for public ownership. The language was the language of efficiency and to a lesser extent of freedom. Once the government started to tackle the core public sector the language of wider ownership became much more important. One of the central conflicts in the privatisation process emerged in the debate between those who wished to keep monopolies whole and those who wished to introduce competition. In my work in 1976 and 1977 I had always seen competition as being more important than the transfer of ownership. If only, I argued, customers and potential employees had a choice between producers in central areas like transport and energy, innovation would flourish, productivity would improve and the nation would be better off. The earlier schemes I outlined were for a completely deregulated bus industry, for a rail system based upon tendering for subsidy rather than a global subsidy to a single monopoly loss-maker and competition in the energy industries. As the idea of privatisation became more acceptable to industry leaders and to the wider public, the chairmen of the industries concerned moved swiftly to argue in favour of privatising themselves whole. They saw the advantages of being free from Treasury controls and of having new ways of raising money from shareholders and banks. Some of them were less enamoured of the idea of full scale competition and came to the government offering privatisation schemes which would permit the industry to be free from intervention whilst leaving the monopolies intact.[10]

The government's response to this was mixed. In the case of the bus industry Nicholas Ridley rightly rejected the idea out of hand and split the industry into dozens of competing companies. At the other end of the scale the attractions of wider ownership, and of establishing a much bigger range of shareholders, proved overwhelming when the government looked at the case of British Gas. Only subsequently have competitive pressures been introduced into the gas marketplace as the public and commentators rightly probe the way in which the gas industry functions.

British Telecom is slowly evolving into a competitve and deregulated animal. Early on, bold moves were made to deregulate equipment added on to the network and value added network services. More gradually competition has been introduced into long line and business telephone services through Mercury, which has had an impact upon service quality and price and is now running public telephone boxes. The system still needs competition on local line and domestic calls: this may well emerge, moving British Telecom on from monopoly to an open, deregulated, fast growing, innovative competitive business. In electricity, different sources of competition will be introduced into generation by splitting the Central Electricity Generating Board into two, by bringing in electricity from the independent Scottish company, from France through the cross channel link and from a new sector of private entrepreneurs entering generation for the first time.[11]

Critics of the scheme for various industries attempted to say that the big conflict in government was between those who wished to maximise the amount of money raised, therefore arguing in favour of a monopoly industry which would have strong pricing powers, and those who were more sympathetic to the arguments for competition. This was a wrong characterisation of the debate. No one ever suggested privatising the monopolies without price controls. In those industries where monopoly elements survived there was always a debate about the strength of price control. Often the Treasury favoured the toughest regime of all even though this would reduce the profits of the industry and therefore reduce the sale proceeds. The argument was really about the political complexity. It is much easier to privatise an industry whole with the complete support of its board of directors and with the acquiescence of its trade-union-organised workforce than it is to privatise it by splitting it. The people at the top of the industry and the trade unions will both be actively against break-up. It was this pressure which led to some compromises in the styles of the early public utility privatisations. As time passes improvements are made by introducing more competition and correcting some of the early caution.

What has all this to do with world politics? From 1985 onwards politicians in many countries abroad began to look at the growing strength and vitality of the British economy, which had been a byword for incompetence and poor performance throughout the 1970s. On their visits to London they began to see that one important element in the economic renaissance was the sharp improvement in perform- ance of many of the core industries that once were nationalised. Some of these overseas visitors saw the significance of the change in attitudes in privatised companies or in nationalised concerns undergoing the process of privatisation more quickly than English commentators.

From early 1983 onwards I began to realise from conversations with visitors from overseas that Britain had an important export in privatisation. It was, after all, Britain which had exported the Morrisonian corporation to the world in the post-war period. Many countries had been persuaded to adopt the independent nationalised corporations ostensibly free of government control only to discover it was under government influence through the lunchtime directive and day-to-day interference with decisions. Many countries had adopted this form of nationalised industry. You can see them today in New Zealand, in Australia, in Canada and in many smaller British Commonwealth countries. Was it not time for Britain to give to the world the antidote, given the problems of losses, low productivity, low morale and Treasury restrictions which characterised nationalised industry performance in many parts of the world?[12] When a French professor came to seek my advice at Rothschild's in the summer of 1983 I knew that the idea was adaptable in the most unlikely of places!

The world was at first hesitant about receiving the antidote. Visitors came to London fascinated by the process, prepared to believe that it was working in the United Kingdom, but full of excuses and reasons why circumstances were different in their country. Some genuinely believed their countries to be in a different position, others were looking for a way out when asked the difficult questions at home as they feared the political complications. The list of objections was long but it soon fell into a fairly routine pattern. Some felt that their nationalised industries were performing well unlike the United Kingdom ones. Examining the evidence usually showed that whilst they might be profitable they were a long way away from being world leaders or from having productivity levels up to the best private sector performance. All were interested in the growing success of the UK, especially in the industrial relations field in both public and private sector industries.[13]

Some believed that their countries lacked big stock markets and therefore would be unable to undertake major offer for sale programmes. They felt that London's pre-eminence as by far and away the largest European stock market, and one of the three largest stock markets in the world, made things possible in Britain that would be impossible elsewhere. Subsequent experience showed that countries with tiny stock markets, like Jamaica, could undertake major privatisation programmes if they had the courage to do so.

Some argued that the political situation in their country was so different that there would be no support for such a radical policy as their politics were still social democrat or socialist. Yet the Labour administration in New Zealand not only carried out a radical restructuring of its nationalised industries but even after its intentions were quite clear went on to win a second term of office, partly because it was perceived by the public to be tackling deep-rooted problems that had caused industrial underperformance for a number of years.

Some argued that their industries had specific legal, technical or business problems that either could not be sorted out or would need lengthy attention before privatisation was possible. I have never yet encountered a single example of a technical, legal, business or financial problem that could not be overcome if people wished to privatise the industry concerned. One of the advantages of privatisation is that it presents a government with a clean sheet for remodelling and restructuring the industry and all its obligations, should it be desirable to do so and should the need arise.

The fatal attraction of the policies was as obvious as the temerity of all those contemplating them. I first addressed a major international privatisation conference in February 1986 in Washington. At this conference USAID expressed its wholehearted support for the idea of major privatisation initiatives in developing countries and assembled delegates from sixty countries overseas to listen to a range of speakers who had direct experience of the privatisation process. I had been invited to give the keynote speech on privatisation as the director of Rothschild's responsible for advising overseas governments on privatisation. I was inundated with requests for more information at the end of the talk and it was on that day that I realised the idea was not only of interest to countries abroad but was going to become a reality.

The idea grew in popularity as governments came to see that it offered a solution to a series of common problems. Many governments were faced with too large a gap between state revenues and state spending. It was not always possible to put up taxes, and cutting spending proved almost impossible everywhere. Privatisation sale proceeds represented a most useful way of bridging the gap. Few countries would ever admit that was their main purpose, although it was quite obvious that the drive for privatisation other than in the United Kingdom was at its strongest where governments had the acutest perception of the need to cut the budget deficit.

Many saw privatisation as offering a way out of the difficulties of microeconomic policy. In many developing countries whole industries were failing to deliver the goods or to work properly. Nationalisation was getting in the way of improved performance and the government was beginning to realise that its own involvement in running the industries might even be an obstacle; certainly it was not a method for delivering greater success. Labour relations were often worse when government was involved: strikes could become political weapons. Very often countries interested in this question wanted to know whether it was possible to capture the benefits of deregulation, improved management and a more commercial approach without going the whole hog and selling the industries. The answer is no for it is privatisation which acts as the galvanising force which makes possible other radical changes. Most countries saw the attraction of the politics of privatisation as it matured in the later 1980s. Privatisation is not and need not be a movement of the radical right. It can encompass the creation of employee based cooperatives, wider capital ownership and democratising wealth holdings; it can include the involvement of small communities or regions in the running of businesses that had been unhappily centralised by more remote national or federal governments. It offered something to politicians of most persuasions. Those to the left of centre could stress the policy as a means of creating genuine participation and broadening employee involvement. Those to the right of centre could stress rather more the efficiency gains and the financial benefits.

Following the election victory of 1987 in the United Kingdom popular capitalism came fully of age. Privatisation had been a struggling infant in the 1970s, threatened with premature death on many occasions. It had an awkward adolescence in the early 1980s and had grown to some maturity in the 1983–7 period. From 1987 onwards it took off and came to encompass a much wider range of economic policies with their genesis in the early Reagan and Thatcher years. What is unusual about the popular capitalism movement is that an economic policy which developed many of its distinctive characteristics in the United Kingdom has been transferred onto the world stage. The 1960s and 1970s have been a period when most of the major fashions have come out of the economic giants of America and Japan. The 1980s saw a successful collaboration between some ideas of the Reagan administration on the one hand and other ideas of the Thatcher administration on the other.

Many countries now look to Britain for the expertise and the experience of privatisation, the methods for building a bigger stock market, the accent upon public budgetary discipline and the movement towards balance or surplus. The movement looks to the US for much of its political leadership, for the accent on deregulation, for many of the moves on debt restructuring. Tax reform, another vital ingredient in modern economic policies, is a combined effort. The United Kingdom administration pioneered wholesale reform of corporate taxes by cutting out allowances and lowering the rates. The Reagan administration undertook the more difficult task of personal taxation reform and has led the world towards much lower personal direct taxation.

How then do all these ideas fit together? Many economies had reached a difficult stalemate in the 1970s. Low or slow growth characterised much of the advanced world. The pressure on the developing countries was intense following the oil price shock, exacerbated by the difficulties they were experiencing with public sector led growth. The 1970s saw a huge build-up in indebtedness. This process continued into the 1980s, with American banks lending billions of dollars to third world countries, who were unable to spend it on productive assets that could, in turn, earn enough hard currency to repay it. Subsequently, in the 1980s, the American government started taking on ever-increasing burdens of debt, as its public deficit remained obstinately high.[14] The world banking system was unstable throughout the 1970s and early 1980s, threatened by the non-payment of third world debt, troubled by the oil crises and by the huge imbalance between the performances and the payments positions of countries around the world.

The new financial technology is based upon a much stronger belief in private rather than public sector solutions and upon the efficacy of enterprise policies. Only if a developing country can lift its rate of growth does it have a chance of breaking free from the vicious cycle of being short of foreign exchange and of investment and being ever more heavily in debt. Experience around the world shows that private sector enterprise policies are the most likely to trigger an expansion in the rate of growth. Policies that favour low direct taxation, deregulation and the opening up of new opportunities to entrepreneurs are the ones that provide the background against which such an acceleration can occur.[15] In central Africa, entrepreneurship is demonstrating that even in extreme circumstances, where major public sector industrial investments have never worked, privatisation can overcome the difficulties and begin to get some return from plants that had failed as nationalised concerns. John Moore has been successful in both Togo and Benin. Ghana is embarking on a major programme of restructuring and privatisation.

An unexpected boost to the whole popular capitalism movement came with change in the communist bloc. When Mr Gorbachev was first chosen as the new leader of Russia the western press made much of his KGB origins and looked forward to a new era of autocratic darkness. It became apparent some months later from his early speeches that there was at the back of Mr Gorbachev's mind a very different idea. Far from being the heir to Stalin or the other advocates of a very strong central administration, using propaganda and control of information to prevent any freedom of expression or innovation, there was in Mr Gorbachev a yearning to be the new Peter the Great. He travelled widely in the west. He came to see the growing disparities in technology, income and wealth between the west and the Soviet Union and he intuitively understood that he had to do something about it if Russia was not to be relegated to the position of being a third world country with rockets. His response was to adopt parts of the agenda of popular capitalism for his own country. His task makes that of Margaret Thatcher in reviving the UK economy look relatively simple. As Mr Gorbachev surveyed his inheritance he must have realised that with practically everything in state hands and with everyone looking to the central party apparatus for their ideas and views, he had to set about the demolition of almost every element in existing Soviet society.

He was soon speaking about the need for incentive, the need to decentralise enterprises, the need to allow limited experiments with private enterprise alongside state businesses and the need to encourage greater free thought to bring in its wake technical innovation and new approaches to business problems. He had to lead a crusade against drunkenness and idleness; he had to allow some families to benefit from their successes. He had to accept wider disparities of income and wealth to introduce to Russian minds the habit of accumulation and self-help. He even had to countenance the transfer of some activities out of state hands into new forms of cooperative or individual enterprise.

In China something similar is happening. China had already liberalised and effectively privatised much of its agricultural system at the end of the 1960s, following a catastrophic failure of harvests on the state-run farms. In the 1980s, the Chinese administration started to look to industry, where it began to permit a bigger private sector of small entrepreneurs who in their turn were able to invest the surpluses generated by the more successful agricultural sector in limited industrial activity. Both countries are going through monumental changes and both are fascinated by experiments with worker control, with small enterprise, with limited amounts of deregulation and even with privatisation. When changes in China triggered a democratic revolt as well, the ageing government called on the troops to try to reassert the old order.

How far, then, will popular capitalism spread? It is too early to say, for whilst it is a mature movement in the United Kingdom it is still only beginning to put down roots in many other parts of the world. It looks as if it is well set. Most people now find it unavoidable. Few can ignore the fact that those parts of the developing world like Hong Kong and Singapore that have gone furthest in embracing economic liberty have prospered the most. Those which went furthest in organising communist austerity or military-based autocracy as in Russia, Eastern Europe, China, Vietnam and most of Africa, are those experiencing the worst problems in modernising their countries or in some cases in Africa even in feeding their peoples.

History tells people the same story. The period of Dutch success in the seventeenth century was based upon a very open trading system through Amsterdam, embracing a variety of peoples and views and looking outward across the seas to trade with many countries.[16] The period of British economic success in the nineteenth century was based upon the principles of free trade and upon access across all the oceans of the world to many varied societies.[17] The period of American success in the twentieth century was based upon the drive of an entrepreneurial capitalism and more open trading with much of the world.[18] Japanese success has been based in recent years upon the myriad of small businesses freely competing one with another to supply the components to the large trading houses who then send the final product abroad.[19] Japan has been less willing than other great powers to abolish all the non-tariff barriers to its own market, but there is now increasing pressure on it to do so as Japan, by virtue of its economic success, is forced to take on the leading role once enjoyed by the USA. As the twentieth century draws to its close we will see the yen replace the dollar as the world's leading reserve currency and we will see Japanese banks replace American ones as the principal financiers for the third world.

Popular capitalism will continue to develop. There has to be a bigger transfer from debt to equity. This will take place by debt conversion programmes in third world countries and by the construction of bigger and better stock markets capable of routeing risk capital into new enterprises via equity issues. Successful economies will develop venture capital and the role of the family and the small business in generating profits and savings for reinvestment will grow. Some governments will try to halt its advance, especially when it is combined with the demand for democracy, but they will find it increasingly difficult to hold it back.

In South Africa the spread of enterprise may help to erode the artificial barriers of apartheid. The successful deregulation of taxis and minibusses has already created a major black-owned transport industry comprising 60,000 vehicles and representing an important part of total economic output. Partnerships between black and white people are growing rapidly in the service sector, whilst the decontrol of some industrial land is giving more opportunities to black enterprise. Popular capitalism is likely to prove a far more effective corrosive to apartheid than sanctions or diplomacy. The logic of the market is beginning to influence behaviour. Nationalised industries are proving more reactionary in enforcing colour bars than the emerging private sector.

There will be reversals along the way. One of the most worrying is the current surge in leveraged buy outs, especially in the United States. Those mounting large scale takeover bids for existing companies and financing them predominantly from debt are forgetting the rules of gearing. Whilst markets continue to expand and stock markets rise, borrowing a large amount of money to buy assets is the way to get rich. If product markets pause and if stock markets fall it is the way to go bankrupt. There will be cases where new private owners do not succeed or do not conduct themselves properly. The only compensation is that the private sector is usually swifter to change management and direction when things go wrong.

The policy of privatisation continues to spread. The idea of popular capitalism is catching on in all parts of the world. It will be adapted to local circumstances, but it is difficult to see many governments now wishing to embark on nationalisation programmes, whilst it is obvious that many governments will want to continue to narrow the gap between spending and revenues and will see privatisation as a helpful part of this process. Canada, the USA, Germany, Italy, Spain, Portugal, New Zealand, Australia, Singapore, Malaysia, several Latin American and Caribbean countries, Austria and some Scandinavian countries are going to pursue this road. China and Russia will develop their own ways of building bigger private sectors as they desperately seek to modernise their creaking economies. For them the danger is the simultaneous break-up of their empires. There is a danger that Africa will be left out, but then Africa seems to be left out of so much, rent by its own civil wars and conflicts and disrupted by its own autocrats.

More and more people will come to be part owners in the industrial and commercial wealth of their own countries. It is a natural development which all developed countries are experiencing. A rising proportion of home ownership can lead on to a rising proportion of share ownership. As public health and hygiene improve and as people live longer, there is a growing need to have a store of wealth for old age. Whether accumulated through pension funds, family businesses or by direct share holdings, more and more countries are looking to private enterprise-based solutions and to claims on private enterprise as the means of sustaining people in their old age.

The health and wealth of the enterprise economy has never been more central to the development of the world. What is fascinating about the current phase is that economic liberalism is beginning to have an impact upon styles of government. We have been living through an era of simultaneous democratic revolutions. The Far East has led the way with Cory Aquino's revolution in the Philippines, the Burmese troubles, the protest movement of South Korea, the successful transition from dictatorship to democratic elections in Pakistan, and the continuing successful fight of Indian democracy against terrorism. Europe now looks safer for democracy following the mid-1970s changes in Spain and Portugal and the evolution of Turkey in the 1980s. Even in Russia some limited choice is being introduced into elections, although we are a long way from the position where human rights are respected and where rival parties are permitted. In Poland the victors in the election have to avoid claiming too much credit, for fear of a clamp-down by the authorities.

Britain has been in the forefront of many of the changes towards economic liberalism. Some of the most vital parts of the popular capitalist movement have been fashioned in Britain before being exported to the rest of the world. What began haltingly in Britain as a possible means of transforming an ailing public sector has become a central part of a wider economic movement.[20] The other economic reforms in the Thatcher experiment including the abolition of exchange control, the encouragement of free capital movements, the enthusiasm for a free common market between the twelve member states of the European Community, the pursuit of lower direct taxes and the deregulation of several industries have also become important examples for the world. Monetary policy, especially shadowing the DM, has been less successful and few will want to follow Britain's 'counter inflation' strategy of 1987–9. The successful partnership between the US and the UK in the 1980s in offering economic leadership is remarkable. It is a rare example of two countries of very different sizes and powers harnessing themselves together, each one developing complementary aspects of common policies and each one contributing to the wider general aim of extending the boundaries of freedom and economic liberalism worldwide. That is the nature of popular capitalism. It is a radical global movement which will do much to raise the prosperity of the world.

Notes and References

*   John Redwood wrote this piece and approved the proofs before being appointed a government minister. The views are personal ones and do not necessarily represent the position of Her Majesty's Government.
1. *Lloyds Bank Review* (April 1976).
2. *Lloyds Bank Review* (July 1976).
3. Richard Pryke, *Public Enterprise in Practice* (London, 1971).
4. Richard Pryke, *The Nationalised Industries: Policies and Performance since 1968* (Oxford, 1981).
5. The problems of control are set out in John Redwood and John Hatch, *Controlling Public Industries* (Oxford, 1982).
6. The origins and early history of the nationalised industries is best charted in Sir Norman Chester, *The Nationalisation of British Industry 1945–51* (London, 1975).
7. A. Nejad, *The Employee Buy-out of the National Freight Consortium* (London, 1986).
8. As described in John Redwood, *Public Enterprise in Crisis* (Oxford, 1980).
9. See John Redwood, *Equity for Everyman* (Centre for Policy Studies, London, 1986), and *Popular Capitalism* (London, 1987) for this evolution.

10. J. Kay, C. Mayer and D. Thompson (eds.), *Privatisation & Regulation: The UK Experience* (Oxford, 1986), argues for the importance of deregulation rather than privatisation to improve micro performance.
11. White Paper, *Privatising Electricity* (HMSO, 1988).
12. See, for example, William Keyser (ed.), *Public Enterprise in the EEC*, 7 vols (The Netherlands, 1978).
13. Martin Holmes, *The First Thatcher Government* (London, 1985) gives an excellent account of the change of climate in handling industrial relations problems 1979–83.
14. T. Congdon, *The Debt Threat* (Oxford, 1988).
15. Gabriel Roth, *The Private Provision of Public Services in Developing Countires* (World Bank/Oxford 1987) sets out a wide range of examples.
16. A. E. Sayons, 'Le rôle d'Amsterdam dans l'histoire du capitalisme commercial et financier', *Revue Historique*, 183 (1938).
17. Arthur Birnie, *An Economic History of the British Isles* (London, 1961): 271 *passim*.
18. R. B. Nye and J. E. Morpurgo, *The Growth of the USA* (Harmondsworth, 1972): 623 *passim*.
19. See the comment on the structure of the Japanese economy in Andrea Boltho, *Japan: An Economic Survey 1953–73*, Chapter 2: 22ff. and especially the comparative table on scale of manufacturing establishments on 26 which shows how much more concentration on large enterprises there is in the UK than Japan.
20. The arguments about state profligacy as set out in David Galloway, *The Public Prodigals* (London, 1976) are becoming more widely understood.

Part VI
Planning: History, Theory and Practice

13 Has Planning a Future?
John Stevenson

Few concepts have had a rougher ride in recent years than 'Planning'. Across a broad spectrum of policy the idea which contributed so much of the apparently bipartisan consensus on the direction of the economy and the provision of social services has undergone a series of spectacular onslaughts and defeats, some the more significant because self-inflicted. The child of collectivism and progressivism, 'Planning' drew together a wide range of concerns in the economic and social spheres to become something of a vogue word in the post-war consensus and as such the most frequent target in recent years of those who have sought to upturn it. Those, however, with an eye to counter-cyclical movements in opinion may well need to ask whether 'Planning' is not about to reappear on the agenda for many of the reasons it was originally favoured.

The term 'Planning', in its current sense, entered the mainstream of British political vocabulary in the early 1930s with the publication as a supplement to the *Week-End Review* in 1931 of *A National Plan for Great Britain* and the formation of the broadly-based pressure-group Political and Economic Planning (PEP). Drawing support from industrialists like Israel Sieff and Laurence Neil, the banker Basil Blackett, the scientist Julian Huxley, architects and town planners such as Maxwell Fry, Raymond Unwin, and Ernest Simon, academics such as Alexander Cairncross, John Maynard Keynes, and William Beveridge, as well as MPs such as Harold Macmillan and Sir Arnold Wilson, PEP's stated objective was 'the reorganisation on a national basis of the political, economic and social institutions of the country'. Essential to this purpose was a 'National Plan' without which 'this country may go drifting on either towards a sharp crisis which might have revolutionary consequences, or to a dictatorship, or perhaps worse still to gradual decline'. Its General Secretary summed up the thrust of much of its work as being to supersede piecemeal treatment of public policy by coordinated policies founded on 'fact-based' and research-based programmes and reliable decision-making based upon accurate and comprehensive forecasting. As a consequence reports were produced on housing, social services and the health service, the press and the location of industry. Its shorter *Broadsheets*, over 150

233

of which had been produced by the outbreak of the Second World War, sought to stimulate discussion on a wide range of concerns.[1]

PEP had a distinctly technocratic 'feel', attracting most of its members and research groups from managers and those explicitly seen as 'experts' in the field, notably in the strong contingent of architects and town planners contained in its ranks. The Next Five Years Group founded in 1933, although less technocratic in tone, included many of those actively involved in progressive causes between the wars, especially in education and the social services. Its membership included some notable figures in the social policy field, including B. S. Rowntree, H. A. L. Fisher, J. A. Hobson, and William Temple. The proposals of the Next Five Years Group included such things as a National Development Board, greater public investment in housing, the coordination of social services to achieve a 'national minimum', the expansion of secondary education, and town and country planning. Harold Macmillan eventually took charge of its periodical *New Outlook*. The views he expressed in *The Middle Way*, published in 1938, pointing towards a managed economy and the expansion of state welfare services, came close to expressing the essential ingredients of what both PEP and the Next Five Years Group wanted.

Covering a broader range of concerns than any single-issue groups, both PEP and the Next Five Years Group were important precursors of much of the policies and legislation which were to characterise the 1940s. Arthur Marwick has stressed the importance of such groups in fostering the development of 'middle opinion', a progressive consensus which emphasised the need for greater state intervention in both the economic and the social sphere. Liberal improvers, progressive Conservatives and socialists found themselves sharing common ground in the assumption that the state was the appropriate instrument to provide both improved social services and economic performance.[2]

The call for greater state intervention and social control went hand in hand with a faith in a more rational and ordered treatment of policy which found its most characteristic expression in the enthusiasm for 'Planning'. What was significant was the extension of this interest beyond those for whom the concept of centralised planning had always played a significant role. Planning, at least in the form of extensive control of the commanding heights of the economy and their utilisation for the welfare of society at large had traditionally occupied a major place in socialist thinking. By the early 1930s there was widespread admiration for the apparent achievements of the Russian Five Year Plans, particularly in contrast to the experience of the depression after 1929. During the 1930s socialist groups such as the New Fabian Research Bureau, founded almost at the same time as PEP, and a range of socialist thinkers such as G. D. H. Cole, Douglas Jay, Barbara Wooton, Hugh Dalton, and Evan Durbin refined the concept.

But while the socialist interest in planning was important, not least in view of Labour's victory at the polls in 1945, it was the wider vogue for planning which was as significant. What was striking was continued and, indeed, growing faith in scientific solutions expressed by an older generation of progressives, the generation of Rowntree, Beveridge, and Wooton, to which was added the enthusiasm of a new generation coming to awareness in the inter-war years. Dissatisfaction with 'Long Weekend' and with the economic consequences of the depression led a number of groups within and without the major political parties to redefine the economic and social role of government. Many believed in the power of central planning to overcome the failures of the market system. Thus in *Reconstruction* in 1933, Harold Macmillan wrote that 'Planning is forced upon us . . . not for idealistic reasons but because the old mechanism which served us when markets were expanding naturally and spontaneously is no longer adequate when the tendency is in the opposite direction'. Others saw it as the means to advance over a wide range of social issues, provoking a desire for greater 'order and logic in public affairs, a higher degree of co-ordination and control, the adequate analysis of problems and the development of strategies to deal with them'.

In this guise, 'Planning' was not a uniquely left- or right-wing cause. Sir Oswald Mosley shared with socialists like G. D. H. Cole a profound contempt for the 'muddle' of existing affairs: both sought to inaugurate a complete reformation of economy and society, one which both would have regarded as more efficient. 'Efficiency' was a key word, for it gave planning an appeal to the growing professional and technical cadres of managers, social scientists, economists, educationalists, architects and town planners. Viewed in this perspective, the planning enthusiasm of the 1930s and 1940s represented the fusion of the still vital forces of optimism and social concern with the scientific and technocratic spirit of the twentieth century. Characterised by a commitment to a greater role for the state, an almost explicit centralisation of control, and a faith in 'experts', the planning movement was poised at the end of the 1930s for its greatest opportunity on the eve of the Second World War. What has been called in the 1930s a 'Young Man's consensus' was about to become what Paul Addison has called 'Attlee's consensus', a bipartisan acceptance of a partly nationalised mixed economy and a greatly expanded state welfare sector.

But, as events were to demonstrate, 'Planning' proved a somewhat ambiguous ingredient. In some areas it was seen as an end in itself, notably in the field of town and environmental planning, in others the means by which changes should be brought about, essentially through well-thought-out rationalisation and reorganisation, or more simply as an almost totemistic commitment to the future – a 'Plan' was the only means of ensuring that desirable social and economic changes could be brought about. For some 'Planning' meant no more than control, for others it meant a genuine attempt to map out a long-term strategy, whether economic, social, or anything else and sticking to it at whatever cost. As Elizabeth Durbin has pointed out, even the socialist economists of the 1930s, while sharing a belief in the power of central planning to overcome the failures of the market system and to usher in a new age of prosperity and redistribution of income and wealth, also disagreed profoundly on the nature of planning and on the appropriate use of economics for socialist planning.[3]

There were also very different views between socialists and non-socialists about the purposes of government economic planning, although many programmes which called for planning represented an uneasy alliance between them. Thus the Next Five Years Group's first manifesto was signed by influential Labour leaders, including Bevin, Lansbury and Dalton. The Next Five Years Group's Final Report was based on two fundamental principles, the planned reorganisation of British industry and, illustrating the broader thrust of planning into areas beyond the economic, an end to war by collective action. In these early efforts the rationale for government intervention was based on microeconomic efficiency considerations. It was only after the publication of Keynes's *The General Theory* that macroeconomic policies were incorporated, as in Macmillan's *The Middle Way*. For Liberals and Conservatives the primary purpose of these programmes was to revitalise capitalism not to replace it; indeed progressive Tories were explicit that their intention was to save Britain from socialism. For many socialist economists, however, planning represented an antithesis to capitalism. In *Economic Planning* in 1935 G. D. H. Cole argued that the fatal disequilibrium in capitalism could be corrected only by planning and that 'planned capitalism' was a contradiction in terms. Others were more flexible, seeing in the adoption of planning within a mixed economy a significant step towards socialism. Hence it was possible for socialists to share some common ground on the desirability of planning as part of a transitional stage. This was facilitated by the distinct shades of emphasis amongst socialists about what planning actually meant in practice. Evan Durbin saw economic planning as being primarily a 'principle of administration', a technique for organising the economic system, not a blue-print with specific objectives. In his view there was to be no 'inflexible budget of production' but 'guidance' on the larger questions of output, prices, investment and costs through which socialist planning would surpass capitalism's economic record by ensuring full employment and socially efficient allocation within – and this was important to Durbin – a still democratic polity.[4]

But planners of all kinds prior to 1939 were far from the reins of economic and political power. The only area in which 'Planning' was being put into practice was in its original field of town and country planning. Although usually considered separately from the field of economic planning, in Britain architects and town planners were prominent in the pressure groups which advocated 'Planning' in general. The rebuilding of the physical environment to create a better world was already firmly on the agenda by the 1930s as the largest slum clearance and housebuilding programme ever undertaken, involving almost three-quarters of a million houses, gave the first opportunities for local authorities to rebuild substantial parts of the urban fabric. To the more ambitious, the 'Garden City' was the favoured model, seen in Welwyn Garden City founded in 1920 and rapidly expanded by 1939, and Wythenshawe outside Manchester where a 'satellite city' was built under the aegis of Sir Ernest Simon, one of the most dynamic advocates of slum clearance and wholesale rebuilding in the pre-war years. Much of the new housing was built in a rather debased version of the 'garden suburb' as extensive estates on the fringes of the main towns and cities or as satellite estates at some distance from the main conurbation. At Speke, near Liverpool, Solihull and Longbridge outside Birmingham, and Becontree outside London, large new council estates were created which were almost miniature towns in themselves. They offered the first experience in Britain of planned environments since the select group of model towns built by industrialists before 1914. For municipal authorities and town planners they represented a genuine hope for a better

future in which a re-shaped physical environment would abolish not
only the slum house but also the slum tenant. The faith in the
therapeutic value of an improved physical environment to cure the
ills of industrial society, to solve or at least minimise squalor,
crime, and ill-health and to create a healthier and more respectable
population remained powerful forces at both municipal and national
level.

It was no accident that town planning, literally building the 'New
Jerusalem', came to occupy a position as the flagship of the new
enthusiasm for planning. By the late 1930s, as the international
modern movement began to capture the imaginations of younger
architects and planners, the language of planning was increasingly
infused with the same technocratic and large-scale ambitions which
animated planning enthusiasts in other fields. Although Planners
looked to the United States for radical solutions to traffic management
offered by major urban highway schemes and clover-leaf flyovers,
European examples were increasingly favoured for their housing and
town planning projects such as the large blocks of workers' flats built
in Austria and Germany. For example, in 1935 Sir Ernest Simon
looked forward to the demolition of some 80,000 houses in Manchester
to be replaced by 'modern houses or flats' and offering a 'splendid
opportunity for replanning the central area on the best modern
lines' – Simon looked to the example of the 'better planned German
cities'. Similarly in the Liverpool of the 1930s Patrick Abercrombie
from the Architecture Department at the University advised the
City's Housing Committee:

> That brilliant Frenchman, M. Le Corbusier, has proposed that we
> should boldly use lifts and so emancipate ourselves from the three
> or four storey block. It would be interesting if some English town
> would attempt this experiment, creating a lofty tenement tower in
> a central park.[5]

But although plans proliferated in the years up to the Second
World War, governments and local authorities had neither the
resources nor the will to carry out redevelopment on the scale
envisaged by either economists or town planners. The Second World
War broke this impasse. The destruction of thousands of acres of
property in the blitz turned the 'rebuilding of Britain' from a vaguely
desirable ideal into a practical necessity. Hardly had the dust
settled on the bomb damage when ambitious schemes for large-scale
rebuilding were pouring off the drawing boards of architects and

planners. The government provided encouragement, just as in the First World War, for the theme of a new Britain arising from the rubble was a powerful weapon in maintaining civilian morale. In October 1940 Sir John Reith was appointed Minister of Works, not only to supervise the repair of bomb damage, but also to supervise plans for rebuilding the cities. The result was a series of plans commissioned from some of the most eminent pre-war architects and planners for rebuilding bombed cities such as Glasgow, Exeter, Hull, and Coventry. But this government-backed programme for rebuilding the cities was only the standard bearer for a new planned future in other spheres. The planning which was seen as essential to Britain's war effort to achieve the most efficient use of manpower and resources was now to be deployed for the creation of a better world when peace came. In *Picture Post*'s 'A Plan for Britain', published on 4 January 1941, when a commitment to wholesale post-war reconstruction was being pressed by a number of groups, the architect Maxwell Fry saw Planning as required in every sphere – summed up in the phrase 'The New Britain must be planned' – plans were required for every aspect of life, industry, employment, social welfare, education, transport and leisure. Planning therefore was to play a central part in the creation of the 'New Jerusalem' which was to arise in post-war Britain.

The lessons of wartime reached apparent fulfilment in the legislation of the Coalition and Labour Governments of the 1940s. The comprehensive overhaul of national insurance, the setting up of the National Health Service, the New Towns Act, and the creation of the National Parks all in their different ways breathed the spirit of rationalisation and reorganisation which had been foreshadowed in the reports of groups like PEP in the 1930s. At the most crucial level of the conduct of the economy, the adoption of planning seemed close to fulfilment. There was a commitment from the White Paper of 1944 to maintaining a high level of employment, implying a degree of government intervention and economic management which came close to fulfilling the ideas articulated in the late 1930s by a broad swathe of 'middle opinion'. Moreover, the post-war Labour Governments inherited one of the most thoroughly controlled economies of the combatant nations. The wartime national emergency which had given the government enormous powers over almost every aspect of life in Britain was followed by the 'economic Dunkirk' of the immediate post-war period in which the government's control over the economy was, if anything, intensified.[6] The operation of a virtual siege economy in the austerity years after 1945 put a premium on the role of the government in allocating raw materials, directing production into exports, and suppressing home consumption by tight economic management.

The late 1940s were, on the face of it, the apogee of planning in twentieth-century Britain. It had not only the support of a triumphant Labour Government but a following wind from many who had experienced the effectivness of wartime control. Sir Oliver Franks in his lectures to the London School of Economics in 1947, published as *Central Planning and Control in War and Peace*, was in no doubt that the lessons abandoned after the First World War would have to be learnt from the Second. He saw Britain's trading position as precarious in the extreme. To survive in peace Britain would have to adopt the methods which had proved successful in harnessing the productive potential of the economy in wartime: 'My reflections have led me to conclude that some form of central planning and control is inevitable'.[7]

Franks outlined what he called 'a general plan for the working of the national economy' to be drawn up by 'experts, statisticians, economists and administrators', but with the crucial allocative decisions taken by Ministers. Franks's proposals were not very far from the real experience of the direction of the post-war economy, but they had a more strategic component than anything carried out by the Attlee governments. Just at the moment when the idea of strategic planning of the economy, with an emphasis on its long-term capacity to compete in world markets, was most openly being advocated, the government was engaged in a hectic battle for economic survival. For better or worse, ideas of long-term economic restructuring were pushed to one side in the almost desperate search for a return to economic viability. Any hopes that the post-war years would see a major effort to modernise the industrial structure of Britain were dashed as existing capacity was worked flat out to meet the demand for exports. The 'ailing giants' of the interwar years, iron and steel, textiles, coalmining, and shipbuilding were actually recruiting labour, not shedding it. Government 'planning' amounted to little more in practice than the application of Keynesian nostrums and the continuation of wartime controls rather than the application of thoroughgoing plans for the reconstruction of the industrial base. In fact, the central feature of Labour's economic 'plans' was nationalisation, and of a particular kind, through the public corporation, which changed little more than nominal ownership. The

nationalisation programme was soon to be regarded as failing to
inaugurate any new thinking about the direction of the economy as
a whole, still less anything approaching an industrial strategy for the
post-war world. The proposal put forward by Keynes and others for
an 'Economic General Staff' responsible for planning policy was
never implemented; nor was Franks's National Plan. Although
some attempts to inject a more strategic element into economic
management were made in aftermath of the fuel crisis of 1947, in
practice they went little further than attempts at greater coordination.[8]
Even at its high tide in the late 1940s, planning in the economic
sphere was more apparent than real.

In the era after the fall of the Attlee Government, the long post-
war boom stilled for a time the impetus behind planning. In contrast
to the crisis years of the depression an expanding world economy
seemed to render demands for planning futile and unnecessary. For
some, certainly, experiments with planning abroad still had an
attraction. France, not the USSR, was now the favoured model and
its *dirigiste* state planning was much admired, not least by the French
themselves – according to J. R. Boudeville in 1966 the French Plan
was 'the best rationalisation of the capitalist system yet arrived at'.
But the centralisation of French planning was usually too much for
Anglo-Saxon proponents to stomach. For example, in one of the
French Plans the administrators were actually forbidden to visit the
regions with which they were concerned in case they became biased![9]
This was far from what British commentators intended when they
called for plans for the regions.

But as disquiet grew about Britain's economic performance in the
early 1960s, planning was still part of the armoury with which the
Labour Party sought to grapple with Britain's economic problems.
A fresh generation of Labour leaders went in search of the Holy
Grail of economic planning. In truth, the spectre had never vanished.
Richard Crossman, for one, was lamenting in 1965 that the opportunities of the post-war era had been missed: 'How much more humane
and imaginative our post-war reconstruction would have proved if
government departments had been invigorated by an influx of experts
with special knowledge'.[10] Harold Wilson's new technocratic image
for the Labour Party provided the impetus for George Brown's
National Plan of 1965 which represented an attempt to recapture the
ground perceived to have been lost since 1945. Blown off-course by
the economic squalls of the mid-1960s and out of date almost before
it was drawn up, Brown's National Plan was more of an epitaph than

a resurrection.

Moreover, just as this belated attempt to revive planning in the economic sphere proved fruitless, disillusion was growing with the major area in which planning had been implememted, the rebuilding of Britain's towns and cities. As well as the schemes to rebuild badly blitzed cities like Coventry, Plymouth, and Exeter, and an ambitious programme of new towns, political demands for more housing and relatively full municipal and government coffers in the 1950s and 1960s unleashed a massive spate of clearance and rebuilding. As large tracts of town centres were razed to build urban motorways and new shopping developments and much of the old, familiar townscape was bulldozed away, 'Planning' for most people had less to do with George Brown and the national economy than with what appeared a headlong race to change the face of every town and city in the British Isles. The reaction against the planners, when it came, was plain. Tower blocks and the new brutalist architecture were increasingly condemned for exacerbating the social problems they had been intended to solve. There was widespread unease at the remoteness of planning from the practicalities of urban life, as well as the threat redevelopment schemes offered to valued areas of towns and cities.

Indications of the turn of opinion lay in the defeat of schemes for the redevelopment of the Covent Garden area in London and after a long battle the final defeat of the Christ Church Meadow Scheme in Oxford, a product of the post-war enthusiasm for facilitating traffic flow at the expense of local amenity. The collapse of the Ronan Point tower block in London in 1968 following a gas explosion was one of those chance happenings which became symbolic of a whole era. Behind the subsequent narrow concern with some of the new building techniques lay a more generalised concern that the planners and architects had got it wrong. Trust in 'experts', in the best modern practice, took a severe blow, reinforced by the economic problems of the 1970s. Soon the tower blocks were tumbling to deliberate not accidental explosions, urban ring roads lay unfinished and grandiose city plans, like that for Liverpool, gathered dust.

By the 1980s the disillusion with what the planners had done had bitten deep. On almost every front, including the one in which planning had been given the greatest scope, it seemed an idea which belonged to the past – to an interventionist and collectivist era, now to be buried once and for all. It was symptomatic of the prevailing sense of disillusion that even when the Labour Party restated its commitment to planning in the election manifestoes of 1983 and 1987 it did so with all the conviction of someone trying to breathe life into a ghost. In spite of the central role which planning had occupied in almost every critique of *laissez-faire* fifty years earlier, proponents of an alternative economic strategy in the 1980s found one of the principal planks in their platform distinctly rotten.

It would be unwise, however, to regard the idea as dead. For one thing, in spite of the battering which post-war planners and architects have taken since the 1970s it would be quite misleading to represent their influence as finished. Planning for environmental and aesthetic purposes has been absorbed into the structure of local government where it retains considerable control over development. Although government may tilt the balance of forces more towards free enterprise, as in the case of the London Docklands development, the structure of planning remains in place. Other results of the high tide of planning, like the Green Belts, while subject to pressure from free-market forces, have by their very existence produced vested interests in their maintenance. Few, in an increasingly conservationist climate, wish to see a return to the unregulated sprawl and endless 'ribbon development' which had been so prominent before the Second World War. Moreover, for every ugly tower block there were scores of low-rise estates of council houses which, if far from perfect, none the less represented an improvement in living standards for many slum dwellers. The New Towns, one of the most ambitious commitments of the planners of the 1940s to relieve conditions in the cities by providing new, overspill communities on green field sites, were a largely untrumpeted success – and widely admired abroad. What conditions in London would now be like without its 'green girdle' and ring of satellite towns, a product of the Greater London Plan of the 1940s, serves to remind us that the successes of planning have been less loudly praised than its evident failures.

In that sense, the planners of the post-war era won part of their battle. What also remains striking is the ability of the concept to attract fresh adherents as new problems appear or old ones recur. One of the key elements in attracting people to the idea of planning between the wars was the growth of road traffic and urban congestion. Increasingly, it looks as though these problems are coming once again to the top of the political agenda. On almost every side there is talk about the need to take strategic decisions about the transport system in the south-east, in other words to formulate a plan. It will be irony indeed if the success of a self-consciously free-market economy in the south-east results in the need to create a plan for London reminiscent of the days of Abercrombie and the LCC.

The much-publicised problems of London and the congested south-east also by implication resurrect the old issue of regional planning. As in other spheres, even a government committed to *laissez-faire* has inherited and operated a complex system of regional aid and subsidy. No-one, to my mind, seriously contemplates its complete abandonment. This raises a question which it is easier to speculate about than to answer definitively: the extent to which a Britain more fully integrated with Europe will, in fact, cease to regard its problems within a national context. To a genuine free-marketeer, nothing could be more absurd than pumping subsidies into declining regions. If market forces encourage industry and services to cluster in south-east England, near to Europe and the Channel Tunnel, why not allow them to do so? Moreover if market forces suggest that British companies ought to set up their new factories or move existing ones to the other side of the Channel what economic logic can oppose them? The answer, of course, is none. The arguments against such a course are political and social. Economic nationalism continues and, one suspects, will continue to cut across commitment to the unfettered operation of the market; so will the political and social consequences of allowing such a policy complete free rein. One suspects that the day is long distant when a British Prime Minister will publicly advocate giving no help to declining regions, welcome the relocation of factories by British companies on the other side of the Channel, or praise the success of the French, Germans or whoever in winning the competition for the siting of some Japanese or Korean plant. Free markets have their limits and they have a remarkable habit of ending at the coastline of Britain.

It might be argued that a certain degree of economic nationalism is inevitable, even after 1992. Governments are, in the end, elected nationally. But there are wider implications to this. One trump card economic planners have always had to play against free marketeers is security of supply for national considerations – defence-related industry is an obvious example. But will Britain after 1992 want to pursue policies which will still speak the language of economic nationalism? Clearly current government policy is predicated upon producing a British economy fit to compete against all comers. But there is no inevitability that economic, geographic, and social factors will favour Britain's economic viability opposed to other parts of Europe, still less the rest of the world over the long term. Perhaps we had better start planning after all.

Notes and References

1. See J. Pinder (ed.), *Fifty Years of Political and Economic Planning* (London, 1981): 6–27.
2. A. Marwick, 'Middle Opinion in the Thirties: Planning, Progress and Political Agreement', *English Historical Review*, 79 (1964): 285–98.
3. E. Durbin, *New Jerusalems: The Labour Party and the Economics of Democratic Socialism* (London, 1985): 266.
4. Durbin, *New Jerusalems*: 270.
5. Council of Social Service, *Liverpool and the Housing Problem: a collection of articles which have appeared in the Liverpool Quarterly* (Liverpool, 1936): 92. I am grateful for this reference to Mr R. J. M. Horrocks.
6. See C. Barnett, *The Adudit of War: the Illusion and Reality of Britain as a Great Nation* (London, 1986): 55–62, 265–75. Barnett, in my view, overestimates the room to manoeuvre possessed by the Attlee Governments: see my review in *Historical Journal*, 30 (1987): 504–8.
7. O. Franks, *Central Planning and Control in War and Peace* (London, 1947): 33.
8. See A. Marwick, *Britain in the Century of Total War: War, Peace and Social Change, 1900–1967* (London, 1968): 336–43; Barnett, *The Audit of War*: 265–75.
9. Cited in G. Hallett, P. Randall, and E. G. West, *Regional Policy For Ever?* (London, 1973): 14.
10. R. H. S. Crossman, 'The lessons of 1945', in P. Anderson *et al.*, *Towards Socialism* (London, 1965): 155.

14 Three Myths of Government*
Oliver Letwin

Most politicians are like children playing at Pooh-sticks: they drop an idea into the water, creating a momentary ripple, and then watch it carried mercilessly on by the larger flow. It is only occasionally that one of the children turns out to be a visionary civil engineer who leaves off Pooh-sticks and attempts instead to dam or direct the stream. The problem for analysts of the political scene, observing briefly a change in the direction of the water, is to determine whether it is merely a ripple about to be carried away or a genuine diversion.

To judge by John Stevenson's argument,[1] Thatcherism is no more than a ripple. The grand flow, as Stevenson portrays it, is carrying us towards rational planning by government. Particular problems may have afflicted previous attempts at planning, but support for a plan will again emerge once the brief moment of Thatcherite *laissez-faire* has passed.

As an analysis, this may or may not prove right. It would be a rash man who prophesied with confidence that ten years of Thatcherism had put paid to the mania for planning. But the analysis nevertheless raises the question, why – if state planning has not worked well in the past – does it remain on the agenda for the future? The answer to this puzzling question lies in the attitude which modern western man, whether consciously or unconsciously, takes towards the state. Cynicism about politicians as people is as prevalent as it is naive; but accompanying this low view of the elected representative is a more touching, and equally naive, faith in the institution of government. Planning by the state remains attractive, despite its past failures, because the western liberal democratic state is seen as a GOOD THING. And this view of the state as a GOOD THING is based – above all – on three prevalent myths: that the state is the beneficent provider of services, that it is morally purer than the private entrepreneur, and that it is omniscient.

THE MYTH OF SERVICE

It is fashionable to describe many activities of government as 'services'. We hear not only about the 'Public Service', the 'Armed Services' and the 'Civil Service', which involves service *to* the state, but also the 'National Health Service', the 'Education Service' and the 'Refuse Service' which are said to involve the provision of a service *by* the state. Politicians use these terms; but they are not alone: civil servants, journalists, academics and others all participate. This is not just an accident of nomenclature. Many people think of government – both central and local – as a provider of services. Indeed, political speeches frequently take this for granted: they assume, without argument, that a service is being provided and discuss only the problems of providing it more efficiently, more cheaply or more lavishly. How and why this description of government as a service arose remains mysterious. But it is certain that, in this case, *tout comprendre* would not be *tout pardonner*. The description of the government's activities as 'services' is a myth.

Like most potent myths, it contains more than a grain of truth. There is an obvious sense in which public medical care, education and refuse collection are services. They are things which people regard as benefits, and for which they would, under most circumstances, be willing to pay. They have little in common with governmental activities such as the administration of justice or the defence of the realm; they are more like private sector activities such as the provision of private education, private health and private cleaning.

But the initial plausibility of the description belies the reality – as is made clear by an amusing Freudian slip. The bodies responsible for providing the so-called 'public education service' are not described as education 'companies' or education 'agencies' or even as education 'managers', but rather as education 'authorities'. Similarly, the health 'service' is run by health 'authorities', and the refuse 'service' is run by refuse 'authorities'. This nomenclature is a slip; but it is by no means an accident. On the contrary, it gives the game away.

A genuine 'service', of the sort to be found in the private sector, is something that people want, and is provided in the way that people want. As a result, it does not have to be imposed upon them by an 'authority'. The public 'services', on the other hand, *do* need to be provided by an 'authority' because – although they are often wanted – they are not always given to people in the way that is wanted.

The principal characteristic of these public 'services' is that they are to some degree compulsory. The authority that delivers them is typically given a statutory duty to administer them and a raft of accompanying statutory powers. The authority typically has, either directly or indirectly, both the power to tax and the power to enforce provision on certain classes of person. Compulsory education for those aged between five and sixteen is the most obvious example, but similar provisions exist under the Mental Health Act and many other pieces of legislation.

This confusion between authority and service is one of the main engines of the belief in the state as a GOOD THING, because it undermines traditional fears about the aggrandisement of political power. For centuries, the possessor of authority has been feared and distrusted as a potential tyrant. But the provider of services is in a different position: he is someone whom free men need not fear, because he is no more than a servant of his customers. When modern western politicians and administrators describe themselves, and to some extent genuinely think of themselves, as providers of a service rather than as authorities, they half persuade themselves and others that plans for the nation drawn up by them will not threaten individual freedom in the way that a blatant expansion of authority would clearly do. A proposal to increase the effectiveness of the health 'service' by constructing a plan for community health does not sound nearly so threatening to the liberal consciousness as a proposal to increase the effectiveness of the policy by building ten new police stations.

But the myth of service is not only a negative force undermining constitutional defences; it also exerts a positive influence, encouraging people to believe that an extension of planning by the state will benefit them. If private taxi companies propose to offer a better 'service' by multiplying their activities, we all rejoice; it is therefore difficult to explain why people should take a different attitude when public agencies propose to offer a better service by constructing a new plan. This spurious but potent analogy of 'service' makes voters welcome planning by the state, even when this leads to increases in the power and scope of authorities that they would otherwise be inclined to fear.

The misdescription of authorities as providers of a 'service' also gives public agencies a powerful rhetorical defence against their enemies. If someone suggests to politicians and administrators that they might withdraw from planning some aspect of our lives and hand over to private entrepreneurs who are adept at providing what the customer wants without the need for a plan, they are in a position to feign amazement: how, they ask, could such a private entrepreneur, bereft of a plan, be expected to fulfil the statutory duties or to administer the statutory powers of an authority? Or if an individual complains that the public 'service' is not giving him what he, as a supposed beneficiary of the 'service' requires, then the public managers ask in return whether the individual has forgotten that their responsibility as an authority is to the plan, which looks to the interests of the 'community as a whole' rather than to the particular whim of a given citizen. Or again, if the administrators are asked why the provision of the 'service' is in some respect inefficient, they are likely to reply that the plan, and the statutory responsibilities which it fulfils, impose upon them difficulties and costs which no mere private entrepreneur would encounter.

In short, the myth of service yields endless opportunities for deceptions and self-deceptions which can help to generate and protect the image of the state as a GOOD THING – a locus of beneficence and good sense, and hence a suitable source for a national plan.

THE MYTH OF PURITY

The myth of service is not, however, the only confusion that helps the state to be seen as a GOOD THING. The myth of purity is almost as important. The two myths are complementary: the first plays on the *similarity* between public and private 'services'; the second plays on the *dissimilarity*.

The accusation of 'impurity' is constantly levelled against private businessmen who attempt to replace rational planning by entrepreneurial competition. Private hospital cleaners, for example, are described as unscrupulous 'con men', out to grab huge profits at the expense of their workforce, the patients and the nation. Public hospital cleaners, by contrast, are regarded as rather charmingly lazy, or even – according to some, more overblown, accounts – selfless heroes in pursuit of cleanliness without earthly reward. This message – the contrast between the despicable impurity of the profit motive and the noble purity of the rationally planned public service – is constantly driven home by public service unions, health service employees and managers, and politicians of several varieties. Even those of us who are disinclined to believe the accusation sometimes experience a nagging suspicion that there is truth in it.

The supposed contrast between selfless excellence of planned public 'services' and the greedy aggressiveness of the unplanned private entrepreneur is at least as much a matter of persons as of corporate bodies. The public servant (as opposed to the elected politician) is, for all his admitted eccentricities, generally painted as an amiable and morally upright character: not too rich, personally disinterested, impartial and apolitical in his judgements, next to incorruptible; at worst, a figure of fun, at best an almost archiepiscopal figure charged with the realisation on earth of the divinely ordered plan. The private businessman, on the other hand, is painted as, at best, a sharp operator and at worst an unscrupulous villain: tainted by wealth, driven by love of profit, seeking whatever outcome achieves his ends and protects his species, if not financially corrupt then at least spiritually so. These caricatures are not accepted everywhere; but they have sufficient currency to be plausible – indeed, to make one wonder whether they are true.

And the suspicion that they may be true lingers despite the manifest evidence that they are radically false. We all too easily forget the private bodies whose existence contradicts the myth – the schools, the hospitals, the building societies, the voluntary associations, the charities, the learned societies, the foundations and institutions – the plethora of private activities which, despite the absence of a plan, are guided by motives other than profit and are corporately at least as selfless, at least as excellent, as the public agencies. Then, of course, one remembers that the people who work, not only in these unplanned, non-profitable private enterprises but also in unplanned standard joint-stock companies, are for the most part not too rich, often personally disinterested, usually reasonably impartial, uncorrupted, apolitical family men and women, on the whole very similar to their counterparts in the public domain. And one recalls, too, that the entrepreneur himself, the private investor, the director receiving share options, who is indeed guided to a great extent by the search for profit, is thereby induced to attempt to satisfy not the requirements of a plan, but the wants, the whims, the wildest expectations of his customers, actual and potential; he is under a stronger pressure to satisfy the recipient than any public servant – a pressure stronger than any plan can create.

At the same time, one recalls that the lack of financial profit in the public 'services' does not guarantee the personal purity of public servants. Indeed, it is an interesting irony that amongst the most frequently cited cases of *private* corruption are those in which the private company or individual has been seeking some *public* favour by means of explicitly or implicitly bribing a public official: where there is no legitimate profit, there may still be *illegitimate* profit. And even when financial probity is absolute – as it undoubtedly is throughout most of the public service – politicians and officials may nevertheless engage in all the self-seeking practices to which ambitious people in private life are prone: empire-building, the concealment of error, attempts to capture the credit for other people's achievements – these vices do not suddenly drop away at the door to the Ministry or the threshold of the public hospital.

The representation of public agencies as centres of a selfless excellence unmatched in private life is, therefore, myth rather than reality. But it has nevertheless been a powerful myth, with a firm place in the socialist consciousness. Herbert Morrison made his view of the mythological ideal quite clear in *Socialisation and Transport*

> The public corporation must . . . have a different atmosphere at its Board table from that of a shareholders' meeting; its Board and its officers must regard themselves as the high custodians of the public interest.[2]

And Bevin talked of this ideal as if it were already reality. In his speech on the 1944 Employment White Paper, he unambiguously derived his boundless optimism about the benefits to be derived from growth of government's power from a sense of the virtues of those in whose hands the task lay:

> I conclude by commending the Motion to the House, with this word: it is not final, it is pioneering . . . it is introducing, as against automatic control, conscious direction. It places a great responsibility upon Parliament and upon the Government of the day, and the integrity of its action: to have in its hands the direction of the economic life of the country as it wills, is not something to be taken lightly. But having taken on that responsibility, then with the great standard that has been built up in our Civil Service, with the standard of our public conduct in dealing with these affairs, and with our great traditions in public life, both local and national, we can with safety start out on this road this week and begin to say that we have left the old vexed disease of unemployment behind us.[3]

That is, surely, the *locus classicus* of the myth of purity. The 'conscious direction' that a national plan appears to make possible is

certain to be the right direction because it is supported by the
'integrity', the 'standard of our public conduct', the 'great standard'
of our Civil Service and our 'great traditions in public life'. The
integrity of private individuals, the standard of private conduct, the
great standards of private schools, the great tradition of private
philanthropy are all forgotten, as is every failure in the public realm:
the plan will be the only perfect method of government because it
will be invented and operated by perfect public servants.

THE MYTH OF OMNISCIENCE

There is, however, an even more powerful excuse for planning than
either the myth of service or the myth of purity – the myth of
omniscience. This third myth is deeply ingrained in political science.
Witness, for example, the standard textbook account of modern
government, given by Max Weber:

> Bureaucratic administration means fundamentally the exercise of
> control on the basis of knowledge. This is the feature of it which
> makes it specifically rational. This consists on the one hand in
> technical knowledge which, by itself, is sufficient to ensure it a
> position of extraordinary power. But in addition to this, bureau-
> cratic organisations, or the holders of power who make use of
> them, have the tendency to increase their power still further by
> the knowledge growing out of experience in the service. For they
> acquire through the conduct of office a special knowledge of facts
> and have available a store of documentary material peculiar to
> themselves.[4]

This account is accepted not only by large numbers of academics,
journalists and ordinary people, but also by many (if not most)
officials and ministers. All sides imagine that government is a machine
primed with huge amounts of useful knowledge that give it immense
power and capacity to plan rationally. Inspired by this image of
government, many journalists and other well-meaning persons consider that one of their main tasks is to 'open up' government by
demolishing the barriers of secrecy. They imagine that they can
thereby prevent plots that are formed within closed doors and that
become *faits accomplis* before the public learns about them. And
they believe that the problem is to find ways of achieving such
'opening up' without unduly compromising either the frankness of

discussion within government or the effectiveness of the nation in dealing with its enemies. This is indeed a real problem, which needs to be thought about. But it has drawn attention away from an even bigger problem. In reality, it is the government that suffers from a lack of information.

For one thing, ministers are seldom, if ever, in a position to observe what really takes place in any of the organisations that they control. The activities of the observer inevitably alter the nature of what is observed: as soon as a Secretary of State announces his intention of visiting a hospital, school or factory, the place is both literally and metaphorically repainted. And when ministers attempt to compensate for this by asking 'people in the know' to come and speak to them 'frankly and openly', they almost inevitably end up by speaking to assorted dignitaries, committee-men and self-publicists who have little or nothing to do with the everyday running of whichever institution is under investigation. Nor is the position much better for senior officials. They, too, cause changes in the places they visit; and they too almost always converse with people other than those engaged in the real work of any enterprise.

Another difficulty is that the division of labour has been carried to an extraordinary extent in government. One can find several different departments that have a part to play in almost any major decision, and within any given department several different branches and divisions will almost certainly be dealing with different aspects of the same problem. This is neither an accident nor the result of a deliberate plot. Rather, it arises from the fact that ministers' concerns constantly shift, and different accumulations of expertise have to be brought to bear as they do so; consequently, a group of officials set up for one purpose one day will be called upon to contribute to some quite other task the next day. The result is that no one is quite sure who is doing what, when.

The chains of command in government are immensely long and complex. A decision emanating from a senior level, even if it is accurately represented in the minutes at the time when it is made, may well be misunderstood by colleagues who were not present and who did not fully understand the context within which the meeting took place. By the time the decision reaches the junior official who is actually responsible for drafting the relevant document, it will have been re-interpreted by a very large number of deputy secretaries, under-secretaries and assistant secretaries in all the departments whose ministers were present at the relevant meeting. The chance of the drafting official having either a clear or a correct view of the real meaning of the decision is therefore slight, particularly because he will not – in a typical case – have met any of the ministers present at the meeting for more than a few minutes in his entire life.

A busy official does not have time for more than a cursory examination of the day's press. He is typically surrounded by colleagues who deal with a relatively narrow range of topics similar to his own; and they too cannot spare the time for much mere journalism. They can therefore be taken wholly unawares by developments which any moderately informed news-hound would have picked up without trying. With luck, their minister may be in a somewhat better position. But even he may find it next to impossible to obtain accurate descriptions of rapidly changing events. During a strike, for example, the attitudes and activities of shop stewards, workers and managers are frequently obscure or incorrectly perceived.

This lack of information is not taken seriously for the single reason that most of the relevant people do not really believe that there is such a lack: they are, to some degree, taken in by the myth of omniscience. And one can all too easily see how such conceptions can make each extention of public control appear sensible, rational, level-headed, the sort of thing that 'anyone in their right mind' would prefer. A government armed with the myth of its own supposedly limitless knowledge is inclined to believe, and leads others to believe, that it alone is capable of 'controlling' and 'catering' for 'demand', of 'coordinating programmes', of 'planning for the nation's future'. The Weberian myth of the omniscient bureaucrat makes the helter-skelter of the marketplace seem an inconceivably slapdash method of conducting businesses – one that cannot possibly produce sensible, predictable, coordinated efforts. The inevitable conclusion must be, in the words of Flanders and Swann: 'all we need, all we need, is a comprehensive system of national planning'.

That was, indeed, what it all came to. On 14 September 1965, George Brown issued a genuine National Plan. As is well known, the Plan did not prove to be quite such an advance as was originally hoped. It was unceremoniously abandoned within a few months of the publication. The reasons for its failure are instructive; above all, its authors lacked the information that they imagined they possessed, and on which the scheme was meant to be based.

Part of the problem was a lack of information on the part of the relevant ministers about the intentions of other ministers in the same government. Writing some years later, George Brown was candid about this:

> One of the assumptions we made was that the Plan would take
> priority and other policies pursued by the Government would be
> made to fit its provisions. In the event this was not done.[5]

But the major difficulty was the inadequacy of the external economic
information needed for the Plan. This was not for want of trying. An
inter-departmental committee sent out a questionnaire, seeking
information from industry about the additional jobs and investment
that would be required to achieve 25 per cent growth between
1965 and 1970. In practice, however, the industrialists (or rather,
bureaucrats in various trade associations) were quite unable to
provide accurate estimates of the growth that would take place in
the absence of intervention, and the planners' calculations of the
measures necessary to stimulate the desired level of growth were
therefore based on shaky foundations.

The government's supposition that it could quickly collect adequate
information for its National Plan, and its subsequent failure to do
so, illustrates both sides of the myth of omniscience: the naive
confidence and the sad truth. But not all the truth is sad. Some of
the evidence about the amateurism that lay behind the planners'
façade of Weberian professional omniscience is pure 'Yes Minister'
stuff. George Brown's own account makes the point:

> Our National Plan – the first attempt at economic planning on such
> a scale that has ever been made in Britain – was related to every
> other aspect of policy . . . The Plan of course had to be presented
> to Parliament, but it seemed to me futile to offer it there unless a
> wide measure of agreement among the people who had to carry it
> out had been obtained beforehand . . . On 4 August 1965, the day
> before the crucial meeting of the NEDC, I suddenly got wind of a
> story that the industrialists were about to go cold on the proposals
> . . . I picked up the telephone and asked one of my secretaries to
> get hold of A – one of the leading industrialists – for me. He wasn't
> in his office, and nobody in his office seemed to know where he
> was. So we telephoned his wife, and she didn't know. Then we
> started on B and C . . . working our way through every single
> member of the group who had represented what was then called
> the Federation of British Industry in our discussions. Not one of
> them was in London, and nobody seemed to have any idea where
> they were . . .

In the end, Pat Kelly, one of my secretaries, rang one of the industrialists for the umpteenth time, and was put through to the man's wife. She, not realising what was going on, said she thought her husband had gone out of London to attend some dinner – it might be a place called Whitchurch . . . With the precious document, the only copy that was supposed to exist, under my arm (I didn't have time even to put it in a brief case) we got out the official car and Sir Donald and I set forth.[6]

Eventually, the culprits were located in Sunningdale where they were holding a meeting. Beer and sandwiches folllowed. And agreement was reached. But all was not over. As George Brown reports:

The Government car we were using then was a magnificent old hearse of questionable age, and coming home the old thing broke down. It was then about 3 a.m.[7]

The problem, as it turned out, was solved by a spot of private enterprise, in the form of a driver who – without any impure hope of profit – gave the Secretary of State and the Permanent Secretary a lift home. Perhaps his garage knew a little more about car maintenance than the aptly named 'Government Car Service'.

Notes and References

* This chapter has benefited from the comments of the members of the Carlyle Club, to whom an earlier version was delivered.
1. Cf. John Stevenson's essay (Chapter 13 in this volume), 'Has Planning a Future?'
2. H. Morrison, *Socialisation and Transport* (London, 1933): 156–7.
3. E. Bevin, House of Commons (21 June 1944).
4. M. Weber, *The Theory of Social and Economic Organisation*, trans. A. M. Henderson and T. Parsons (New York, 1945): 359.
5. George Brown, *In My Way* (London, 1971): 119.
6. Brown, *In My Way*: 104–5.
7. Brown, *In My Way*: 105.

15 Government Investment in Universities and Science
Terence Kealey

In 1963 Lord Robbins and his committee published their famous Report on Higher Education. The Committee, which was appointed by the First Lord (Treasury Minute dated 8 February 1961) consisted of ten men and two women; and it was the very stuff of the educational establishment. Between them, they could muster a peerage, three knights bachelor, a KCMG, a DBE, a CB, four CBEs, an OBE, an FRS and two professorships. Their report not only embodied the wisdom of its time, it moulded that of the next twenty-five years. The changes it heralded can be recognised by the foundation dates of the rash of universities that it spawned: Aston (1966), Bath (1966), Bradford (1966), Brunel (1966), City (1966), Cranfield (1969), Dundee (1967), Heriot-Watt (1966), Loughborough (1966), Salford (1967), Stirling (1967), Strathclyde (1964), Surrey (1966) and Ulster (1965).

The Committee reflected the spirit of the times. A number of universities were already being built: a University Grants Committee (UGC) minute of 1958 had initiated the universities of East Anglia (1963), Essex (1964), Kent (1965), Lancaster (1964), Sussex (1961), Warwick (1965) and York (1963). A further seven universities had only just been founded: two, Keele (1962) and the Open (1969) *ab initio*, and five by the manumission of London University colleges: Exeter (1955), Hull (1954), Leicester (1957), Nottingham (1948) and Southampton (1952). Out of a total of forty-five British universities, therefore, over half (twenty-three) were founded during the 1960s and a further four during the 1950s. The established universities, too, expanded massively over that time: there were 5,000 tenured British dons in 1938/39; 11,000 in 1954/55; 15,682 in 1962/63; 25,839 in 1967; and 32,738 in 1976/77. It now stands at 31,432.[1] Staff/student ratios have remained at approximately 1:8 over that time, which indicates the considerable expansion there has also been in students' numbers.

Why did the government spend the taxpayers' money on this

expansion? Robbins gave two justifications: the committee believed that university expansion would not only ensure economic growth, it would also promote higher cultural standards. Let us, therefore, examine these premises, and let us judge Robbins on their successful attainment.

ECONOMIC GROWTH

Robbins gave two reasons why the expansion of the universities would promote economic growth. First, productivity depends on trained manpower: Britain would need more scientists and technologists, and these are produced by universities. Secondly, Britain needed more technological and scientific research to ensure a continuous flow of new discoveries that industry could then exploit. Robbins recommended, therefore, that the UGC and research council budgets should be expanded.

Robbins's advice was followed. We expanded the research and teaching of science and technology manyfold. What happened?

Since the war, Britain's science has flourished. We are, in fact, a major science nation. Consider, for example, the number of scientific papers published per million population in 1982. The figures are: Canada, 483; USA, 465; UK, 432; West Germany, 295; France, 279; and Japan, 174.[2] Not only do we produce many papers, but they are good. We have won more Nobel Prizes *per capita* than anyone else: since their inception in 1901, 363 prizes have been awarded in science, and their national allocation has been: USA, 132; UK, 62; Germany, 50; France, 22; etc. Throughout the post-Robbins period, moreover, we have continued to publish good papers, as judged by the numbers of citations they attracted per thousand population in 1982, the last year for which we have comparative data: USA 2.27; Canada 1.66; U.K. 1.60; West Germany 0.96; France 0.78; Japan 0.49.[3]

This scientific distinction has not been surprising: governmental support for British academic science has been good. In 1982, for example, the percentage of GDP that was being spent on academic science was: West Germany, 0.49; France 0.44; UK, 0.38; USA, 0.31 and Japan, 0.25.[4]

But where was the growth? The years 1945 to 1980, the very period of the great post-war academic expansion, witnessed Britain's worst relative economic performance in three hundred years. At the turn of the century we were a great world power, one of the very richest nations on the globe. By the early 1980s we had sunk to 14th in GDP *per capita*, a position we contested with Italy. Our economy, in fact, started to recover only during the mid-1980s, the years of academic austerity and government science cuts.[5]

Robbins assumed that academic science would create wealth. His model proposed that (1) academic science made discoveries, (2) these were converted into technology, and (3) this creates wealth. There is, in fact, no historical reason to suppose that academic science generates wealth. Indeed the opposite appears to be true: academic science depends on the wealth created by industry. Industry's wealth, clearly, depends on technology, but it seems that it is technology that underpins academic science, and not the other way around.

Consider our history: as neolithic man progressed, he moved through ages named for technology: the stone, bronze and iron ages. These ages witnessed huge technological leaps: the discovery of fire; the harnessing of wind and water through sails and mills; and the development of animal and plant husbandry. Those leaps must have stretched mens' minds as much as any ever have, but there were no universities around in those days. Their equivalents such as Plato's Academy emerged only as the centuries of technological development finally flowered into the classical civilisations. But the intellectuals of Greece and Rome spawned very little new technology, or little wealth.

A similar pattern was repeated during the first half of this millennium. Medieval Europe grew increasingly rich as it developed its agricultural and commercial technology; but neither the doubling of agricultural productivity between 1200 and 1400, say, nor the development of double-entry book-keeping, owed anything to the universities, which were then engrossed in such economically useful activities as the justification of the burning of Joan of Arc. The wealth of medieval Europe flowered in the Renaissance of Galileo, Vesalius and Newton – from whose science, however, little further technology flowed.

The agricultural and industrial revolutions repeated the pattern yet again. During the eighteenth and nineteenth centuries, England had only two universities, Oxford and Cambridge, then notoriously stuporous. Edward Gibbon (1737–94), writing in his *Autobiography* of his undergraduate months at Magdalen College, described his tutors as 'monks . . . easy men, who supinely enjoyed the gifts of the founder'. Of his own tutor, Gibbon wrote that he 'well remembered he had a salary to receive, and only forgot he had a duty to perform'. Gibbon described his fourteen months at Oxford as 'the most idle and unprofitable of my whole life'.[6]

It was only after the industrialists had created their wealth that the English universities were revitalised. Consider, for example, the dates of some of the major events of the industrial revolution: Darby's discovery of coked iron-smelting, 1709; the invention of the flying shuttle, 1738; the development of the spinning jenny, 1767; Crompton's invention of the mule, 1770; the building of Ironbridge, 1777. Now consider the foundation dates of England's great civic universities: Manchester, 1851; Newcastle-upon-Tyne, 1852; Birmingham, 1900; Liverpool, 1903; Leeds, 1904; Sheffield, 1905.[7] The history of other countries is similar. Japan has grown spectacularly in the near-absence of basic university science; it is only now that its country is rich that the Japanese government has started to spend money on university science, and it still spends less than ours (see above). The Americans have a similar history: America's domination of science is recent – essentially post-war. Allan Bloom wrote in *The Closing of the American Mind*: 'if all of America's universities had been closed in 1930, the loss to international research and scholarship would have been negligible'. Yet, by 1930, America had long overtaken Britain in GDP *per capita*.

Our history shows, therefore, that university science is the product of wealth: but it also confirms that it is technology that breeds wealth. This latter relationship has been quantified: Robert Solow won the Nobel Prize in Economics in 1987 for his studies on the factors that underlay the doubling in gross output per hour of work that the USA enjoyed between 1909 and 1949.[8] Of all the factors that might have been responsible, such as the capital–output rates, the rates of savings or the rate of growth in the work force, Solow showed that seven-eighths of the economic growth was attributable to 'technical change in the broadest sense'. Only one-eighth was attributable to increased capital injection which will, after a certain point, yield only diminishing returns. But, if technology spawns both wealth and academic science, whence does technology come? This question was answered by J. Langrish *et al.* of Manchester University.[9] They studied the origins of 84 technical innovations in industry and they found that although 'scientific discoveries occasionally lead to new technology, this is rare'. Generally 'technology builds on technology'. And that building occurs in the workshops and laboratories of capitalists.

Harrison's chronometer provides a good eighteenth-century example of the capitalist building of technology on technology. The Royal Navy, like all navies, had long needed an accurate chronometer to measure longitude. In 1713, therefore, the Navy offered a reward of £10,000. After much development of pre-existing horological technology Harrison, a skilled watchmaker, produced one and claimed his money in 1765. But is modern technology different? Thirty years ago C. P. Snow suggested that we were now living through a second industrial revolution, one in which technological change had become so sophisticated that it could grow only through intellectual advance – an advance that had to come from the universities. Let us, therefore, ask the question: does current economic growth depend on academic science?

Figure 15.1 correlates the number of scientific papers published *per capita* in 1973 by the major industrial countries with their annual real change in GDP over 1979–83. This time gap was chosen to allow the fruits of academic research to be translated industrially. Figure 15.1 shows that there is no positive correlation between scientific output and the growth of national wealth. We British publish lots of papers but our economy does not grow as fast as other countries who publish less. A similar result emerges if scientific output is measured by quality, not quantity: a graph comparing national citations with economic growth would show a similar shape to Figure 15.1.

It appears, therefore, that the traditional relationship still holds: namely, that technological developments are industrially-led, not curiosity-led, and that the wealth they create then supports academic science. But academic science cannot, itself, promote economic growth. This was recognised by Sir George Porter, the President of the Royal Society, who wrote in the *Independent* of 23 March 1987: 'In those industries where countries like Japan and Germany are so successful, it is usually because they make better products. And they make better products because they do more research and development *in the industry itself*' (Porter's italics).

Academic science is not economically worthless, of course. The discoveries of Newton or Leibnitz or Faraday underpin much later technology. But these discoveries, too, were funded by industrial technology. Faraday, for example, discovered electromagnetic induction in 1831 while working at the Royal Institution. This was then, as now, a private body funded by industrialists. It appears, therefore, that healthy industry will satisfy its own scientific requirements. It does not need government support and, as Robbins's experiment showed, unhealthy industry should not enjoy government support for its research either, because it will not exploit it usefully.[10]

Robbins's hope of creating wealth through government-funded

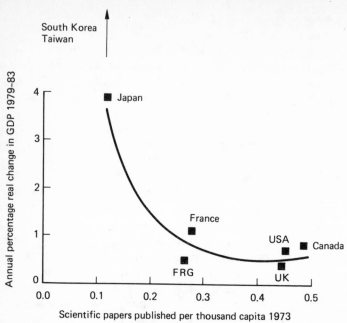

Note:
Economic data came from OECD *Economic Outlook: Historical Statistics 1960–1983*
(1985). The horizontal axis was calculated by the author from population data provided
by OECD *Economic Surveys 1983–84* (1984) and the publication counts were provided
by the ABRC Science Policy Studies, 1 (1986).

Figure 15.1 The correlation between the annual real change in GDP and
the number of scientific papers published.

academic science appears to have been foredoomed. But Robbins
did not hope to generate wealth through science alone: he wanted to
train more scientists and technologists so that they might, in their
turn, create industrial wealth. Was Robbins right? Does the training
of scientists by the universities lead to growth? At first sight that
might appear to be so: Langrish *et al.* may have suggested that
academic science *per se* was rarely of economic value, but they
concluded that 'the most important benefit . . . of basic research is
. . . the output of highly qualified men and women educated in
science and its methods. This is because discoveries and techniques
cross international boundaries more easily than men'.

Solow, moreover, may have shown that seven-eighths of the
economic growth of the USA between 1909 and 1949 was 'attributable

to technical change in the broadest sense' but he included the better education of the workforce within that category.

It appeared in 1963, moreover, that British education in technology had lagged behind that of our richer competitors. Between the First and Second World Wars, for example, less than 10 per cent of British university students read technology, 10 per cent read science, but no less than 46 per cent read the humanities. At that time Germany or Switzerland had over ten times as many technology students per head of population.[11] The forerunners of Germany's superb technical universities, the *Technische Hochschulen*, were founded in the 1820s, but France had already created the *Ecole Polytechnique*, the first of the *Grandes Ecoles* for the education of engineers, in 1794. Zurich set up its famous *Polytechnikum* in 1855, the Massachusetts Institute of Technology dates from 1865. Yet it was another forty years before the first comparable British institution, Imperial College, was founded; and it was not until the 1956 White Paper that we created the ten Colleges of Advanced Technology (places like Aston or Salford that Robbins reorganised as universities). And, as Robbins noted (paragraph 66), none of the seven new universities that the UGC had initiated in 1958 taught technology.

There is no doubt that our relative economic decline over the last one hundred years has been due, in part, to our lack of technology. This has long been bewailed. Indeed, over a century ago, no less than four Royal Commissions (Newcastle, 1861; Clarendon, 1864; Devonshire, 1875; and Samuelson, 1884) had warned that our lack of technological education was crippling our economic growth. Why, then, was Robbins's attempt at correcting that decline through the expansion of technological education foredoomed?

There was, in fact, considerable evidence available to Robbins that an expansion in technology education would not be economically fruitful. There was, for example, no evidence that British industry actually wanted more technologists: since the turn of the century, the Board of Education (1909), the Balfour Committee (1929), the Malcolm Committee (1929), and the Deputy Under-Secretary at the Board of Education (1942) had all reported that the supply of technologists had fully met, if not actually exceeded, industrial demand.[12] There was, furthermore, no evidence of an unfulfilled demand for places at university to read technology. As will be discussed below, the Colleges of Advanced Technology were so undersubscribed that, despite their pretentions to university status, they were admitting in 1961 a quarter of their students with no 'A'-

levels at all – just ONCs. A further 15 per cent only had one 'A'-level. Despite this, Robbins still recommended an expansion in university places in science and technology and, sure enough, by 1969 no less than 1,500 such university places were unfilled.[13]

What was happening? British industry was declining for lack of trained technologists, yet it did not actually want more technologists. And, in the event, there were no more anyway.

Britain had not, in fact, considered herself as primarily an industrial power for over one hundred years. She might have fostered the Agricultural and Industrial Revolutions, and she might as late as 1851 have called herself the workshop of the world but, by 1901, the national genius was increasingly channelled into imperial administration. Britain controlled one-quarter of the earth's surface and one-sixth of its population and she took her new imperial responsibilities very seriously. At one time Balliol College, Oxford, for example, was sending one-quarter of its graduates into the Indian Civil Service alone. For such graduates, the study of the literature of those earlier imperialists of Greece or Rome would have seemed of greater relevance than the study of thermodynamics. The British universities adapted, therefore, to Britain's new non-technological, imperial needs by teaching the humanities.

These post-industrial, imperial, influences did not operate so strongly in Germany or France. Those countries, scarred by a collective sense of inferiority to Britain, and largely spared the haemorrhage of imperial administration, could concentrate on catching Britain up in technology and commerce.

The great source book for tracing our industrial decline is Frances Trollope's *Domestic Manners of the Americans* published in 1832. Frances, the mother of Anthony, was shocked by the Americans' disregard for culture, scholarship or charm. They only wanted to beat the British at making money. And by 1835 Richard Cobden could write 'Our only chance of national prosperity lies in the timely remodelling of our system, so as to put it as nearly as possible upon an equality with the improved management of the Americans'.

Robbins is not the only technocrat to have promoted the government funding of science and education as an economic investment. In paragraph 194 he quotes with approval the Russian authorities who justified their own huge investment in education, particularly of science, with the phrase that 'the Soviet Union would always have use for people who had been trained to the limit of their potential ability'. Certainly, the Russian investment in scholarship and research has been huge. They spend, for example, 3.73 per cent of their GDP on science as opposed to our 2.3 per cent. India, too, invests hugely in science and technology. But these nations are not rich, although they can boast of many under-employed engineers.

Non-commercial cultures cannot be led to wealth creation simply by training technologists at university. Wealth creation depends upon a commercially-minded populace. We were that once and it appears that we may be becoming one again. If we do, our universities will re-adapt to meet industry's technological requirements. But the cultural process cannot be educationally-led.

THE PROMOTION OF HIGHER CULTURAL STANDARDS

Robbins believed that one of the aims of higher education was 'the transmission of a common culture and of common standards of citizenship'. He believed that education 'should be fostered to produce good men and women'.

Has the universities' expansion achieved these ends? Have we transmitted a common culture and common standards of citizenship better than have previous generations? Robbins reported in 1963 and his recommendations were implemented immediately. By 1968 the universities were ablaze with riots, sit-ins and direct action. For several years during the late 1960s and early 1970s higher education was in thrall to violence, promiscuity and Marxist *chic*: 'property is theft'. There is every reason to believe that the universities' chaos was caused by the Robbins expansion, and that their recovery was effected by the halt of that expansion: there is also every reason to believe that the universities have not only failed to transmit 'a common culture and common standards of citizenship' but that they have helped brutalise their own society: the intolerance, violence and drug abuse of the students' unions will have legitimised, for many a young thug, direct action and brutality. The anti-police sentiments, sexual licence and drug dependence of many offenders still echo the fashionable *mores* of the 1968 university intellectual.

How did the universities fall so low? Robbins's defining axiom, the famous rationale that underlay his entire report, was that 'courses of higher education should be available to all those who are qualified by ability and attainment to pursue them and who wish to'. This might appear to be an unexceptionable, even obvious axiom, except that Robbins's definition of those 'qualified by ability and attainment' encompassed all those who passed 2 'A'-levels at grade 'E'. Robbins produced statistics which showed that, whereas 90 per cent of all schoolchildren who had attained at least 3 'A'-levels were embarking upon full-time higher education, only 62 per cent of schoolchildren with 2 'A'-levels were entering it; but most of that 62 per cent training to be teachers. Only 22 per cent of schoolchildren with 2 'A'-levels were actually going on to university. Robbins believed that these statistics, coupled to the upcoming effects of the post-war baby boom, justified immediate expansion. Robbins complained that 'there has been increasing competition for entry to university' and that it was 'most undesirable that this should increase in future . . . in fact it should be reduced' (paragraph 156). Robbins actually believed that even two 'E's were too demanding an entrance requirement. At his instigation the ten Colleges of Advanced Technology, places like Bradford, Loughborough and Salford, were promptly converted into universities, yet at the time 15 per cent of their students had only attained one 'A'-level at admission – and a further 25 per cent did not even have that: they were admitted on ONCs.

Most dons would agree that students with two grade 'E's at 'A'-level are simply insufficiently prepared to benefit from a British university education as it is generally understood. Three grade 'C's might represent the minimal acceptable preparation, although few dons would really want to teach an undergraduate who had not attained at least a grade 'B' in the 'A' level that approximated most closely to the degree subject. Robbins knew all that: he was in fact trying to destroy the British tradition.

His report advocated the German *Abitur* or the French *Baccalaureat* systems as ideal models. Continental universities are different from our own: whereas ours only admit undergraduates competitively for a limited number of places, continental universities admit all applicants who have passed the government *Baccalaureat* or its equivalent. A continental university, in consequence, is a huge impersonal diploma factory while one of ours, traditionally, is an *alma mater*.

Some continental universities, frankly, are slums. The French, for example, regard their own with such horror that they direct their best pupils to the *Grandes Ecoles*. These have stiff entrance requirements, high academic standards, close tuition, low failure rates and no riots. Yet Robbins wanted to convert our high quality *Grandes-Ecoles*-type universities into continental-style ones. And for a time he nearly succeeded.

Robbins has proved to be the greatest purveyor of *anomie* in

British intellectual history. He took an entire generation of youngsters and pushed them into an environment where they simply could not survive. Two grade 'E's just do not equip an eighteen-year-old to flourish at university. Quite properly, university life is unstructured: students have hours, even days, to negotiate alone. Well-stocked, robust minds love it, of course, but ill-educated, ill-informed minds find it frightening and purposeless. Inevitably such minds will leap at the crude certainties of international revolution or drug-induced mind expansion. To use the then-fashionable terminology, the sit-ins, marches and demos of the 1960s and 1970s were cries for help from young people bewildered by an environment they could not master.

Our students were, in fact, alienated. All adolescents have to fight insecurity, but the adolescent at university with two 'E's knows that he is academically inadequate in the one place which values academic achievement most highly. That insecurity, coupled to the loneliness of the long, empty campus hours, will provide precisely those conditions that Durkheim predicted would breed alienation. He, at least, would not have been surprised by the mess, silliness and sometimes pure wickedness of the average students' union.

Were the Robbins universities actually designed to breed alienation? Why do so many of them look so grim? Their grey windswept concrete towers shelter, only too often, low, grey, ill-lit cemented corridors. And they are isolated. The concrete University of Bath, for example, occupies an exposed hill top some five hundred feet above the lovely mellow-stoned city that nestles in the cosy valley of the River Avon.

Robbins anticipated that his expansion would increase the wastage rate (the percentage of students who fail to complete their courses). The French or American rates are about 50 per cent, but ours are only 14 per cent. Incredibly, Robbins was contemptuous of our low rate, dismissing it with 'an average wastage rate of 14 per cent in universities as selective as ours is nothing to boast of' (paragraph 576). Robbins did not think that wastage mattered. He believed that even some exposure to higher education was better than none. But wastage is synonymous with failure, and there are few worse things with which to burden a young person launching into adult life than a sense of failure. An inadequate exposure to philosophical ideas such as Marxism, moreover, may do more harm than no exposure at all. It is curious how glibly Robbins ignored the wisdom of Pope's *Essay on Criticism:* 'A *little learning* is a dang'rous thing; Drink deep, or taste not the Pierian spring: There shallow draughts intoxicate the brain, And drinking largely sobers us again'.

As well as stuffing our universities with poorly prepared students, Robbins then gorged them on second-class dons. The 1960s expansion was so precipitate that the universities simply could not find good people to appoint. Britain, in 1939, possessed just 5,000 university dons. Several centuries of natural university development had flowered in just 5,000 scholars; but of such quality! One Cambridge college alone, Trinity, could boast of the overlapping fellowships of Bertrand Russell, Wittgenstein, G. E. Moore, G. M. Trevelyan, F. A. Simpson, Littlewood, Hardy, Ramanujan, A. E. Housman, Gow and Adrian. By 1962/63, following some dramatic post-war expansion, Britain had 15,682 dons. The reservoir of talent must have been fairly exhausted by then, but within five years we had increased that number to 25,839. Whence were 10,000 university dons to come? In five years we were somehow to generate twice as many academics as the universities had managed to produce after six centuries of development.

It could not, of course, be done, and the universities found themselves appointing as lecturers and professors men and women who were little better educated than the students they were expected to teach and to guide. No wonder the universities collapsed into chaos.

Second-class people propagated second-class ideas. Take the academics' obsession with tenure (jobs for life). Good dons need not fear its loss subject to proper safeguard. But the mediocre dons who now pack the British universities cling onto tenure desperately – and they infect their students with the same timorous expectations of life-long, index-linked bureaucratic employment. Consider, moreover, the academics' traditional disdain for commerce. This was once, at least, expressed elegantly, if snobbishly, by Newman in *The Idea of a University*, 'liberal knowledge or a gentleman's knowledge . . . as it tends more and more to the particular and practical . . . ceases to be knowledge'.

This is, of course, simply not true. What is a classical education but the particular dissection of ancient texts? The grammatical and literary skills that the classical student acquires are his practical tools – just as the student of thermodynamics learns calculus. Each tool trains the mind, but neither, surely, is inherently superior to the other? Yet, by the late 1960s, Newman's snobbery had mutated into the crass socialism of Malcolm Bradbury's *History Man*, a man who taught his students to despise industry, courtesy and decency.

The universities are better places now, but only because their expansion was halted around 1970. Following the arrest of their expansion, the universities' standards have risen. Only 15 per cent of undergraduates are now admitted with less than three grade 'C's at 'A'-level. Even this remains too high, although some unreconstructed Robbinsonian dons will still frighten television viewers with their persistent claims that there remains a shortage of university places.

As academic standards rise, so have standards of behaviour. It is instructive that the remaining troublesome universities are the least good ones: Aston, for example, has barred Conservatives from holding meetings on campus because it cannot afford the costs of security; and Swansea recently had to provide no less than five security guards to protect Ian Grist, MP, Under-Secretary of State for Wales.

The worst excesses are now reserved for polytechnics, another legacy of Robbins. Although few were ever as degraded as the North London Polytechnic, whose horrors were chronicled by Cox and Marks in *The Rape of Reason*, they can still be unpleasant places. A recent lecture by the South African diplomat Louis Mullinder at the Wolverhampton Polytechnic was aborted by a mob that stormed the hall.

The polytechnics admit the students who could not get into university, and there is now an excellent case for restricting their courses to those that are strictly vocational. This would, in fact, raise their prestige: the Oxford Polytechnic, for example, is rightly celebrated for its teaching of architecture, but it earns no lustre for its teaching of English literature or philosophy.

It is not fair to blame Robbins for everything that has gone wrong in British higher education. The student riots of the 1960s and 1970s were international – not only because they were *chic*, but also because everybody expanded their higher education after the war. The Continental and American universities expanded as did ours – the French named theirs *l'explosion scolaire* – and if their violence exceeded ours it was because they started from a higher base.

But Robbins can be blamed for joining that particular merry-go-round. One of his major justifications for a British university expansion was the Continental and American one – 'Almost everywhere we have travelled we have been impressed by an urge to educational development' (paragraph 129). The Europeans and Americans, in turn, were probably expanding to emulate us. This sort of argument might have seemed sophisticated to the Gadarene swine, but it is surely not unreasonable to have hoped for a little better from a Royal Commission?

Curiously, the most public warning against Robbins did not come from an academic, but from a novelist, the vagaries of whose career had driven him to teach temporarily in one of Britain's more mediocre university colleges, Swansea. It was Kingsley Amis who warned that 'more means worse'. It is strange how often the novelists have warned, unsuccessfully alas, of the academics' ambitions. Amis's *Lucky Jim* (1954) exposed only too well the inadequacies of some provincial universities and their dons, while Tom Sharpe's *Wilt*, though set in a technical college rather than a university, beautifully chronicles the sheer irrelevance of educating students beyond their abilities.

Violence, drug abuse and promiscuity have always dogged the universities – for obvious reasons. Medieval Oxford, according to some chroniclers, was little better at times than a drunken brawl spread across its brothels. Young men will always be naughty, and the excesses of the 1960s embodied much tradition. But over the centuries the universities developed defences: Oxford, for example, threw up proctors, selective admission and rustication. But the Robbins Committee was so hell-bent on expansion that it over-whelmed the new universities' defences with a flood of new students. Those students were remarkably privileged. Predominantly middle class, paying no fees, and in receipt of mandatory grants, those students could hardly have believed their luck. In return for very modest academic attainment, they were being invited by the taxpayer to have a ball – as of right. So they did.

Brideshead Revisited is the universities' least popular novel because it describes only too well the antics of over-privileged upper-class undergraduates. Now, thanks to Robbins, we have all heard the sound of the newly-privileged middle-class baying for the sound of broken glass.[14] But have we learned the lesson?[15]

Notes and References

1. Figures provided by the University Grants Committee annual reports.
2. Data calculated by the author from the *Evaluation of National Perform-ance in Basic Research*, ABRC Science Policy Studies, 1 (1986) and the *OECD Economic Surveys 1983–1984: United Kingdom* (OECD, 1984).

3. Ibid.
4. Source: *International Comparison of Governmental Funding of Academic and Academically Related Research*, ABRC Science Policy Studies, 2 (1986).
5. It should be noted that, despite what is popularly believed, the universities have not actually shrunk over the last ten years. There were 40,246 full-time university academics in 1977, and 47,038 in 1987, the last year for which the UGC has yet collated the statistics. But this growth has come from non-governmental sources and reflects a healthy, consumer-led growth in universities that harks back to their traditional origins. These figures are further discussed by T. Kealey in *Science Fiction: and the True Way to Save British Science* (The Centre for Policy Studies, London, 1989).
6. The Scottish universities never quite plumbed the depths of Oxford and Cambridge, and they played some part in technological development. James Watt, for example, was for a time a technician at Glasgow University. But, in practice, even the academic Scots' contributions to the industrial revolution were small.
7. These are the dates of the Royal Charters. Many of these universities developed from earlier institutions, but even those post-date the great developments of the industrial revolution.
8. 'Technical Change and the aggregate production function', *Review of Economic Statistics*, 39 (1957): 312–20.
9. *Wealth from Knowledge: A Study of Innovation in Industry* (New York, 1972).
10. Government funding for science is a recent event. The forerunner of the MRC was founded in 1913, the SERC in 1916 and the UGC/UFC in 1919. These institutions were founded for defence and strategic reasons. The economic justifications for government science funding were invented later as a *post hoc* rationalisation. It should be noted that during the two centuries that we led the world through the Agricultural and Industrial Revolutions, British science enjoyed no governmental support. But, as that has increased since 1913, so our relative rate of industrial decline has accelerated.
11. Summarised by Correlli Barnett in *The Audit of War: the Illusion and Reality of Britain as a Great Nation* (London, 1986).
12. Barnett, *The Audit of War*.
13. Barnett, *The Audit of War*.
14. This is an adapted quotation from the Oxford scene in *Decline and Fall*. Actually Waugh stole it from Belloc.
15. The government now (1989) proposes a doubling of the number of students in higher education.